Ancient Middle Niger

The cities of West Africa's Middle Niger, only recently brought to the world's attention, make us rethink the "whys" and the "wheres" of ancient urbanism. These cities present the archaeologist with something of a novelty: a non-nucleated, clustered city-plan with no centralized, state-focused power. *Ancient Middle Niger* explores the emergence of these cities in the first millennium BC and the evolution of their hinterlands from the perspective of the self-organized landscape. Cities appeared in a series of profound transformations to the human–land relations and this book illustrates how each transformation was a leap in complexity. The book ends with an examination of certain critical moments in the emergence of other urban landscapes in Mesopotamia, along the Nile, and in northern China, through a Middle Niger lens. Highly illustrated throughout, this work is a key text for all students of African archaeology and of comparative pre-industrial urbanism.

RODERICK J. MCINTOSH is Professor of Anthropology at Rice University and visiting Professor of Archaeology at the University of Pretoria, South Africa. His recent publications include *The Peoples of the Middle Niger. Island of Gold* (1998), *The Way the Wind Blows: Climate, History, and Human Action* (2000), and *Geomorphology and Human Palaeoecology of the Méma, Mali* (2005).

T0370781

Case Studies in Early Societies

Series Editor
Rita P. Wright, New York University

This series aims to introduce students to early societies that have been the subject of sustained archaeological research. Each study is also designed to demonstrate a contemporary method of archaeological analysis in action, and the authors are all specialists currently engaged in field research. The books have been planned to cover many of the same fundamental issues. Tracing long-term developments, and describing and analyzing a discrete segment in the prehistory or history of a region, they represent an invaluable tool for comparative analysis. Clear, well organized, authoritative and succinct, the case studies are an important resource for students, and for scholars in related fields, such as anthropology, ethnohistory, history and political science. They also offer the general reader accessible introductions to important archaeological sites.

Other titles in the series include:

Ancient Middle Niger

Urbanism and the Self-Organizing Landscape

Roderick J. McIntosh

CAMBRIDGE
UNIVERSITY PRESS

CAMBRIDGE
UNIVERSITY PRESS

University Printing House, Cambridge CB2 8BS, United Kingdom

One Liberty Plaza, 20th Floor, New York, NY 10006, USA

477 Williamstown Road, Port Melbourne, VIC 3207, Australia

314-321, 3rd Floor, Plot 3, Splendor Forum, Jasola District Centre, New Delhi - 110025, India

79 Anson Road, #06-04/06, Singapore 079906

Cambridge University Press is part of the University of Cambridge.

It furthers the University's mission by disseminating knowledge in the pursuit of education, learning and research at the highest international levels of excellence.

www.cambridge.org
Information on this title: www.cambridge.org/9780521012430

First published 2005

A catalogue record for this publication is available from the British Library

ISBN 978-0-521-81300-6 Hardback
ISBN 978-0-521-01243-0 Paperback

For Alex and Annick
The most precious companions in the field

Contents

Illustrations

Permissions

Cover: Aerial photograph of Jenne, Mali, kindly provided by G. Tappan

Original art work, commissioned for this book or used with permission, by:
   Matt Prater: Figs. 1.3, 1.6, 1.8a–d, 2.4, 2.12, 2.14, 4.12, 4.14, 5.5, 6.4
   Tera Pruitt: Figs. 1.4, 1.7, 3.1–3.4
   Matt Harvey: Figs. 4.2, 4.3
   Edwin DeVries: Fig 2.8
   Annick McIntosh: Figs. 2.10, 4.5
   Harry Rowe: Fig. 2.11
   Kate Ziegler: Fig. 2.12
   J. LaRocca: Fig. 4.10
   M. Kirtley and A. Kirtley: Fig. 4.13
   T. Togola: Fig. 5.1
   A. Schmidt: Fig. 5.3 (right side)

Satellite imagery kindly provided by G. Tappan: Figs. 2.2, 2.6, 2.7, 2.15

Map 1. "The Middle Niger" superimposed over West Africa, kindly provided by the Rice University GIS/DATA Center

Fig. 2.3 (upper left and center). From *Archaeological Landscapes of the Near East*, by T. J. Wilkinson, Fig. 5.6a and b (after R. McC. Adams,

Preface

The core approach taken in this book emerged from two conversations. At first glance, the two conversations could not have been more different – one, in the shadow of a ravine cut deeply into the heart of Jenne-Jeno, with my long-term Malian collaborators, Drs. Téréba Togola and Boucacar Diaby – the other around a campfire in a national forest in Texas, with a field class of my Rice University students. One with my source of many insights into the deep-time, evolving landscape of the peoples who built the ancient city we were in the process of probing. The second with one segment of this book's intended readership, with those open to learn about motivations of peoples very different than themselves, curious to know how archaeologists massage such knowledge from dry stone, brittle bone. At the confluence of those two conversations emerged this book and the self-organization approach to origins of complex systems cascading throughout its pages – a concept fundamental to the enduring Middle Niger vision of causation in the world and one that sits very comfortably with those frighteningly numerate undergraduates. (Just how many calculus jokes can one professor take in an evening?)

It has been a lifetime privilege to excavate the cities of the ancient Middle Niger. I sometimes walk through the vast fields of these towering *tell*s in a state of awe. They are also a source of frustration. No kings, apparently no armies, no palaces nor citadels – for the longest time we were frustrated in our attempts to imagine the social glue holding together these vast populations. The archaeological mounds, or *tell*s, themselves are vast and each frustratingly resides as a city within a larger urban cluster. From a purely selfish stance, how many lifetimes would it take even to scratch the surface of this, the most recent of the world's major urban civilizations to be discovered? Yet there have been many joys and the deep satisfaction of working with the many colleagues and institutions that made this book possible. Greatest satisfaction has been in the partnership in discovery with Susan McIntosh, always one of the most original minds in the business. In addition to my friends and co-directors, Drs. Diaby and Togola, over twenty-five years I have generated a list, too large for me to mention everyone on it by name, of Malians without whom the research, frankly, would simply have floundered. Topping the list, of course, are our friends in Jenne, principally our phenomenally dedicated workers (led by our foreman, Baoukassou Traouré), whom it has been a privilege to learn from. Never say "Abana" ("It's finished."). Thank you, a thousand times, to those many who have adopted us, especially Dani and Yama Traouré, Jaje Traouré, Petit Baba Traouré, and Hama Bocoum. Our deepest respect and thanks for three decades of support go to El Hadj Ba Hasseye Maïga, the Chief of Jenne, and to the Imam of the Great Mosque, El Hadj Alman Korobala. The staff of the Mission Culturelle de Djenné (Dr. B. Diaby, Director) supported the research in innumerable ways; thanks go also to the Jenne mayor's office, the office of the Deputé (formerly Commandant du Cercle), all the Amis de Djenné, and members of Patrimoine Djenné. Jenne lives (!) because of their efforts. I am pleased to acknowledge with gratitude and personal affection the continuing interest in the Middle Niger research (where he dug with us in 1977) of His Excellency Dr. Alpha Oumar Konaré, former President of Mali and now Chairman of the African Union, and of his wife, the distinguished historian Dr. Adam Ba Konaré. (As together we've often pledged, we'll get you back in the field ... someday.)

Research permission and encouragement for the various Middle Niger campaigns has been granted over the years by the Director and Assistant Director of the Institut des Sciences Humaines, Drs. Kléna Sanogo and Mammadi Dembélé, and by Dr. Mamadou Diallo, Director of the Centre National de la Research Scientifique et Technique. Thanks, especially, go to the many staff members of the ISH, the Direction National des Arts et de la Culture (Dr. T. Togola, Director), and the Musée National (Samuel Sidibé, Director) who lent their various technical skills to our missions. I am particularly happy to heap praise on our Malian field supervisors, M. Cissé, B. Sékou, and M. Samaké – the work continues! Thanks go also to our many workmen, officials and friends at Dia, Kayes, Nampala and Timbuktu who have made possible some twenty years of survey and excavation at urban sites within the larger Middle Niger. With too many to mention by name, I would particularly wish to thank the mayors of Timbuktu, Nampala and Dia for their personal kindnesses, as well as for officially facilitating the research.

Funding for twenty-five years of Middle Niger research has come from the National Science Foundation, the National Geographic Society, the Olive Branch Foundation, the American Association of University Women, and the Fulbright Senior Scholar program. Over the years we have enjoyed the support and friendship of the official American community in Bamako, that of many ambassadors (I mention the particular friendship of Dr. David Rawson), heads of the USIS bureau and of the Peace Corps. Too many Peace Corps volunteers, expatriate students and specialists (Senegalese, European, Canadian and American) have contributed to be acknowledged individually (but are in the monographs on each "mission") – but I would have a mutiny of Malians were I not to mention Karol Stoker, a participant in every campaign since 1977. Scores of specialists and laboratories in the US, the UK, France and elsewhere have analyzed materials from the Middle Niger. To the many Rice University graduate and undergraduate students who contributed in innumerable ways to the vetting and production of the research results, many thanks – particularly to Matt Harvey, Tera Pruitt and Matt Prater for the graphics that contribute so much to the creative heft of this book. Many of the satellite and aerial images (including this book's cover) were generously provided by Gray Tappan of the EROS Data Center. And to Kriss Barker, thanks for patience when the creative juices just aren't flowing, unaffected praise when they are.

Rita Wright suggested this book; our many conversations together about alternative urbanisms and heterarchy nurtured it. Simon Whitmore of Cambridge University Press professionally and with good humor brought it into existence. I am grateful for the comments of the anonymous reviewers of the manuscript, but particularly need to apologize to the many, many friends, colleagues, and collaborators who have contributed to my vision of the dynamics of the ancient Middle Niger landscape, all of whom cannot be mentioned individually here. I dedicate this book to my patient – and exhilarating – children.

Chronology

	Present	
	AD 1750	
"SOLITARY" CITIES REMAIN		Urban clusters eviscerated
	1500	Regional abandonment of "live" basins
REGIONAL ABANDONMENT		Abandonment of Jenne-jeno
	1250	
		Regional abandonment of "dead" basins
	1000	
CLIMAX OF URBAN	750	
CLUSTERS		
	500	
HETERARCHICAL URBANISM		
MATURES	250	
	BC–AD	
		Founding of Jenne-jeno urban cluster?
	250	Founding of Jenne-jeno
EMERGING CITIES		
	500	Permanent occupation – "live" basins
	750	Metallurgy – Fe, Cu
	1000	
	1250	
	1500	Elaboration of niche specialization
CORPORATE GROUPS IN		
FULL ACCOMMODATION	1750	
		Small, seasonal clustered hamlets
	2000	Permanent occupation – Méma
	2250	Domestication rice/millet/sorghum
	2500	Emergent pulse dynamics
	2750	
INCIPIENT SPECIALIZATION		
	3000 BC	Azawad peoples under climate stress

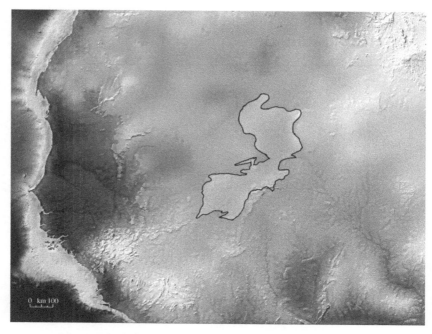

Map 1. Map of the Middle Niger

1 Discovery

Jenne-jeno "discovered" to the world

It can be said, without much fear of contradiction, that the ancient Middle Niger is the most recent of the world's major urban civilizations to be discovered. Sadly, this discovery only dawned upon the archaeological world in the late 1970s. Why sadly? Independently developed. Enormous in size and population. Sophisticated in crafts. Voluminous in production of their manufactures. And with dominion over the granary of West Africa, the Niger River's vast interior floodplain that, at its heyday, covered more than 170,000 square kilometers. (Compared to Pharaoh's 34,000 square kilometers and the maximum cultivable 51,000 square kilometers of Mesopotamia: Lehner 2000: 283; T. J. Wilkinson 2003: 76.) These Middle Niger cities comprised, by anyone's definition, a major and indigenous world civilization. Yet they were occluded from the archaeological eye until very recently (to put it delicately).

In fact, not until 1977, with the initial excavations at and regional survey around the first *discovered* of these cities, Jenne-jeno, was the world alerted to this highly original species of urbanism. *Discovery*: a word minted expressly to make archaeologists squirm! It is a word that archaeologists accept as connoting, for the larger public, the romantic in the archaeologist's job description; but it is a word they also cringe to hear directed at themselves (perhaps only rarely for false modesty!). *Discovery?* After all, these cities were hardly unknown before the first archaeologists walked their surfaces. The townspeople of the descendant city (Jenne) certainly knew of Jenne-jeno. Those same townspeople directed the archaeologists to the tall mound (a *tell*, or artificial hillock, a city site built up of centuries, millennia of trash and rain-melted mud buildings) marking the ancient urban settlement. "Discovered to the world," perhaps, is a better description of the archaeologists' role. But hardly discovered.

Nevertheless, the reason for the delayed appreciation of these Middle Niger cities by the archaeological world also has much to say about why their very originality has begun to shake up the conduct of pre-industrial

Fig. 1.1. Panoramic view of the Jenne-jeno mound, viewed from the north (east–west dimension, c. 800 m)

urban research in places as distant as Mesopotamia and northern China. That shake-up will be the last item to savor from this book's menu – dessert, as it were, for those of us who long have thought that Africa has received short shrift in the Grand Accounting of the world's prehistoric accomplishments (R. McIntosh 1999a)! (After all, we are all of us Africans, all *Homo sapiens sapiens*, whatever our mass, hue and flavor – shouldn't we all be more acknowledging of our homeland?) As the appetizer, however, let us turn to the entry (with annotations in brackets and italics) from my field journal for early 1977. This was the moment of "discovery" of Jenne-jeno as a small group of archaeologists (a Malian and three expatriates) trudged up the steep northeast slope of the Jenne-jeno mound for the first time (fig. 1.1).

3 February 1977: In the morning we went out, at last, to Djenné-djeno. [*We had arrived in Mali's capital, Bamako, on 22 January, but official visits and delayed permissions, purchases, nursing a cranky car (forgive me!), and the two days needed to crawl the 400 kilometers of neglected national highway had delayed, and delayed, and endlessly delayed* . . .] It's about three kilometers over the floodplain to the southeast of the city of Djenne [*The spelling of the town and ancestral site will change over time, at the insistence of the government, as will our mode of transport from cranky car to even crankier donkey-cart – funding for Middle Niger research has never quite reached Mesoamerican, or even Mesopotamian, proportions!*] [fig 1.2].

The site is absolutely incredible – it defies description. It seems to be divided into two parts, the larger of which must be almost a half-kilometer in length. [*I laugh now at my incredulity-driven underestimation – the "larger of which," the Jenne-jeno mound itself, is in reality over a kilometer long. The smaller of the pair, linked to Jenne-jeno by a causeway, is the separate satellite mound of Hambarketolo, itself a respectable 290 meters in length. In fact, the urban site of Jenne-jeno is divided into fully seventy physically discrete parts! And* THAT *is the core story of this book!*]. It is literally a mound of potsherds. [*It is this blanket of millions of sherds on the surface of all Middle Niger sites that most immediately strikes the tourist. A visitor, a Palestinian archaeologist who had once dug at Jericho with Kathleen Kenyon, said it was this overburden of broken pottery that astonished him even more than the site's enormous size.*] We found at least twenty funerary mounds exposed, roof tuyeres, pottery bedsteads, Muslim burials. There seems to be definite regions of concentrations – a function of erosion or not, I don't know. All pretty staggering.

Staggering and, frankly, discouraging. In a short time, this site would utterly transform our thinking about the origins of cities in Africa south of the Sahara. However, what this entry in the field log of my first day's impression of Jenne-jeno does not mention is just how overwhelming, and, frankly, terrifying that first impression was for this green, excited (and impoverished!) graduate student. As my partner in "discovery," Susan McIntosh, puts it, "Months of preparation. All that sampling

Fig. 1.2. Donkey-cart, the only reliable transport over the tortured clays of the Middle Niger floodplain. Note the extremely flat alluvium, interrupted vertically only by *tell* archaeological sites

theory, all those pages upon pages of exquisite gridding and random number strategy design in the grant proposal – to see it all disappear in a puff of smoke the moment I topped the rise of the mound!"

Scared, yes, because here were graduate students visiting the site for the first time in the company of the newly appointed head of Mali's national bureau for heritage, Direction du Patrimoine, Dr. Alpha Oumar Konaré. How much more terrified would we have been had we, at the time, but known our colleague's political future! In 1991, Dr. Konaré would spearhead the overthrow of the country's twenty-eight-year dictatorship, then serve two terms in the 1990s as the first democratically elected President of Mali, before stepping down to become the Chairman of the African Union (successor body to the Organization of African Unity, where he has spearheaded the initiative for a continent-inclusive *Etats Unis de l'Afrique*, a United States of Africa). But that is a story for later in this book (chapter 5). Dr. Konaré had been trained in Poland in medieval, ecclesiastical archaeology and was anxious to witness firsthand some techniques more appropriate to the kind of sites for which he had responsibility in Mali. The pressure was on!

The immediate source of our anxiety was that we had to make some initial sense of a settlement that stretched out before us at a scale that defied our wildest imagination. Not only that – we had to make sense of Jenne-jeno quickly, so we could select the best places for our preliminary test units. Dr. Konaré only had a week to stay with us (most of that eaten up by travel). He could not wait around while we walked and walked the site in a daze of indecision! We had to tickle out patterns to the distribution of the mass of features and artifacts littering the surface. Superficially, there seemed a tornadic chaos of furnaces, houses built of clay bricks – round and square – burial urns, burials in urns, and skeletons planed off by sheet-wash erosion – all exposed to desecrating view etc., and of the thousands of smaller items: ceramic bed rests, roof tiles, furnace blow pipes, copper bits, iron slag, animal bones, etc. Of course, we cannot forget the tons upon literal tons of broken pieces of pottery – all at a site unresearched previously and set in a vast region unexplored, in any systematic manner, by archaeologists.

Between the two of us, Susan McIntosh and I had logged over a dozen seasons of archaeological experience at a variety of sites in the United States, in three European countries, and in the forests of Ghana. No previous experience, however, could have prepared us to grasp the sheer vastness of this ancient settlement. And here is the more critical point: Beyond sheer scale, there was nothing *erected on the surface* of this site to direct the eye, to focus the archaeologist's mind, on the vast cityscape arrayed before us. Details about where and why we selected the first four test units must await a later chapter (chapter 4, where the strategies by archaeologists for making sense of a deeply stratified *tell* sequence are explained). Here we must explore the more fundamental question of why Middle Niger cities were so ignored by archaeologists and historians, so neglected by the outside world, for so long. Let us return to this freighted concept of archaeological discovery.

Does this mean that the site of Jenne-jeno had been previously undiscovered? Hardly. As mentioned before, the site was well known to the locals. But even beyond that, it had even been walked over by otherwise quite competent colonial-era prehistorians. But its importance as a city and as a pre-Islamic center of trade, wealth, and population was obscured to them. To understand why this should have been, we need to understand the history of scholarship (classical Arabic and Western) concerning West African cities and society.

It is a strange thing, but ultimately not a mystery, that neither Jenne-jeno nor, indeed, any of the hundreds of Middle Niger cities deserve any mention in the first Arab accounts of trade, towns, and states of West Africa south of the Sahara (see S. McIntosh and R. McIntosh

1980, I: 41–45; R. McIntosh and S. McIntosh 1981: 2–8, 19–22). These sanctioned, authorized court geographies, being second- and third-hand compilations of travelers' accounts written to a template of received, canonical views of the world with an intellectual lineage going back to Ptolemy, began to appear in the eighth century AD (Levtzion 1973; Levtzion and Hopkins 1981; Levtzion *et al.* forthcoming). At that time, Jenne-jeno and the other Middle Niger cities were arguably at their apogee and had certainly been in existence for over a millennium – yet, silence. Trade across the desert in West African gold, that commodity wantonly lusted after by all states north of the Sahara, was already centuries old. Jenne-jeno and other Middle Niger cities were principal southern termini in that commerce – yet, silence. And the travelers and merchants from whom the court geographers heard of these exotic African lands and peoples would surely have themselves had heard (if not actually traveled there themselves) of the hundreds of cities along the Middle Niger – yet, silence still.

Silence in the written records until Jenne (the descendant town, 3 kilometers away), or "Geni," was discovered to the world across the Sahara in the fifteenth century by an Italian commercial spy. In 1447, the Genoan Antonio Malfante was poking around for intelligence about the sources of West African gold in the North African city of Tuat. Predictably, he was getting little out of the suspicious local merchants. But he did learn of fabled towns, of Thambet (Timbuktu) and of "Geni" – a city he calls a "*civitate*," with the clear implication, for a northern Italian of this epoch, of a mature city-state with a larger administered hinterland, or "*contado*" (R. McIntosh and S. McIntosh 1981: 4). Would that we knew just what his southern merchant informants in Tuat had told him to occasion use of this highly freighted term. "Civitate," with its implications of a self-administering city-state and hinterland, goes to the very core of our definition of a city.

If the modern town of Jenne remained so obscure to the world (even under the intense glare of interest from the Islamic and European worlds in this center of the trans-Saharan gold trade), what chance was there of any mention of the ancestral Jenne-jeno? Little. For that, the ancient city must wait two more centuries.

Around AD 1656, the imam and notable of Timbuktu, al-Sa'di, wrote a personal history in Arabic, a *ta'rikh*, of the important towns, states, and historical events of the Western Sudan (al-Sa'di 1900; by the Western Sudan we mean, roughly, northern West Africa, the southern fringe of the Sahara). In his *Ta'rikh es-Sudan*, al-Sa'di recalls the oral traditions of his natal town of Jenne:

Jenne is one of the grandest markets in all the Muslim world. There, one will encounter merchants bringing salt from the mines of Teghazza, who meet merchants bringing their burden of gold from the mines of Begho ... Everyone conducting business in Jenne is blessed by God with great profit and, indeed, only God Himself (may His name be blessed!) keeps a true accounting of the fortunes that have been made there. It is because of this blessed city that caravans flow towards Timbuktu from all points on the horizon, from the east, from the west, from south and from north. (al-Sa'di 1900: 22–23, trans. R. McIntosh)

According to al-Sa'di, Jenne was founded by pagans in the middle of the eighth century AD. Its king and all its inhabitants converted to Islam around AD 1200 (1900: 23). But al-Sa'di is very explicit that the "founding" spoken of was not of the present town, but of its ancestor, Jenne-jeno (that is, "ancient Jenne" in Jennéké, a Songhai language dialect). First site of the city is the mound of Zoboro (or Djoboro) (or "ancient Jenne" in the local Bozo language), located just south of the present town (1900: 23). Sparse enough reference, but an eighth-century date for the foundation of *any town* was so impossibly early, given received wisdom about when and why states and towns should have appeared in the Western Sudan, as to have created considerable skepticism amongst historians. That is, until proper excavation revealed the true dates for the settlement's founding.

This is the first surprise from al-Sa'di: His founding date is, frankly, too early for a scholarly world convinced that states and cities could not have appeared amongst the "backward" people of black West Africa until there had been sufficient contact with the civilized peoples of Islamic North Africa and metropolitan Egypt and other Islamic nations (R. McIntosh and S. McIntosh 1988; R. McIntosh *et al.* 1989). But wait! – al-Sa'di provides another strange tale about Jenne that will come to have enormous implications for understanding the originality of urbanism here. He is not terribly specific about when this anecdote took place. By the time of the gold trade to the far Akan forests (the Begho of the last quote, far to the south in West Africa) at the very latest, Jenne held authority over a large territory. The territory's size may have been fully one-tenth of the entire Middle Niger, a possible 17,000 kilometers square (al-Sa'di 1900: 25; R. McIntosh 1979: 15). What really catches the archaeologist's attention is the statement that, throughout this territory, the land is fertile and was well populated; so densely populated, in fact, that 7,077 villages were packed close together. This allowed a curious form of communication:

If the head of Jenne, for example, has occasion to call on an inhabitant of one of the villages located near Lake Debo [approximately 160 kilometers away], his messenger will simply avail himself of one of the city gates. From there, he will cry out the message that he has been charged to transmit. From there, and from village to village, the people of the hinterland will repeat this message until it arrives, almost immediately, to the person sought. That person then rushes to the desired audience. There is no need further to illustrate how densely peopled is the territory of Jenne. (al-Sa'di 1900: 24–25, trans. R. McIntosh)

Sadly, after these tantalizing suggestions of great antiquity and of enormous regional importance, the ancient city of Jenne-jeno is, once more, lost to history. There are some later elliptical mentions, as when in the fifteenth century an invading Songhai army garrisoned the site during its siege of Jenne lasting seven years, seven months, and seven days (R. McIntosh 1998: 285–92)! Amongst classical Arab or local Islamic scholars there appears to have been no further curiosity about its foundation date or the town's role in the earliest history of the Middle Niger.

In fact, the first colonial achaeologists shared with their Islamic predecessors a disbelief in the ability of West Africans to discover for themselves the fruits of complexity – cities, long-distance trade, states, and the like (R. McIntosh et al. 1989; R. McIntosh 2001). But with French colonialism came renewed interest – albeit not always of the most selfless, uplifting kind.

The archaeological mounds around Jenne were, in fact, objects of the first interest shown by prehistorians in the Middle Niger – unfortunately, an interest in the prehistoric that has made true, scientific archaeology literally a race against time – and against art. Art, specifically, statuettes: Terracotta statuettes are for the legitimate archaeologist here the mixed blessing that gold is for archaeologists elsewhere. On the one hand, they provide an important testimony to the activities and interests of the past population, and thus are necessary to record and publish. Sadly, on the other hand, however, the act of publishing can bring the valued commodity to the attention of the unsavory world of collectors and looters. Colonial figures stationed in Jenne found anthropomorphic terracotta statuettes eroding out of several of the mounds surrounding the city and further down river (Ligers 1957; Masson-Detourbet 1953; Monod 1943; Mauny 1949; "Sculpture soudanaise" 1947). The first recorded "archaeological" episode (of the Indiana Jones vintage!) was occasioned by schoolteacher Vieillard (1940), who sank robber pits into Jenne-jeno in 1938, without, as he complained in an unpublished letter, "any other result than finding some stone beads, pendant fragments, and bits of iron that were impossible to identify" (from Mauny 1961: 102). By the early 1970s, long before serious, legitimate excavation began at any of the *tell*s of Jenne, battalions of peasant looters in the employ of international art thieves had started to turn scores of Middle Niger sites into ghastly, eviscerated cadavers. All the more reason to try to understand why the Jenne *tell*s had not earlier attracted more legitimate scientific attention. Unquestionably, the archaeological obscurity of these ancient sites aided the clandestine activities of the looters and their patrons in the rarified world of the international art and antiquity trafficking.

To the best of anyone's knowledge, the next colonial personality to walk the surface of Jenne-jeno was a truly admirable prehistorian and polymath, a larger-than-life personality, Raymond Mauny. Unsung champion of the richness of the Western Sudanese past, Mauny was an administrator-turned-archaeologist–linguist–historian–historical architect–preserver of cultural heritage. Largely self-taught in many of those disciplines, he nevertheless provided, in his magisterial *Tableau Géographique de l'Ouest Africain* (*A Geographical Overview of West Africa* – 1961), a synthetic picture of the Western Sudanese "medieval" (post-Iron Age) past.

Every prehistorian's vision of the past is viewed through a particular lens. Mauny's lens was clouded by the prejudices and Eurocentric conceits of his time (more on these later in this chapter). But he was avidly curious, visiting and sometimes excavating into as many kinds of sites throughout francophone western Africa as he could. (Getting ahead of our story, somewhat, when the true age and urban significance of Jenne-jeno was first presented to him in the late 1970s, long after his field days were over, he was amongst the first enthusiastically to accept and to trumpet those results. This, despite the fact that the new interpretation stuck a dagger into the very heart of his customary explanatory paradigm for the appearance of states and cities. Before accepting the early Jenne-jeno dates, Mauny full expected urbanism along the Middle Niger [and, indeed, anywhere in sub-Saharan Africa] to be late and derived, blocked as it was by the great desert from the "centres of radiation" to the north and east [Mauny 1970: 76].)

It is curious, but highly instructive, to read Raymond Mauny's personal thoughts as he walked the surface of Jenne-jeno. Mauny recalls his frustration, and admits, openly, to being aimless and confused:

The archaeologist is utterly at a loss, lacking any useful diagnostic artifacts – likewise, the examination of surface ceramics, the rare statuette, beads, or tobacco pipes (indicating occupation after 1600) recalls just how little help we receive from local oral tradition or from the Arabic *ta'rikh*s. We are on fickle land here and we are left with the impression of being only at the very beginning of the pioneering stage of archaeology. (Mauny 1961: 95, trans. R. McIntosh)

It is difficult to find the precise English rendering of "fickle land" (the original is "... en terrain mouvant"). The translation could be the far more evocative "quicksand" – in the sense that Mauny felt swallowed up, drowning in the sheer immensity of the site without a conceptual lifesaver to make sense of what he was seeing (Mauny, pers. comm. 1976). The translation could even be the prescient "earthquake" – in the sense (and he alluded to this feeling in private conversations some twenty-five years later) that a site of this size, clearly urban, clearly important, simply lacked the *urban signatures* he was looking for. Lacking those urban signatures, Mauny and the colonial archaeologists to follow departed the site without further investigation or commentary, allowing it to languish in the sullen Sahelian sun, the surface eroding away millimeter by millimeter with every monsoonal rainy season, naked but for the dire attentions of the terracotta thieves.

What were those urban signatures? What had even so wise and experienced an archaeologist as Mauny expected to grace the surface of every archaic city – in West Africa, North Africa, or Mesopotamia? This question goes to the core problem, the principal conundrum that had to be solved before the originality and deep age of Middle Niger urbanism could be accepted: City without Citadel!

City without Citadel

This book is about a simple problem – a concise conundrum, really: City without Citadel. When is a city not urban? When there is no king to call it so. Kings need their citadels – if a city has no citadel, no manifestations of kingly presence and power... our conundrum, City without Citadel. Or do we need a logic adjustment? By one way of thinking about circumstances leading to cities, anywhere, the three words of our conundrum simply should not go together. The weight of well over a century of our archaeological experience blowing the dust of memory loss from prehistoric cities throughout the world tells us so. Traditional archaeological theory about the origins and the functioning of the ancient city tells us so. At least that is the message of customary, majority archaeological theory and expectation: In order to have a city, particularly in prehistoric times and, emphatically, those grounded in pre-industrial economies, one also has to have a demonstrable seat of power, with all that implies about social and political relations.

Citadel: seat of coercive power (fig. 1.3); signature of the power of the state. The fantasy in figure 1.3 is the prehistorian's received dream – citadels of monumental scale, of every imaginable cultural variety, but all remote, Olympian, lording the uncontested power of the local despot over the figuratively (and, here, literally) enslaved populace. Thus, our conundrum implies the requirement of Citadel as signature of despots with a monopoly on force and at the apex of a bureaucracy that functions

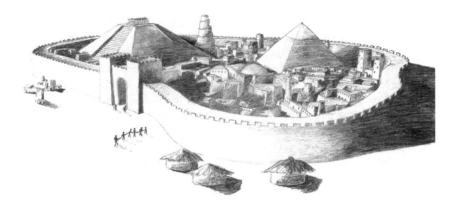

Fig. 1.3. Fantasy of the Eponymous City, with citadels

to promulgate through the society the decisions of the leader. The City must possess the Citadel, the Seat of Power. The physical remains of the citadel may be (but rarely) at a small remove from the city. But the cityscape (the urban landscape near and including the largest or principal settlement of the region in question) must have some awe-inspiring physical presence of the ruler. In most cases, the city functions directly as the seat of power. The city and the coercive kingdom or state are complementary and, most importantly for the coherence of traditional theory, the latter is thought to be a necessary condition for the former. If so, what are we to do with the emerging number of prehistoric cities lacking any good evidence, at least at the beginning of the evolution of the cityscape, of a parallel or antecedent state structure? Thus, our conundrum – City without Citadel. It just should not be!

Take this recent summary of the foundational conditions for ancient urbanism, principally in Mesoamerica, this particular author's area of expertise, but broadly applied to early urban societies, anywhere:

A basic feature that . . . was critical to a definition of urbanism was the existence of a state level of organization. Such an organization is central to the complex infrastructure of city life, and the two go hand-in-hand. Thus when we speak of the rise of the first cities, we also mean the emergence of the state. (Manzanilla 1997: 5)

And Manzanilla is just the most recent expression of a widely held expectation (held so widely that it is often accepted uncritically) that cities and states occur simultaneously and causally, "that cities are found only in societies that are organized in states" (Fox 1977: 24; see also Adams 1966: 90; Adams and Nissen 1972; Trigger 1972: 592; Zeder 1991; discussed in M. Smith 2003: 12–13 and R. Wright 2002).

Now, it is very true that modern urban archaeology is not a monolithic, myopic "palace archaeology," that is, exclusively the search for "large civic-religious structures, palaces, massive sculptures, paintings and the elaborate tombs of the rich and famous" (Andrews 1995: 11). It is also true that recent standards for investigating the life and birth of prehistoric cities insist that all segments of the population (peasants, craftsmen, merchants, even visiting tribal herdsmen) be searched for, not just the elite and the powerful (Trigger 2003: 40–52). And, as we will see in the concluding chapter (chapter 6) of this book, even the fantastical, fero-cious facades of the Egyptian and earliest Near Eastern urban civilizations have begun to crumble, showing a far more human face to the polity behind. Yet the Citadel retains, for us, a doubly freighted significance. I would go so far as to argue that the Middle Niger cities, such as Jenne-jeno, were "undiscovered" as true cities, even by fine observers such as Mauny, because – specifically – the Citadel was lacking. The Citadel – symbol of the coercive power of the ancient state, unfettered by western, recent sensibilities of democracy, civil society and the *philosophes'* mew-ings about abstract rights of the governed. What makes the Middle Niger urban experience so unusual – and provocative – is the apparent lack here of a state-level organization at the core of urbanization. Provocative enough (as we will see in chapter 5) that an archaeologist Head of State (our friend, Dr. Konaré) has used presidential addresses to the nation purposefully to promulgate these cities as proof to his citizens of the deep roots of Malians' democratic instincts. But we get ahead of ourselves.

We get ahead of ourselves; yes, but this brings up another, intimately connected dilemma in the study of emerging social complexity in West Africa south of the Sahara. In one such speech, Dr. Konaré also invoked the "empires" of Ghana and Mali (of the late first and early second millennia AD, respectively) in his acclamation of his countrymen's deep democratic leanings. "Empires" – with all the associations of the word with despotic emperors, state terrorism on a grand scale, expansive militarism, and the like – how could someone just experiencing – indeed, orchestrating – the overthrow of a modern despot even use that word in the same sentence with "democracy" or "decentralization"? In point of fact, in the popular memory of Malians, and now in a major scholarly revision to Levtzion's classic *Ancient Ghana and Mali* (Levtzion *et al.* forthcoming), even these eponymous centralized states come in for a dramatic reassessment.

We saw above that Jenne and the major gold-trade towns within the spheres of Ghana and Mali are not even mentioned in the classic Arabic sources about those "empires." Now, after decades of search by archaeologists (S. McIntosh and R. McIntosh 1984), we have yet to find the capitals, much less palaces, audience halls, monuments and pleasure gardens, or any of the other expected purple-prose manifestations of power. (Koumbi Saleh, in Mauritania, convinces fewer and fewer archaeologists of its claim to be the capital of ancient Ghana, as more archaeolology is done there.) Could it be, as an analog to the European colonial need to find the chief or king in their new overseas territories ("Cherchez le chef"), that the Arab chronicles describing the far western pagan lands needed to find empires and states, familiar political entities, in order for their narratives to be convincing, credible, and not overly "fantastic" to the audiences back home? "Cherchez l'empire"? There is a deep historical tradition among Malians that ancient Ghana and Mali were not mere clones of political styles experienced in the European and Islamic worlds, that one need not demonstrate despotism, militarism, state terrorism and the like in order to demonstrate past greatness. If so, perhaps our traditional equation of state with urbanism just does not apply. Yet the equation rests deep within the soul of archaeologists.

Let us delve more deeply into how fundamental the prior presence of the state continues to be to our thinking about the circumstances giving rise to the ancient city. Consider two brief quotes from the recent, authoritative book *First Cities*, from the prestigious Smithsonian Books series Exploring the Ancient World (Andrews 1995). In the initial, theoretical, chapter of this work, summarizing city beginnings around the world, from Mesopotamia, to Egypt, to the Maya and the Andean civilizations, Andrews captions a picture of the pioneer of attempts to systematize and codify a definition of the city (past, present and future): "V. Gordon Childe . . . was the first archaeologist to establish criteria for defining a truly urban society. These criteria included a class structure, a system of taxation, an organized labor force, long-distance trade, *and most importantly, a state organization that included a bureaucracy and a military apparatus*" (1995: 11, emphasis mine).

Andrews goes on to demonstrate his continuing conviction, one still shared by many modern urban archaeologists, that a state level of organization was obligatory, a necessary precondition (or contemporary pairing) for the "complex infrastructure of urban life":

Thus, when we speak of the rise of the first cities, we also mean the emergence of the state. Simply put, pre-state-level societies, such as tribes and chiefdoms, do not have true cities. Within this context, then, it is possible to provide a more formal definition of that oft-misused term, "civilization"; most scholars would likely accept the notion that a true civilization is one with a complex level of cultural development, which includes fully formed urbanism and a state level of organization. Still, some scholars use the term "civilization" to describe less complex societies, such as those of the Olmec, Chavín, or Preclassic Maya, which had simple regional polities governed by complex communities that were not fully urban. (Andrews 1995: 12)

End of discussion. But what if the following neat and tidy equation, posited by the standard formula of urban origins, is not necessarily true?

State {= centralized decision making + bureaucracy + (coercive) military apparatus} + specialized labor force → urbanism

What if we can demonstrate not just an alternative City without Citadel, but also a logic – a calculus, if you will – of emergent urbanism not in need of an exploitative, extractive (and cruel) economy, nor of a despotic, rigid, and bureaucratized social and political structure? How intellectually liberating to find that our problem of the City without Citadel was no conundrum after all!

It is the purpose of this case study to focus upon the urban story coming out of research, merely three decades old, along the Middle Niger of West Africa – where we appear to have scores, hundreds (and who knows – survey has just begun – thousands) of eponymous cases of City without Citadel (R. McIntosh and S. McIntosh 1983; S. McIntosh and R. McIntosh 1993); eponymous in the sense that these Middle Niger cities have quickly become exemplars of and classic cases cited in the larger literature (eg., Stone 1997; Stone and Zimansky 1995; R. Wright 2002: 9–10) of urbanism in the absence of the state. The analysis of these cities has developed in lock-step with the study of a larger social phenomenon, the heterarchical social structure – horizontal social complexity in which "each element possesses the potential of being unranked (relative to other elements) or ranked in a number of different ways"(Crumley 1979:144). Only in the mid-1970s was this very different cityscape "discovered" by professional archaeologists in the Middle Niger. As we have seen, these massive ancient *tell*s (mimicking in size those of the Middle East) had even been walked over by colonial-period prehistorians. But the originality and the potential of these Middle Niger cities vastly to alter our way of thinking about the foundation causes of urbanism, here and far away, were unappreciated by these archaeologists of another age. In that age, of course, one recognized the "citiness" of a large settlement by its monumental manifestations of the state.

What were they looking for, those archaeologists who could not imagine a City without Citadel? In the first place, they were looking for signposts of permanence. The term derives from Jacobsen's (1976: 180) exposition of the Mesopotamian creation epic: "Marduk's first demand upon the gods was that they build him a city and a house to serve as a permanent royal administrative center and a place for them to stay when they gathered for an assembly: a signpost to permanence." This meant monumental art and architecture, the kind that would reinforce to the lesser of the population the elites' contention that they had a "natural" (gods-given) right to rule and the right also to take the best the land and artisans had to offer. That right might come baldly from force (something that might easily be seen by archaeologists as, for example, the war-machine of the Aztec, the state terrorism of the Inca or the scores of headless sanctifying the rammed-earth palace foundation of Shang Chinese royal cities), visible in looted and destroyed settlements, in abuses of corpses, and in the great asymmetries of wealth and diet. That right might more subtly be the will of the gods – with the beneficiaries anxious to record their special relationship to the gods, or to their personal ancestral god, in public art or in the ceremonial architecture of temples.

Those older archaeologists who passed briefly through the Middle Niger were also looking for signs of the coupled hierarchies of the political sphere and of the social. In the first sphere, a state bureaucracy with the kingly decision maker at the apex has a series of intermediary administrative tiers. The middle men and toadies at these intermediate tiers serve the hierarchy by channeling decisions down to the rest of the population, while limiting many of the worries and concerns of the peasants from overtaxing and polluting the mind of their master. When thinking about decision flows through the hierarchy, we call these middlemen gatekeepers. We shall see that the role of the gatekeeper in a vertical, centralized hierarchy is not always positive. Gatekeepers too often clump as scleroses in the arteries of state decision making and information flow. Under their influence, decision makers become ever more removed from the generators and receivers of subtle information of change impinging upon the polity. That change may come from climate shifts or landscape alterations, or may come in the form of new internal demographic developments, or as hordes upon the horizon. Cut off by the gatekeepers from those with their ears to the ground, the state becomes less and less resilient. So, the hierarchy in politics (and its expected social triangle of a few well off and many barely getting by and those in the middle jostling to better their access to the very privileged) may not be the best model for urbanism after all!

Think, after all, about what, under this despotic model, the critical functions of the ancient city might have been. There is not a little circular reasoning in the arguments of those, such as Andrews (1995), who state that the city's foundation had to follow that of the state because only the state could provide the bureaucratic organization (and coercive

lubrication) needed for the complex infrastructure of the city. By infrastructure we can presume they mean the warehouses (for redistribution of
surpluses in times of want), the corps of non-productive specialists
(craftsmen charged with manufacturing the luxury trifles and the sumptuary signatures of status, scribes, religious functionaries, and the bureau-
crats themselves), barracks for the state police and soldiers enforcing the
king's will, and the regional representatives of the centralized states – the
ambassadors, governors, tax collectors, etc., etc. But the complex infrastructure they talk about is the infrastructure *of the state* based in the city.
Take away the state, and does the infrastructure come due for a radical
rethink? Or can we ask in another way the question about what constitutes
the ancient city's function?

What must happen in a city for all its citizens to function in peace,
security and some degree of harmony? I would argue that the essential
function of the city is to reconcile corporate diversity. Here, we use the
term "corporate" in the anthropological sense. A corporation is a self-
defining social group (or a community, if you will) that holds property in
common (Cochrane 1971; R. McIntosh 1993: 188). That property can
be material; it can be ideological or symbolic; or that commonly held
property can be territory or even the memory of a historical event.

That is, a discrete group of people can consider themselves to be a unity
separate and distinct from their neighbors because of their exclusive, but
shared, possession of goods or wealth (stockholders and worker stake-
holders in an industry; a blacksmithing clan with exclusive access to an
iron-smelting furnace). A discrete group can derive communal self-
definition because of a shared belief or purpose (the First Baptist congrega-
tion; a "sodality" such as an age-grade regiment in Shaka's Zulu army or a
Pueblo kiva society). Or the group self-definition can come about because
of a memory (real or fictive). Such corporate memory can be of an origin
from a common homeland (the Irish in America) or dramatic/heroic
event (the Afrikaner character forged by the collective body blows suffered during the Great Trek – but, interestingly, the battle of Blood River
serves an equally celebratory role for the Zulu nation in post-apartheid
South Africa). There is a special beauty in being human. We are flexible
in our definition of self: One can take on, without sinking into spiritual
schizophrenia, multiple allegiances, multiple identities. One individual
can simultaneously have a family (lineage, clan) affiliation, conform to a
religious or ritual creed, have an exaggerated ethnic pride, work as part of
one or more artisan or industrial corporations, and go to the Elks or the
Shriners (sodalities) to meet with the guys, reminisce over a beer about
the war days, and plan the upcoming charity fund-drive. Oops, conflict
tonight with the Jefferson Democratic Club . . . If one lives in a city is one

necessarily only and exclusively defined in terms of one's allegiance to the king? Obviously not necessarily.

In fact, what the city does supremely – today and in ancient times – is to create many, many new domains from which the individual can derive plural self-identification. And plural self-identification, under the right circumstances, can be a powerful engine of expanding the sphere of others with whom one maintains good relations and can exchange goods and ideas. The city, lest it spiral into hostility, chaos, and non-functionality, must also provide mechanisms to reconcile this corporate diversity. This includes ensuring peaceful and relatively open access by all to the manufactures, services, and "intellectual creativity" of the multi-plying, ever-elaborating corporate groups that make up the city. Now, the mechanism to ensure peaceful access, to reconcile corporate diversity, might well be the state. Indeed, the state's hierarchical bureaucracy can function to facilitate the movement of goods and decisions, with its hierarchical rules about just who has how much access to just which goods and freedoms, and with its apparatus of force to enforce this hierarchical organization. But we now are coming to appreciate that hierarchies have some pretty serious built-in inflexibilities as well. Before we talk further about those inflexibilities, let us just ask a simple question. Is the state, the hierarchical, centralized organization, the *only imaginable mechanism* to reconcile corporate diversity? It is fairly clear from the archaeology conducted thus far that we have to consider an alternative possibility.

Look at the problem from an archaeologist's point of view. What do we see on the ground, as it were? Much ink has been spilt since V. Gordon Childe's attempt way back in 1950 (when he coined that classic, the "urban revolution") to generate a catch-all trait-list of the city. Many have attempted to come up with a universal definition of the city that archaeologists can actually use in the field. Few are better, from the perspective of applicability to the broadest numbers of cases throughout the world, than the two-part definition proposed by Bruce Trigger (1972: 577): "Whatever else the city may be, it is a unit of settlement which performs specialized functions in relation to a broader hinterland."

We can expand that core definition to emphasize the corporate diver-sity "problem" (and this issue will be revisited again in chapter 4). The city is a settlement with a heterogeneous population that provides a variety of specialist manufactures, functions, and services to a larger hinterland. Note: There is no quantification of settlement size or of numbers of population. One could well imagine a city of diverse specia-lists providing those services to homogeneous agricultural settlements in the hinterland that were, each of them, several times larger, in terms purely of numbers of people. Note: There is no specification of the total numbers or relative ranking of the "artistic sophistication" of the specialist corporations. We are talking about the patterns of flow of specialist goods and services (and not to forget information) within a hierarchically patterned, integrated set of settlements in the hinterland. And note: There is no attempt to dictate how large the city's hinterland should be, or the number of tiers of dependent settlements functioning within that hinterland.

Critical here is the fact that, when the city appears from a prior landscape of relatively unspecialized and certainly less heterogeneous villages and hamlets, there appears a radically transformed landscape of diversity. New corporate groups appear. The resulting new corporate loyalties could never have been supported and never have been predicted by the old order. Old corporate groups defined by ethnicity or lineage, that never would have lived together before, now live (ideally) in harmony. And the city itself is a boiling, roiling cauldron for the brewing of newly invented corporate belonging.

By the older way of thinking, only the state could keep a lid on that pot! Left to its chaotic self-devices, anarchy would soon take over and all would collapse. Here I would like to propose a term for this top-down, coercive, state-dependent concept of the cityscape: *ex astra*. Out of the stars. Celestial; remote; detached; organized from on high – so high, in fact, that the lives of the rulers and most elite were a purposefully hidden mystery to the common folk. Purposefully hidden – very often with justification for rule articulated in terms of a celestial authority (fig. 1.4). The king is secure in his role as living representative of supernatural, celestial authority. *Ex astra* is the broadcast of the gods' desires. The king represents the gods' will. The king is the personal representative of the city-god. The king is god. *Ex astra*. (Peachy if you are in the power-crowd. Not so nice for everyone else.)

Take a moment to examine the complexity humorously depicted in figure 1.4. It is a complexity that shows the essential tension between the horizontal and vertical attributes of authority in civilization. The social and productive base, the lowest tier, is the most complex horizontally. In figure 1.4 one sees the representation of different subsistence "corporations" (depicted by the fish, grain, and livestock symbols), as well as the more elusive (in the archaeological record) marginally integrated and/or mobile segments of the population (appropriately, at the margins). Then one climbs vertically up the hierarchy, through tiers with progressively more authority (and power) and greater legitimation through proximity to the apexial figure. The figure at the apex is the font of decisions, in evolutionary theory, the pacemaker (the few who command and

Fig. 1.4. *Ex astra*: an idealized state hierarchy, its apex merged with its celestial legitimization

coordinate decision making for the many in any command system: Johnson 2001: 14–15). That ruler with his (or her) head in the stars also has his or her head in the clouds (!), figuratively, because of the doubly freighted influence of the gatekeepers (represented in fig. 1.4 by keys). It is an absolutely fundamental premise of this book that gate-keepers in hierarchies selectively filter the welter of information bubbling up from the base to the apex. But, in so doing so, they can and too often do deprive the decision maker of knowledge critical to the long-term flexiblity of the system. In a complex society, a long-term sustainable trajectory requires flexibility and resilience. A corollary premise of this book is that, in the traditional rigidly hierarchical states of the ancient past, life was quite nice for those at the top; not so nice for everyone else. Another key to sustainability, so I will argue, is a co-evolutionary will, on the part of all participants, that the system should continue and flourish. Nice for those at the top; not so nice for everyone else – and the *ex astra* system rests poised, perpetually, for that meteoric tumble.

Just to drive home this last point, consider a key moment in the story of the violent birth of kingship, the *Enûma elish*, the Babylonian creation story. Marduk, the first god-king, has vanquished the avatars of primevalness, chaos, formlessness, and of the Void – especially Ti'amat, the "begetter, and the 'matrix',", Ti'amat, "she who gave birth to them all" (Jacobsen 1976: 168). Recognizing the god-warlord as king, the other gods swear to him an oath of "Benefits and Obedience" (setting themselves in hierarchical position beneath Marduk). The more privileged of the gods help in the administration of heaven, the others to look after things on earth. In recognition of this Obedience (the manifestation of which was for the subordinate gods to build Marduk a citadel), and "to ease things for them, a great new benefit," he decided to create man.

> Arteries I will knot
> And bring bones into being.
> I will create *Lullu*, "man" be his name,
> I will form *Lullu*, man.
> Let him be burdened with the toil of the gods,
> That they may freely breathe.
>
> (Jacobsen 1976: 180–81)

Pity poor *Lullu*. Those at the apex, touched by celestial authority and exuding earthly, naked power, benefited enormously. For those further down in the hierarchy – still, good work, if you can get it. Life for everyone else at the bottom was not to be so nice! Poor *Lullu*.

Not so nice for everyone else and, many archaeologists have come to appreciate, not so nice for posterity. These state-driven cities are fragile, if one looks just behind the facade of temporal power (coercive force) and of the monumentality of eternalness (ideology in symbols). They are fragile, and their society is prone to collapse, because their hierarchical infrastructure is rigid. They lack the flexibility to deal with the unexpected. The unexpected can come from internal forces (revolts of the under classes; undermining efforts by disaffected soldiers or eclipsed aristocratic factions) or it may come from the outside (those pesky nomads; uncooperative weather; plagues of locusts).

It is the premise of this book that cities lodged within a state apparatus lack an essential element of sustainability, one we can inelegantly call "over-engineering." Hierarchies that are elaborated on the vertical (control) axis typically have no alternative pathways should one section be effaced or if there are radical changes in the baseline condition for which the bureaucracy was constructed in the first place. And perhaps most importantly, because all but the privileged minority benefit hugely from the despotic state system, few feel a responsibility to the whole that might push the whole to be greater, more balanced with the ever-changing world about it, than each of its parts. Lacking flexibility; rigidly engineered; not self-generating an "enlarging responsibility": is this our only option? This book is an argument for an alternative ancient urbanism: Permanence not pomp. Sustainability not sumptuary. (Pluri-) Corporate not Citadel – the heterarchical city! But before we present this radically alternative course towards urbanism, we need to ask, where did such academic allegiance to this somewhat tortured, not entirely savory, representation of the state-based ancient city come from? Why do academics quiver at the mental image of our city prostrate beneath the feet of the citadel?

Ex astra (a brief history of values)

I do not intend the above to give the impression that there has been no dissatisfaction whatsoever with the expectation that the state served as a precondition for ancient urbanism. One only need look at a recent collection of essays on *The Archaeology of City-States* (Nichols and Charlton 1997) to see the first glimmerings of unease with this monolithic model. There one finds an outright condemnation of archaeologists' acceptance of the precedence of despotism by Morris (1997), which he (after Gellner 1983) calls the "agro-literate state" model. Arguing that the flow of authority in, for example, Athens radically undercuts the "agro-literate state" model, Morris asserts that most archaeologists nevertheless at least implicitly subscribe to some version of that model. The model has a decided neo-evolutionary, stadial (step-by-progressive-step), "upwards-and-onwards" slant: Ruling classes, consisting of elites, use writing and religion to underwrite an asymmetrical social structure and rigidly to separate themselves from the great majority of producers, the peasants. But if Morris is correct that most urban theorists have ignored city-states because they tend not to conform to expectations generated by the "agro-literate state" model, there surely must be a deeper, historical, values-driven reason for this particular tunnel vision.

Let us spend just a moment conducting an archaeology of the hidden, the deeply buried and deeply stratified values behind the prevailing view of pre-industrial urban despotism. David Thomas (1979: 141) argues that every social science (and, equally, every historical discipline) is steeped in its own metaphysic, its own underlying validations of the knowledge base of every interpretive theory. These metaphysics are, in turn, deeply rooted in the unspoken or unexamined values deriving from implicit assumptions about human nature. At root, those values underlying the *ex astra* model of the state-within-city generate a terrifying vision of the cityscape, a newly invented space of asymmetrical power (R. McIntosh 1991: 203 and 1999c; see Lefebvre 1991: 235–53).

Divorced from the freedom and piety of life in the country and of an existence linked to the soil, city life is bondage, rootlessness, namelessness, and depravity. The city creates a new order of human nature forever dedicated to the control of the many by the few: to hierarchy. This is a control that robs one of essential freedoms and of the essential connectedness of (kinship-based) community. Also, and most importantly, the urban existence deprives one of any chance for a covenantal relationship with God that is the very core of a venerable Western tradition of biblical exegesis called Yahwism (Gottwald 1979; Matthews and Benjamin 1993). At the root of this biblical tradition is the Covenant (*berîth*) that only a free individual (i.e., the tribal, pastoral Israelites) can enter into with their God. The resulting relationship is called Covenantial Piety (Albright 1953: 271), and the rightness of this relationship remains a deeply seated, if unexamined, value held by Western archaeologists. For our purposes, the important issue is that of the asymmetrical, despotic power that makes a misery of those living *outside* Covenantial Piety. The ancient city, necessarily and almost by definition, is the arena of control of the many by an elite few. And from whence comes the right of rule of those few? The right to rule in the city comes not from God, but from the pagan gods' relationship with the despot celebrated in *ex astra*. Such pagan, barbaric control is reflected in the monumental constructions that came to be viewed as the signature of the city, especially the Citadels oppressively serving those Oriental seats of despotism. Sites without large-scale construction could not, in this view, be candidates for urban status. Such is the calculus of urbanism according to the logic of Yahwism.

The West African sites rendered invisible by this cognitive occlusion are massive. As high *tell*s, they pop up unmistakably from the flat Middle Niger floodplain. True, the density of field archaeologists, in the colonial Western Sudan as in present-day Mali, has always been discouragingly low. But how could such distinguished observers of the ground as, for example, our friend Raymond Mauny (1961: 101–2) or the geographer-polymath Théodore Monod (1943, 1955) have been able to walk over the site, yet dismiss so massive a settlement as Jenne-jeno with barely a mention? And these are only the most distinguished of cohorts of pre-historians and natural scientists who, during perhaps a century, have yawned their way over the high and extensive *tell* remains of many early Middle Niger towns. I contend that, because of unexamined Yahwist values, they lacked the intellectual toolkit to recognize and process the evidence under their feet. They failed to recognize the town they trod upon because they could not see the expected signs of pre-industrial urbanism. In the Yahwist formulation, such expected signs – namely, an encircling wall and citadel (or palace or temple) – serve as preeminent monuments to coercive political organization and to a state ideology (R. McIntosh 1991: 203).

Surely, some of these elements of monumentality would be visible if Middle Niger urbanism had come about because of a preexisting condition of elaborated (vertical) social stratification and (coercive) state formation? That is why I argue that we must take just a moment to step back and look at the process by which these expectations came to have such a defining role in the search for pre-industrial cities, not just along the Middle Niger, but in global archaeology writ large. Therefore, we must take a brief excursion to the realm intellectual genealogies – in order to identify the implicit social values that can intrude in a major way upon the nitty-gritty decisions of fieldwork. Later chapters of this book are, in fact, a roadmap through the fieldwork decisions that led to the discovery of anomalous urbanism along the Middle Niger.

Major classes of West African cities long remained invisible to archaeologists because of the occluding veil of a mainstream Western representation of the early city. Happily, whole new urban vistas, new and alternative pathways to urban origins, can be seen once the underlying social values (Covenantial Piety) of an older model are made apparent. In order to do this, we need to visit historical scholarship about the social world of biblical lands. At the core of this scholarship were the dichotomies of Yahwist values: pastoral vs. urban, piety vs. ideology.

What were the assumptions about the moral life of the pre-industrial city, assumptions that drove the writings of social thinkers and that resonated with their scholarly and educated-lay readership? A historical criticism of a dominant tradition of Bible exegesis, Yahwism, shows clearly why the primitive town was represented as dark moral exemplar. Yahwism was subscribed to by several generations of biblical scholars and, most importantly, by many social theorists of the origins of cities beyond the Greco-Roman world. (The Greco-Roman cities presented their own challenges to the early theorists of the city, because [unlike the morally depauperate Oriental cities] these were considered to be ancestral to Western urbanism – and hence had to be held up to a more positive light. Greco-Roman cities were, after all, the birthplace of enduring Western political and moral forms: see R. McIntosh 1999c.) In

Yahwism, the positive value attributed to an idealized, pastoral piety – and the condemnation heaped upon the impious lifestyles of non-white, Oriental urban dwellers – are dichotomies that underlie much of this Old Testament biblical tradition.

The story from the urban archaeological dirt of Mesopotamia and the southern Levant was one of impermanence, decay, and waste, and of great states and cities stricken down because of impiety and Oriental despotism (Kuklick 1996: 8, 38). Just how the monotheism of the Hebrews and the transcendent spirituality of early Christianity emerged from all this was not entirely clear! The German "pan-Babylonians" attempted to get around this problem by the invention of an *ur-Semitic* (for some, "Aryan"), Sumerian homeland of a (non-Israelite) race responsible for the first flickerings of monotheism. This was rejected as rank invention by influential synthesizers of the newly uncovered Mesopotamian and Egyptian evidence, especially by James Henry Breasted of Chicago, Albert Clay of Yale, and Hermann Hilprecht of Penn. Each argued, in his own way, for a Greco-Roman distillation of the best elements of earlier or adjacent Egyptian, southern Levantine, and Mesopotamian civilizations. As influential as these secular, compromise interpretations were, they were ultimately unconvincing to the majority of scholar-excavators of the biblical lands (such as William Foxwell Albright) and world civilization synthesizers (such as Arnold Toynbee). For these latter scholars, profoundly immersed as they were in Old Testament sentiments, there was a fundamental discontinuity between ancient Near Eastern religions and morality and Hebrew belief in the absolute transcendence of God (Kuklick 1996: 185–87).

The focus of these scholars' attention (in excavation and exegesis) were the southern Levantine, Syrian, Egyptian, and Mesopotamian cities of the Bible. An influential interpretative school developed that argued that the shift to monotheism (Albright's "evolutionary mutation") took place *physically exterior to* and *morally in contrast to* the impious, despotic Oriental city.

In this Yahwist tradition, the clearest commandments of Judeo-Christian piety are etched onto the lenses that scholars held up to the continuing revolt of early Israelites against the iniquitous and impious cities of the Mediterranean coast. Israel was founded in that revolt. In the period of roughly 1800–1200 BC (and especially after c. 1550 BC), the southern Levant coast Bronze Age ended in a jumble of famine, political turmoil, and plague stories (Gottwald 1979; Matthews and Benjamin 1993: 3–5; Mazar 1990: 191–300). Yahwist scholars interpreted this chaos not (as increasingly do modern revisionist archaeologists of the southern Levant) as the result of climate change, outside interference by Hittites, Hurrians, Hyksos, and Egyptians, or of random local political adjustments; for the early biblical archaeologists, such as Albright, later Bronze Age urban culture collapsed as an expression of divine retribution.

Yahweh was not only signaling his extreme displeasure with Canaanite urban culture. He was also offering a covenant to those willing to leave the material security of a centralized urban existence for the spiritual fulfillment of a life on the margins, where the pious individual commended himself voluntarily into Yahweh's care. Serve in thrall the city despot or serve God in freedom.

Those who elected to pioneer this new relationship with Yahweh would sacrifice much. They would sacrifice the security of life behind thick city walls. They would sacrifice the surplus harvests and abundant pastures of the coastal plain. They would sacrifice the potential to work their way into the higher citadel or temple bureaucracies. But, this is precisely the Yahwist lesson: Only by sacrificing these apparent advantages would the pioneers of a new way of life and a new piety be in a position to become the chosen of an all-powerful God. The early city was the physical seat and the metaphor of all the surpluses, riches, and the iniquities that would be sacrificed by the move to the marginal existence in the Judean hills. Thus, by fleeing the material security of their former homes in the coastal cities, the early Israelites fled the values that have persistently characterized the Western representation of the primitive Oriental city. These same values gave rise to archaeologists' expectations of what they should expect to find at the earliest cities of the southern Levant, or Mesopotamia – or West Africa.

In Yahwist exegesis, the values of the urban dweller are the values of the unfree. Only those relatively few with kinship ties to the monarch were free; all others were the king's bondspersons. The king's power rested upon a centralized, surplus economy supporting the standing army needed both to protect the city from covetous neighbors and to maintain a degree of state terrorism within the city walls. The surplus economy depended upon the administratively directed labor of an unfree populace, be they *de jure* slaves or the *de facto* servile urban peasantry.

Despotic power reinforced the urban kings' distinctive form of authority that so enraged Yahweh. The unfree craftsmen and laborers built security in the form of the city wall. And they built monumental public structures, secular palaces and cultic temples that glorified the ideology of monarchy and idols of the god(s) from whom the monarch derived his authority to rule. They built the Citadel, preeminently.

Thus, according to the Yahwist interpretation, the state-based authority prevailing at the earliest cities was based upon the exclusive, personal relationship of the despot monarch with the city's god. This is Weber's (1968: 241–43) "anointed" right to rule at the dawn of *Gottesgnadentum* (divine right of kings). The right to head a brutal, exploitative social structure derives from what Weber labels "charismatic authority ... by virtue of which he [the monarch] is considered extraordinary and treated as endowed with supernatural, superhuman, or at least specifically exceptional powers or qualities" (1968: 241). The state (and all corollary institutions, such as the city – seat of the king) exists as an expression of the exclusive relationship between a god and a monarch. All relationships of power in the social structure are reckoned by distance from that essential node. Piety is equated with absolute submission, absolute loyalty to the monarch's person. Because of the exclusive, anointed relationship of monarch to his god, there can be no higher check to the power of the state. Power is celebrated in the absolute. Cults elaborate their affronts to the austere Yahwists' God – and the town way of life sinks "to extremely sordid depths of social degradation" (Albright 1953: 77).

Historical exegesis uses this representation of the city as its springboard to exhortation to piety. Dichotomous with primitive urban despotism and degradation are the Yahwists' free-will covenant with God and the harsh strictures of the pastoral life on the Judean hills. The city must appear before the Israelites can reject its temptations for true Covenantial Piety. Here, it is not our purpose to critique the history of this idea of piety as a personal covenant with God. Here, we are concerned only with how archaeologists' expectations for the kinds of artifacts and features that would serve as signatures for the earliest cities derived from this Yahwist moralizing upon impious urban life.

Interestingly, the Yahwists concentrate on the prophets' criticisms of urban life, but tend to ignore the theocratic urbanism central to the evolution of Judaism with David and Jerusalem (M. Maas, pers. comm. 1998). All scholars are selective of evidential pertinence!

The early city's role is cast mechanistically (R. McIntosh 1991: 203). A complex, surplus economy is made possible and is massaged by a hierarchical, centralized administration. The first demand of that administration is that everyone affirm their allegiance, vertically, to the hierarchically flowing font of authority. Everyone must accept the single-sourced, sacred-based charismatic nature of that authority. *Ex astra*! In time, and with evolving control of the economy and material/monumental props of ideology, the hierarchy becomes ever more elaborated, ever more rigid. Perceived threats to its authority are dealt with ever more brutality. Centralized state administration necessarily precedes or emerges simultaneously with urbanism.

In plan and in monumentality, the city is a unity focused on the Citadel complex: the temple – palatial physical seat of the monarch and his font of authority. Its wall is as much to keep in the subject population as to keep out threats from rival powers. Plan and monumentality reinforce state ideology in their implied statement that the social condition is eternal, inevitable, and without recourse. All are locked into their condition. Just as physical freedom is just a dream for most of the population, so too is piety expressed (under pain of torture, formal enslavement, or death) in terms of the relationship of the individual to monarchy. To flee this requires much more than slipping away from the city's walls. To flee, in Yahwist terms, means to have the ability to make the free-will choice to enter into a covenantal relationship of piety with Yahweh. The formerly oppressed now voluntarily marginalize themselves in order to eschew (Weber's) charismatic authority.

The city as dark moral exemplar and the underlying, unspoken values of Covenantial Piety are integral parts of the Western intellectual tradition. So integral are they, in fact, that we must acknowledge and analyze their influence if we are to understand the history of archaeological investigations of cities, whether in Africa or in the Near East. Few of the founding scholars who formulated our canon of historical sociology of the early town could have escaped the endless scriptural descriptions of bondage, despotic rule, and urban impiety that came out of Yahwist exegesis. But are *we* necessarily locked into this calculus for the originating conditions of ancient urbanism? Could there have been alternate routes from the undifferentiated village and hamlet landscape to the city?

Co-evolution: an alternative path

In the end, what is wrong with hierarchy and state-based urbanism? After all, there are broad *theoretical* advantages to hierarchy, whether in social or political systems, ecosystems, biogeography, or molecular systematics. In all these fields, hierarchy and its alternatives are being intensely scrutinized. Certain theoretical commonalities have presented themselves, such that scholars now talk of a pan-disciplinary arena of Self-Organization and Complexity studies. So we shift gears, briefly, as we now turn to tap into a larger, terribly exciting literature about dynamics of systems' organization. Cities are, lest we forget, dynamic and highly unpredictable systems, with multiple alternatives for pathways to evolve their complex organization.

Hierarchy has some undoubted organizational advantages over simpler systems. Our task here is to determine whether, in all – or even most – cases, those advantages are greater than those derived from alternative calculuses of complex organization. For the moment and for the sake of facilitating interdisciplinary thinking, hierarchy can be thought of as a form of symbiosis. The hierarchical structure (for example, fig. 1.4) is asymmetrical (vertically) to be sure, but represents a symbiotic system nonetheless. In any symbiotic system, individual elements or subsystems partially or wholly sacrifice autonomy. The leitmotif linking our *ex astra* discussion to that of the Yahwist Covenantial Piety is, of course, autonomy. Who has it and who can prevent whom from exercising it? Indeed, what is the coercive apparatus of a despotic state all about if not to perpetuate one particular iteration of that asymmetrical symbiosis? So why do hierarchies appear in the first place, if constituent elements must sacrifice autonomous action, their freedom to decide?

The overall advantage of participation in any superordinate system (that is, plural systems in which two or more strata are linked functionally, a system that has passed into complexity), of which hierarchy is just one and the heterarchies of the Middle Niger are another, is that the system itself enjoys a new order of autonomy in the environment (Jantsch 1982: 346). In other words, an agent lodged within the hierarchy can, in certain spheres, accomplish more than it could as a participant just in a simple system. And so, in the discipline of ecology, just to give one example, there is a vast literature and a history of debate at the conceptual level about the "hierarchical concept of ecosystems" (e.g., O'Neill *et al.* 1986). Key to this concept is tracing the trajectory and "dampening" of output flows (energy, information, etc.) between vertical tiers and between the different scalar manifestations of the hierarchy (e.g., O'Neill *et al.* 1986: figs. 5.1 and 5.3).

The problem comes when one deals with a so-called fused hierarchy, one in which the autonomy of the subsystems is virtually totally abandoned. This is precisely the kind of hierarchy expected by prehistorians dealing with the ideal state-based, citadel-embossed city. In fused hierarchies, the subsystems (each vertical tier or all horizontal components within each tier) are not free to respond to change with any degree of flexibility or autonomy. Nor are there mechanisms allowing them to provide messages to any linked partners (messages about the nature of new inputs or about past strategies that worked in analogous situations in the past) – beyond or outside the rigidly vertical information-flow channels of the hierarchy. Equally serious, as we will see, there is little motivation for any lower member to work for self-interest combined with superordinate interest. That can be the source of fundamental malaise within the system.

So depauperate of subsystem autonomy and motivation are these fused hierarchies that they often fail. Indeed, because fused hierarchy is a major part of our conception of the ancient civilizations, *collapse* has become a dominant part of the popular (and scholarly) conception of civilization trajectory (Allen *et al.* 2003; Tainter 1988). Say "Mayan civilization" or "Roman Empire" and the man-on-the-street is likely first to make the association " ... collapse of ... "! One of the curious facts of speaking to other scholars about the 1,600-plus-year steady success of Middle Niger urbanism is the initial wonder and mild envy at that record of sustainability. I hope that, by the end of this book, the reader will not find that record so astonishing!

Ironically, then, decades of research into the great world civilizations show that they are remarkably fragile (when one gets beyond the glitz and bombast, aspects that are conspicuously lacking at the Middle Niger cities!). They lack flexibility. And, if truly rigid in their despotism – that is,"fused"– they are prone to sudden, catastrophic, and cascading collapse because they lack redundancy of subsystems. In terms we used above, they are not "over-engineered."

Perhaps the appeal to scholars of writing about the collapse of fused-state hierarchies and the source of great difficulty in comprehending the origins of complex systems (be they polities, cities, or expansive social formations) is reductionist thinking. There is a habit of mind amongst archaeologists and historians of complex society – a classic "normal science" (shared with most of the classical sciences – after Thomas Kuhn 1962) – that is implied in my use above of the term *ex astra*. That habit of mind is reductionist: a belief that explanation of causation will follow naturally from a reduction of our vision of the complex world to a description of its most simple, basic elements (Prigogine and Allen 1982: 3). The habit of mind is deterministic: Focus on the actions, interests, and roles of the elites – the pacemakers (Johnson 2001: 14–16) – because the histories and the motivations of the other, subordinated elements of a fused hierarchy are fundamentally irrelevant. Again, we are mired in expectations about autonomy. And this habit of mind, therefore, has had a natural tendency to focus on the apex – to investigate in epigraphy, dirt archaeology, and in armchair musings the behavior, ideology, monumentality, and even the depravities of the elite.

Let me provide an example of reductionist thinking – and its failings – about urban origins from my own work. Not to skip ahead too far, but we shall see that one of the striking points of thinking about the origin of Jenne-jeno is that the site is multi-componential. There are some seventy separate now-abandoned settlement mounds comprising the city. Which came first? Was there a single founding settlement or, from the first moment, was clustering of different specialists the order of the day? Did one specialist occupation, such as iron working, play a privileged role in the regional settlement pattern?

From a very functionalist perspective I once toyed with three hypotheses about which settlement came first, displayed as a classical classification tool, cladograms (diagrams illustrating rates of origination and extinction of lineages) (R. McIntosh 2000a: fig. 1.3, p. 30) (fig. 1.5).

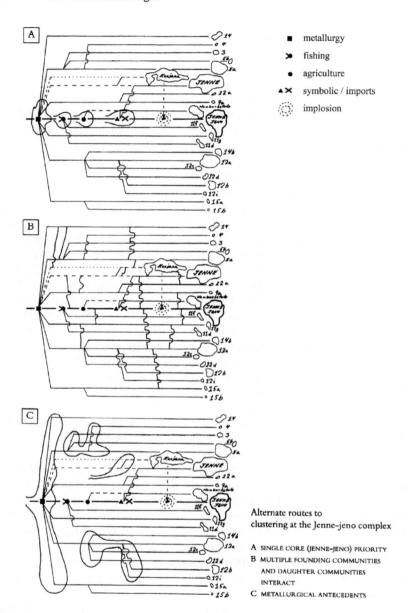

Fig. 1.5. Alternate routes to clustering at the Jenne-jeno Urban Complex: expressed as cladograms

Cladograms are brilliant tools to aid the researcher's parsing of the inter-locking history of a complex phenomena's many parts. The three alter-natives in figure 1.5 illustrate three entirely plausible starting conditions: (a) Jenne-jeno as the sole ancestor, with specialized daughter communities hiving off at various times; (b) multiple early specialist communities, each spawning off daughters; and (c) metallurgical antecedents: an initial iron-working community (most probably Jenne-jeno) fissions into daughter metallurgical communities, each of which is the focus of sub-clusters-within-the Urban Cluster. The complex cluster of urban satel-lites reduced in this form may alert us to the fact that there is a long history to the relationships amongst the constituent element. But the cladograms fail, miserably, to explain either the nature of the ongoing symbiosis between the parts or anything about why this complex form came into being. Nor do any of the cladograms even begin to direct archaeological investigation of why urbanism, clustered or otherwise, emerged as a different beast altogether out of a previous landscape of far simpler, less differentiated villages and hamlets. Explanation patently does not follow naturally from reduction.

In the end, and after centuries of painstaking digging at all elements of the Urban Cluster, it may be that any one of the three alternative cladograms in figure 1.5 will adequately describe the urban trajectory. Proceeding by reductionism, most assuredly, means that we will only get to that point by pure brute force. Despair not! Hope comes from archaeology's sister sciences.

Here we see the structural analogy of this failure to explain the origins of ancient urbanism with the failings of reductionism in physics (e.g., non-equilibrium thermodynamics) or chemistry or evolutionary biology or ecology or a host of other disciplines. "For many problems involving interacting populations ... additional global concepts are required" (Prigogine and Allen 1982: 3; see Kauffman 1995: 18). Out of a pluri-disciplinary frustration with the failing of reductionism in the face of the challenge of complexity has come an exploration of the organizational properties (and origins) of collectivities that *are more than the sum of their individual parts*; more than the sum of their parts *and* something quite unpredictable from any preceding form. A quick example: No mind experiment can imagine the linear, "logical" development of the first photosynthetic organism from preceding cellular structures or biochem-ical brews. Yet that radically new complex process did appear, apparently evolutionarily "abruptly," and apparently out of a dynamic of co-evolutionary "self-organization" of antecedent elements. Once functional, of course, the process of photosynthesis has put life on earth on an entirely unprecedented plateau of dynamism. A pluridisciplinary frustration with the failing of reductionism in the face of the challenge of complexity has led to an exploration of the organizational properties (and origins) of collectivities that are more than and are radically different from the sum of their individual parts. There is an acceptance that, etched in nature's many faces, there are coherent, self-organizing phenomena, such that the structure's essential properties are inherent to the collectivity and cannot be explained, understood, or inferred from a dissection of the whole into its individual elements (Prigogine and Allen 1982: 7, 21). In Stuart Kauffman's ringing words, "If, instead, core phenomena of the deepest importance do not depend on all the details, then we can hope to find beautiful and deep theories" (1995: 18).

What are the new insights about complexity to have wrung such poetry from a physicist? The growing literature may give it different labels emphasizing different aspects – Self-Organization, Dissipative Structures, Self-Transcendence, Emergent Structures, Morphogenesis. But here I wish to concentrate upon the co-evolutionary aspect of spontaneously self-organizing landscapes – which I will argue is at the core of understanding the emergence of ancient urbanism in the Middle Niger (and very probably many other places as well).

If we are dealing with evolutionary phenomena, whether chemical, physical, or social, for which the whole can be greater than the sum of the parts, then we need to be able to explain the appearance, spontaneously, of new forms and new dynamics. Co-evolution often lies at the heart of such spontaneous, often abrupt, appearances.

Co-evolution: Some of the most interesting thinking about emergent structures and self-organization has been done by evolutionary biologists and ecologists dealing with the co-speciation. Humans co-speciate with the best of them! Co-evolution can be defined as the co-related character changes, the reciprocal adaptations and reciprocal selection (that is, co-speciation) that take place out of the prolonged mutualistic symbiosis of two or more species in a bio-physical environment that is also transformed by their association (see Page 2003: 1–5). Evolutionary ecologists speak in terms of molecular systematics and of speciation systematics when describing the processes and history of co-speciation. I hope to show that urban archaeologists can speak in terms of "accommodation systematics" when describing the emergence of non-hierarchical urban landscapes (chapter 4). But that's getting ahead of the story. What is critical here is to introduce the idea that separate, self-identifying communities in the Middle Niger (we will call them corporations) and the bio-physical environment nurturing them "co-evolved" into a larger whole, a *self-organizing landscape*. Indeed, the process passed through several distinct phases of self-organized landscapes to reach its climax in a multi-satellite, multi-corporate Urban Complex by the middle of the first millennium AD.

Back to insights from our sister sciences: As we evolve, so do our competitors, our hosts, and our prey and to remain fit we must adapt to their adaptations (Kauffman 1995: 27). The environment is an agent of external stimuli to new adaptations (through climate change or tectonic deformations of landmass, or intrusions of newcomers, for example). But the environment is also transformed in complex ways by the new co-evolutionary dynamics, as new niches open for new explorations of possibilities (Kauffman 1995: 28; Jantsch 1982: 346). Enormous dynamism always involves a degree of destabilization and incomplete mutual adaptation.

And because of this co-evolutionary state of perpetual destabilization, leading (at first blush, paradoxically) to unprecedented order, the study of co-evolution falls squarely within the larger – and terribly exciting – field of self-organization dynamics. Life poised on the Edge of Chaos.

Different authors, reflecting their backgrounds and research interests, attempt to describe self-organization in different ways. Our friend Stuart Kauffman is perhaps the most eloquent:

> I suspect that the fate of all complex adaptive systems in the biosphere – from single cells to economies – is to evolve to a natural state between order and chaos, between structure and surprise. Here, at this poised state, small and large avalanches of co-evolutionary change propagate through the system as a consequence of small, best choices of the actors themselves, competing and cooperating to survive . . . we all do the best we can but will eventually be hustled offstage by some unanticipated consequences of our own best efforts. (Kauffman 1995: 15)

Kauffman evokes the destabilized (pregnant) state of high possibilism, the cascade of unintended consequences, and (useful for thinking about human systems) the agency and intentionality of the individual. One of the originators of the theory, Prigogine, speaks of system "bifurcation," or abrupt appearance of new paths not predicted by the former state(s) of the system, moments of instability when small fluctuations are not dampened, but may carry the system to a new (unprecedented) configuration – a new emergent state (Prigogine and Allen 1982: 4).

Here the emphasis is upon systems far from equilibrium which enter spontaneously into new and self-organized, self-transcendent states, in which the larger number of actors causes the larger number of auto-catalytic reactions – "typical of large, nonlinear systems operating far from thermodynamic equilibrium" (Prigogine and Allen 1982: 7). Here the emphasis is upon large, energy-positive systems showing definite non-linearity in their trajectories (what we will soon come to call "phase transitions"), trajectories that leap and bound from one implausible morphology or mode to another. And another *éminence grise*, Erich Jantsch, emphasizes self-transcendence. By this he means the unpredictable, often abrupt emergence of self-organizational dynamics that could not be anticipated from the morphology or from the state of the prior condition. Jantsch uses examples of pre-cellular evolution or of emerging eukaryotic (nucleated) cells (out of prokaryotic cells; giving way, eventually, to multicelluar organisms) as examples on the microevolutionary scale and of division of labor in human communities as an example on the macroevolutionary scale (1982: 345, 350). From pre-cellular, then to prokaryotic, then to eukaryotic, then to multicellular – an earlier tradition of reductionism in biology could give these discrete phases, or modes of organization, a name (and could link them in elegant cladograms), but could not even begin to explain the self-emergent dynamics leading from leap to leap to leap!

What is needed is a way for us to visualize all these aspects of self-organizing modes of discrete emergent behavior, as applied to the emerging urban landscape in places as remote (and analogous) as the Middle Niger, the Huanghe floodplain, and perhaps even Mesopotamia. We have a ready tool: the phase transform diagram. The need for these diagrams has arisen in disciplines such as climate physics and meteorology, where giants such as Edward Lorenz (1970, 1976, 1990) and H. Flohn (1975) began to think of non-linear, non-deterministic climate change in mathematical terms. What they call "intransitivity" has all the hallmarks of the autocatalytic, self-transcendent, emergent systems we have been talking about here. But they have taken the construction of phase (intransitivity) diagrams to a new level, one very useful indeed for our purposes here. Indeed, the phase transform diagram should apply to all complex phenomena in which linear change of one (or more) variable results – abruptly and "cascadingly" – in a non-linear change of state (or mode).

Let us look, just for a moment, at an idealized phase or intransitivity diagram, a very simplified form of the two-dimensional diagram that Lorenz might construct to describe interannual rainfall variability. (There is a method of connectedness to all this non-linear madness. In the following chapter we will see that the chaotic structure of climate variability on several temporal and spatial scales has to be a major consideration in the long, non-linear evolutionary path of Middle Niger social accommodations and cities.) The Lorenz phase transform diagram classically is set up so that, in two-dimensional Cartesian space, the X and the Y axes represent change in some variable of condition (progression through time, ΔT) or some mathematical function expressing change

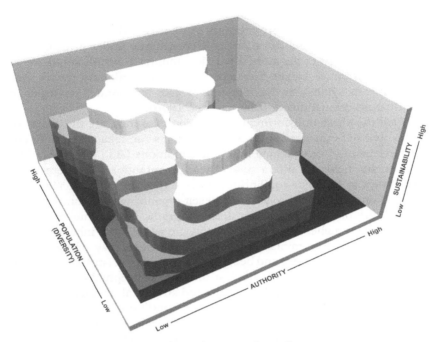

Fig. 1.6. Idealized Lorenz phase transform diagram

$(f(1), f(2), \ldots)$. Figure 1.6 takes this a step further into three-dimensionality. One dimension describes a scale of states of AUTHORITY: from low (ultimately, the chaos of nihilism!) to high (George Orwell's nightmare). The second dimension describes a composite condition of POPULATION (a function of density, absolute numbers and, critical to this argument, of complexity and interconnectedness of corporateness – the diversity that is the signature of the city). The Population range is from low (the always-fissioning small band) to high (the high-population, high-diversity urbanisms of an imperial Rome or a present-day Yoruba city). The final, vertical, axis is SUSTAINABILITY – and we shall spend considerable time in a later chapter defining this term. (Here, suffice it to call it a measure of the succcess of a community in maintaining its present transform mode.) Clearly seen in figure 1.6, the shifts across the field are in abrupt blocks, or phases, with relative plateaux ("normalcy," little movement about "normal conditions": see R. McIntosh *et al.* 2000a: 15). The real intrigue is at the abrupt frontiers, the shifts between phases. That is where all those astonishing cascades take place.

Note that the functions defining the axes of cartesian space are not "either-or," "yes or no" propositions. Authority is described as a spectrum, along which one can plot one's community under investigation. This is in contrast to the more usual dichotomous conception of authority, the dissipative versus hierarchical of neoevolutionary theory (see S. McIntosh 1999b), or the "network" versus "corporate" strategies of the dual-processual theory (Blanton *et al.* 1996).

What the phase transform diagram purports to show are the variety of paths that self-emergent, autocatalytic systems can take, given different "environments," or changing base-line conditions (ΔT, $f(1)$, etc.). The phases are fields of interacting ("near" symbiotic) subsystems that are always in far-from-equilibrium states – that shift episodically from one self-organizing state to yet another self-organizing configuration. The great value of these phase transform diagrams is that one can make the point that higher levels of complexity are possibilities inherent in the process, a non-deterministic upward spiral (which may under certain conditions reverse course and become more simple – or, in archaeological terms, collapse). One of the hardest things to conceptualize about self-organizing systems is that the outputs and structural interactions of one (simpler) phase can create the autocatalytic conditions leading to the next intransitivity shift "up" towards greater complexity (or, indeed, "down" towards collapse). This is the case as long as there is a considerable surplus of energy (and matter) entering the system.

Hence, we have seen that phase transitions are typical of self-organizing or dissipative (in an energy surplus: Prigogine and Allen 1982) systems where stability of the existing state of relations/interactions between subsystems comes to a bifurcation, to a breakdown frontier. There is often the amplification of small or random fluctuations (in human complex systems these can be called innovations or social deviations!). The phase shift is spontaneous (not deterministic and not directed by some supervising "pacemaker" agency) – that is, autocatalytic – and the turbulent motion, the cascading effect created in one domain, can propagate through many other aspects of the superordinate system. All authors echo Prigogine and Allen's (1982: 14) words that "life is sandwiched between the dangerous uniformity of equilibrium and the dangerous chaos of turbulence." I will argue that Middle Niger urbanism came into existence, spontaneously and "autocatalytically," at this edge of chaos – and that it provides a brilliant solution to the problem of proving innovative and flexible in the face of change, yet maintaining a long-term sustainability of complexity.

Here again I will risk getting a bit ahead of the story. Figure 1.7 shows four abstract states of interrelations among specialist groups such as early

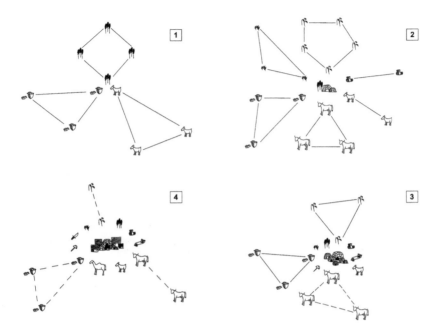

Fig. 1.7. Four transforms of Middle Niger clustering

farmers, fisherfolk, blacksmiths, etc. These co-evolutionary states (or trans-form modes) appear to have been taken by Middle Niger societies on their pathway from simple, autonomous movement and interactions of bands (specialized or otherwise) (not shown) to the fully urban "accommodation systematics" of many, many corporate groups living together in a large, densely populated agglomeration. Proceeding clockwise from the upper left in figure 1.7, one sees a step-wise increase in complexity, but there is no stadial imperative here, no inevitability that one phase will eventually lead to another. And the core integrative calculus, the melding of rules of authority with details of numbers of people, with corporate sense of belonging, is quite different in each case. Each of these stages will be explained, in turn, in chapters below. The point I wish to make here is that one can better visualize and understand the radically self-organizing dynamics at play if these same states are inserted in their appropriate positions on the three-dimensional Lorenz phase transition diagram of figure 1.6.

This brings us to figure 1.8a to 1.8d, an attempt to present graphically the various phase transforms and potential pathways that urbanism could have followed in the Middle Niger. Perhaps at some level this diagram can

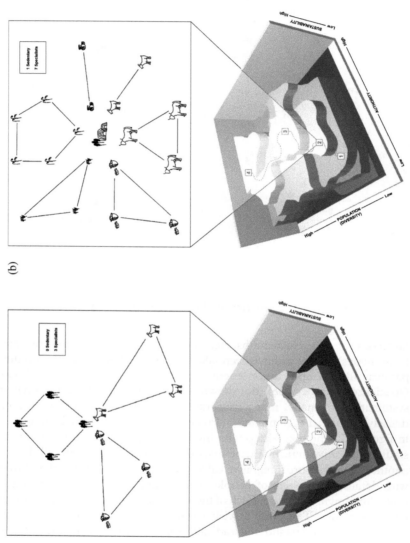

Fig. 1.8a–d Middle Niger urbanization dynamics represented as a phase transform diagram

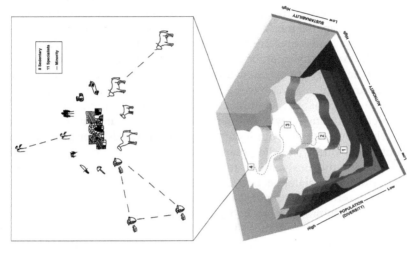

(c)

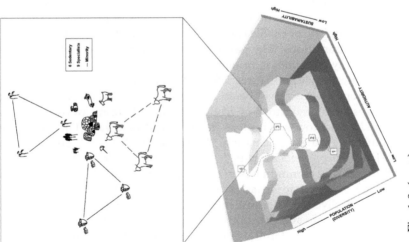

(d)

Fig. 1.8. (cont.)

illustrate the quite different urban pathways we see in the other major ancient civilizations, and some of these (China, Mesopotamia, Egypt) will be visited in this book's final chapter. In these figures, we see the classic phase transform diagram representation of well-differentiated, if hypothetical, spatial modes, each "phase" of which may be called a landscape. Some landscapes are "pacemaker"-driven (that is, on the "high" end of the Authority axis), because no one can deny that some pathways to the ancient city are precisely those described in an older urban theory, state-bound and *ex astra*. Yet this is the value of self-organization theory: It reminds us that any complex system, urbanism included, can also exhibit a higher intensity or frequency of phase shifts and an autocatalytic, entirely spontaneous evolutionary trajectory towards ever greater complexity due, simply, to the greater frequency of subsystem interactions and the (in the best cases) attendant increased rate of innovations. "Evolution is a dialogue between fluctuations leading to innovations and the deterministic response of the interacting species already existing in the ecosystem. Thus, an ecosystem rich in resources will tend to be occupied by a large number of specialized species, while a system with sparsely scattered resources will be filled with generalists" (Prigogine and Allen 1982: 30). This book, then, is an exploration of the deterministic and the "stimulative" aspects of the Middle Niger environment that came into play during the long, indigenous emergence of urbanism. Complementarily, the book looks at the phases of urban evolution, not in a deterministic or rigidly stadial fashion, but by focusing principally on the phase transitions. The pathway to urbanism here could have meandered in any direction, in principle.

One last element of figures 1.8a to 1.8d remains to be explained. And this, I hope to show, will be absolutely the key to following the unique (perhaps not?) trajectory of Middle Niger urbanism away from fused hierarchy and towards a more heterarchical pathway. The Population axis needs further explanation. "Population Diversity" could also be labeled "Corporate Diversity," which simply describes the number of self-identifying communities in proximity and available to interact. I am tempted to revert to an admittedly somewhat bloodless term such as "corporate diversity" because one individual can self-identify, depending on circumstances and situations, as a member of any number of corporate bodies (immediate family, lineage, secret society, religious sodality, occupational specialist or trade group, etc.). Further, the axis called "Authority" can be defined as a spectrum ranging between "coercion" (terminating in the extreme of absolute "fused") and, on the other end, "persuasion" (with, I suppose, the extreme of the chaos of absolute mistrust, radical unpersuadability!). Somewhere in the middle between persuasion and coercion lies an ill-defined realm that I label "contractual." Contractual, not in the modern legal sense, but in the sense of a society that functions on the authority of a deep-time election to subscribe to a few, often simple, core rules. This is a key point.

A major thrust of this book is the assertion that the peoples of the Middle Niger achieved their non-despotic urbanism and sustained that urbanism well over a millennium and a half, because of the Mande complex of core rules. Mande refers to a large group of West African peoples with affiliated languages who share a core of beliefs about causation and about the legitimate sources of authority and social rules (R. McIntosh1998: 305 and 2000b: 144). Most of the Middle Niger peoples are Mande; those such as the Songhai, Fulani, and Dogon who are not have assimilated many of the core concepts and social metaphors over the course of centuries or millennia of close Mande contact. With these rules, we have the classic self-organization conditions for amplifying (indeed, rampant) mutual enhancement instead of the dominating self-enhancement of, on the one hand, a classically acephalous situation and, on the other, of the fused hierarchy. These simple core rules are ways of looking at rightness and of causality in the world. In a very real sense, they allow the freedom of action as well as the ubiquitous systemic interconnectedness (Jantsch 1982: 347) of every urban dweller. And they allow the system to stay in that condition of creative non-equilibrium that allows (self-spontaneously) ever greater intensities of corporate diversity and corporate co-evolution to take place.

These rules provide the framework for accommodating ever-increasing densities of complex interactions and allow the increased flexibility (over-engineering, if you will) that allows the new organism to deal with change. For the Middle Niger peoples who embarked in the millennia before the appearance of their first cities on that pathway (potentially, those multiple pathways) that would lead there, the rules frame "responsibility": responsibility in the sense of a self-reflective image of Self-in-World (Jantsch 1982: 351) that would allow a whole series of self-transformative, self-organizing landscapes to emerge within the Middle Niger environment. Not irrelevant is the fact that these core Middle Niger rules precisely parallel the recent "solution" to the classic Tragedy of the Commons dilemma (Millinski et al. 2002). (We will take this issue up again in chapter 3.)

Tragedy of the Commons describes the breakdown of collective benefit derived from a common resource (the village Commons) if everybody is free to overuse that resource. Many Mande and those of us who work today amongst the Mande (and other ethnic groups) of the Middle Niger have always felt ill at ease with the pessimism of the Tragedy of the

Commons theoreticians, at least before the recent "solution," because of the pervasiveness (and persuasiveness) of these simple (and, I and others have argued – R. McIntosh 2000b; McNaughton 1988 and 1991 – core) rules. Now we find that the "solution" to the Tragedy of the Commons is as simple as "reputation," the indirect template for reciprocity, the "give and you shall receive," that can sustain a high level of cooperation and, indeed, can generate new canons of reciprocity. As summarized by Millinski *et al.* (2002: 426), "the Tragedy of the Commons was no longer a tragedy, instead the commons became productive and could be harvested"! Yet, when this reputation was abused and indirect reciprocity not sustained in practice, then "contributions to the public good drop quickly to zero." Sounds a lot like Life at the Edge of Chaos to me!

In the end, the idea of the self-organizing landscape provides many of the essential elements of emerging urbanism along the Middle Niger. The pathway is anything but deterministic or inevitable, but neither is it derived (as earlier Africanist archaeologists pessimistically assumed) from outside sources (the failed Arab Stimulus thesis: see R. McIntosh and S. McIntosh 1988). To date, the Middle Niger evidence frustrates our academic analytical tendency to look for "pacemakers" (top-down, hierarchically embedded, decision makers, such as Weber's charismatic prince) (Johnson 2001: 14–16), working with powerful and coercive command structures. Instead, let us take it on faith that cities, like other complex, emergent systems, might emerge spontaneously out of simpler, often apparently chaotic landscapes. What is needed is a trajectory in which a few repeating patterns and a few simple core rules of interaction come together.

The city emerges as a pattern-amplifying machine: Here we have higher densities of patterns of behavior and movement and individuals' decision making that feed back, ever altering the participants' subsequent behavior and decisions. In this landscape of stability and change, individuals are encouraged in their corporate capacity for open-ended learning – as long as the many subscribe (not absolutely and rigidly, but "on the whole") to a constellation of a relatively few simple rules. Following these rules over time, there emerge distinct macrobehaviors with specific shape and pattern – a coherent phase personality that self-organizes out of many individual decisions and many local interactions. Co-evolution.

Archaeologists of distant periods and of non-literate peoples often lament their lack of information on the personal motivations, on the larger group intentionalities of the past. Here, however, we have a solution. Each solo actor makes decisions and acts based on his or her own assessment of the changing conditions of existence. These decisions are made in terms of culturally generated schemata (R. McIntosh *et al.*

2000b: 27–28, and *passim*), to be sure. But the beauty of thinking about the freedom and the greater corporate integration made possible by the heterarchical city is that we have a role for the individual. That individual functions as a member – potentially – of multiple corporate groups to participate in the emergence of a highly flexible, highly "over-engineered" (or redundant) self-organized landscape. This urban landscape along the Middle Niger, demonstrably, was sustained over a millennium and a half (and arguably is still thriving at a shifted phase!).

There is no need for the king, the pacemakers, the gatekeepers, or any of the other appurtenances of the state-based town. The City without Citadel can emerge by itself.

Finally, to bring the discussion back to the self-organizing genesis of Middle Niger cities, what is so distinctive, so useful for imagining evolutionary dynamics, about phase transform diagrams? Why the emphasis upon the abrupt transitions (cliffs) between the discrete states (plateaux) of figure 1.6 and the iterations of figure 1.8 – a standard representation of how a linear increase in energy in any self-organizing system can produce a non-linear change? And why the emphasis on the seemingly trivial solution "reputation" (that is, paying attention to how one's acts are perceived by one's neighbors, in a socially reinforced web of beliefs about the "common weal") to the Tragedy of the Commons? Because melded together, all of these help to resolve a common paradox of emergent, co-evolutionary behavior that is, simultaneously, the paradox of urbanism along the Middle Niger.

For Steven Johnson, this paradox is shared by all emergent systems with the capacity to "develop ever more baroque bodies out of impossibly simple beginnings" (2001: 14). These emergent systems may be water molecules coalescing into ice, or the unaccountable appearance of northern Italian late medieval cities out of a radically simpler anterior landscape. If, in any self-organizing system, individual agents (H_2O or swarming ants or Lombards) "pay attention to their immediate neighbors rather than wait for orders from above" ... PARADOXICALLY ... "they think locally *and* act locally, but their collective action produces global behavior" (Johnson 2001: 74, see 79). Incidentally, this is a better way to think about heterarchy, from the inside out, than by always comparing it to hierarchy. Heterarchies are preeminently those complex systems that can evolve out of simpler forms because their constituent agents share a few simple rules about how to learn from and provide information to their neighbors. In heterarchies, individuals are acutely attuned to the states of surrounding elements and surrounding environmental inputs (bio-physical and social), rather than passively awaiting directions from the pacemaker. For Johnson, the resolution of the paradox takes place in "neighborhoods"

(2001: 86–87) (what we will call cityscapes) – the coherent albeit decentralized arena where neighbors, working together and abiding by a few simple rules, can achieve horizontal specialization of tasks within a complexifying larger context.

So, the neighborhood, or urban landscape, is a place abuzz with information.

But cities have a latent purpose as well: to function as information storage and retrieval devices. Cities were creating user-friendly interfaces thousands of years before anyone even dreamed of digital computers. Cities bring minds together and put them into coherent slots. Cobblers gather near other cobblers, and button makers near other button makers. Ideas and goods flow readily within these clusters, leading to productive cross-pollination, ensuring that good ideas don't die out in rural isolation. (Johnson 2001: 108)

In other words, cities function as "emergent intelligence" – with the unorganized but efficient ability to recognize, store, access, and process (into innovations) information, be that information patterns in human behavior or changes to the physical world. The argument of this book is that the discrete-state progression of the Middle Niger cityscape was a progression driven by a linear increase in information about landscape variability (expressed as a non-linear, phase transformation in the style of settlement). The non-linear trajectory of heterarchical complexity in the Middle Niger is shown in figure 1.7: From the seasonal gathering place for subsistence specialists in the Late Stone Age, to the first sedentary agglomeration of farmers, fisherfolk, potters, and blacksmiths of the early Iron Age, and finally to the full Middle Niger Urban Complex of corporate satellites.

The Middle Niger cities evolved a distinctive signature of multiple satellites in motion around each other – but not particularly in search of a gravitational master body (a pacemaker, a citadel). Not from the stars, but planets unto themselves! And the gravitational attraction of the planetary cluster itself draws in ever more planets in ever more diversity. Surprisingly (but perhaps not) this feat of self-organization into the urban landscape takes place in a physical landscape of stress and surprise (not always pleasant, but always ripe with risk and opportunity). If, as I argue above, cities are devices for acquiring and processing environmental information, then we must now turn to the nature of those surprises the Middle Niger always has thrown at its human complement. In this we are aided enormously by a new and radically different analytical lens to train upon the local geomorphology, Niger River paleohydrology, resource base, and climate change – Historical Ecology.

2 Transformed landscapes

Historical Ecology

The Middle Niger is a landscape of mystery folded upon mystery – mysterious, that is, for those approaching its study from a purely functional, deterministic, and reductionist perspective. The mystery lies in the other, the non-material, the *perceived* dimensions of the landscape that allowed the peoples of the Middle Niger to create a highly successful, highly flexible and sustained urban field out of a particularly stressful and surprise-ridden natural environment. It is precisely situations such as the long-term complex environmental dynamism – some have called it "chaos" – of the Middle Niger that has recently led to the abandonment by historical geographers and geo-archaeologists of traditional Human Ecology.

Human Ecology (and its counterpart in anthropology, Cultural Ecology), as the study of human response to environmental stimuli, served us well for many decades. However, as practiced customarily, the approach had an implied assumption of humans reacting mechanistically to change going on about them, an assumption that placed humans and their communities in far too passive a role (Crumley 1998: xi–xii). An eminent climatologist (Shukla 1995: 44) comments despairingly on Middle Niger climate (and Sahelian climate writ large), "there is no other region on the globe of this size for which spatially and seasonally averaged climatic anomalies have shown such persistence." Given such a reality of unpredictability, imagine the difficulty human geographers, historians, and prehistorians have had conceptualizing the kinds and subtleties of social strategies that would allow these communities *passively* to respond to climate change! Historical Ecology (Balée 1998a; Crumley 1994; R. McIntosh *et al.* 2000b), the recent replacement of traditional Human Ecology, goes to the very heart of two recent revelations about virtually all human landscapes, the Middle Niger certainly not excluded:

(1) As long as there have been modern humans (and perhaps long before), the bio-physical geographies they occupied have been thoroughly and intelligently transformed by human action. Even eminent

paleoclimatologists have begun to contemplate the radical idea of an "anthropogenic era" to climate change beginning, not 150 years ago with the Industrial Revolution, but thousands of years ago (Ruddiman 2003). There are no "pristine" landscapes.

(2) The deep-time histories of transformed landscapes cannot be understood without an appreciation of how humans, individually and as communities, acted according to their culturally conditioned perceptions of the bio-physical world and of causation in that world (R. McIntosh et al. 2000b).

We can make this last argument, one that is absolutely key to understanding why self-organization is a reasonable description of the Middle Niger process of urbanization, more immediate by an example. Let us consider a simple east–west transect through two of the six Middle Niger basins (the Upper Delta and the Méma) and extend that about 65 kilometers further to the west. Let us look first at this hydrology at three scales (figs. 2.1a, 2.1b, and 2.1c). At the scale inclusive of West Africa (fig. 2.1a), not surprisingly, the options for human occupation would appear to be stark. The rivers Niger and Senegal frame, to southeast and southwest respectively, a vast Saharan geo-synclinal basin devoid of through-flowing surface water. Our transect tickles the southern part of that basin.

At a scale comprising the Western Sudan (fig. 2.1b), we can appreciate a far denser, far older superimposed web of paleohydrology (now dry rivers, old seasonal stream channels, paleolakes and seasonal pans or playas) considerably complicating the scene. At this scale, one could still be forgiven for supposing that a creeping, progressive drying of the Sahara might be the primal causative factor for human exploitation.

Now consider how complicated things become when one looks at a more detailed scale (fig.2.1c) (still a scale too gross for most human geographies). Using this map we can roughly approximate the kinds and chronologies of settlements found, during real-time archaeological surveys, organized by the three coherent hydrological unities depicted on this last figure. Beginning to the far east–southeast (in the Jenne vicinity, the Upper Delta and the Dia vicinity of the Macina) one finds many abandoned classic Iron Age (late first millennium BC and first millennium AD) sites. In contrast, here one finds fewer but sizable historical and present-day settlements (often to an order of magnitude fewer: R. McIntosh 1983: 195–96), and not one Late Stone Age (pre–mid-first millennium BC) occurrence (S. McIntosh and R. McIntosh 1980, II). To the west, still within the Middle Niger, but representing one of the so-called "dead" basins (the hydrologically senescent Méma) one finds some modern settlements. These are, however, tiny and highly atrophied, certainly compared to present-day Upper Delta towns and villages. In contrast to the Jenne region, however, the Méma can boast Iron Age cities

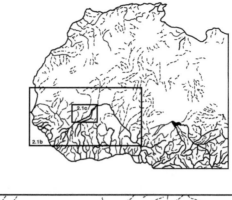

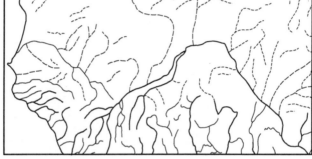

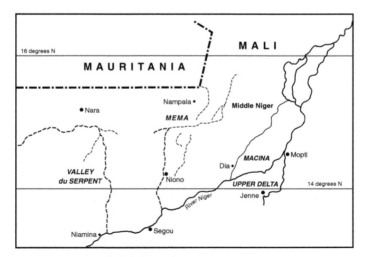

a. Pan-West-African representation of the continent's hydrology

Fig. 2.1a–c Three scales of Middle Niger and Vallée du Serpent hydrology

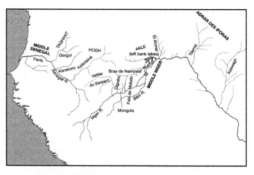

b. Western Sudanese hydrology and paleochannels

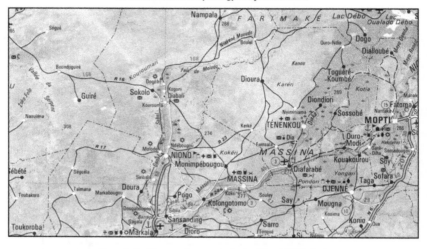

c. Longitudinal traverse from approximates 16 to 14° N latitude

Fig. 2.1. (cont.)

of vast number and size and an equally impressive network of clustered Late Stone Age hamlets and villages (MacDonald 1994; Togola 1993). We will speak at length of this critical period and critical region below (chapter 3).

But then consider the Vallée du Serpent at the western margin of the Middle Niger. Because this paleovalley is on higher ground to the west of the Niger's floodplain, it is, strictly speaking, just outside our area of concern. However, the Vallée du Serpent rests well within the trade and migration corridor feeding the Middle Niger with subsistence goods, exotics, and excess populations (MacDonald and Allsworth-Jones 1994). The Vallée du Serpent is just one of many north–south-trending paleochannels scarring the pristine face of our desiccated geo-syncline of figure 2.1a. Where survey has been done on banks of other West Africa paleochannels, all are rich in Late Stone Age and early Iron Age settlement. Archaeologists swoon with the embarrassment of riches of, for example, the Gorgol (Baro *et al.* 1987) and Kolimbiné trending north from the Senegal River, the Baoulé west of the Middle Niger (Huysecom 1990), the El-Ahmar and other Azawad channels north of Timbuktu (R. McIntosh and S. McIntosh 1993; S. McIntosh and R. McIntosh 1986a), and the Azawagh of Niger (Bernus *et al.* 1999; Paris *et al.* 1993). But not the Vallée du Serpent!

Curiously, and from a purely functional perspective inexplicably, in the Vallée du Serpent one finds an abundance of very early "macrolithic" sites (dated by MacDonald and Allsworth-Jones [1994: 76–77] to the mid-Holocene of c. 7000–4000 BC) and a smattering of nineteenth-century pottery scatters (perhaps dating to the brief passage through the valley of Tukulor invaders, originally from the Middle Senegal Valley, in 1862?). And, eerily enough, one finds nothing between. Not the expected thick clusters of Late Stone Age sites; not the Iron Age villages or temporary pastoral sites so common at other Western Sudanese paleochannels of exactly the same latitude, the same rainfall, and with the same mineral, plant, and animal resources.

Something anomalously else appears to be going on. Rather a mystery. There will clearly have to be a dedicated research project to examine this and other, more mundane and functional explanations. However, it is highly intriguing that, to most Mande Malians, the Vallée du Serpent is considered to be the manifestation on the ground of a subterranean pathway taken by the great snake, Bida, on his transverse from Wagadu southwards to the Niger River (R. McIntosh 1998: 144–45). Wagadu (or Ghana) was the location of one of West Africa's earliest consolidated "empires" (Dieterlen and Sylla 1992; Levtzion *et al.* forthcoming). Bida was the horrendous snake that consumed his annual virgin in tribute, but who, when sated, was the key to the wealth and stability of the Ghana empire. When asked why the Vallée du Serpent should have been devoid of settlement, even recently and long after the purported killing of Bida, Malians look at the questioner pityingly: Who in their right mind would live just above the passageway of so horrible a beast?

And the problem for the archaeologist, then, is: Did this "causative" perception of the Vallée du Serpent suffice to prevent all occupation of the banks of this potentially and otherwise highly desirable riverine landscape? Does one find settlements of period X, Y, and Z? ... Presence or absence? Verification at this level is purely empirical. If avoided, can we make the leap and say, therefore, that this culturally conditioned prohibition reached way back into the mid-Holocene? How, empirically, can the archaeologist prove this explanation? And what proof would be valid at a remove of several millennia, without the investigator making just so many assumptions of unchanging mental constructs, timelessness, and uniformitarianism?

Despite these issues of ultimate verifiability of our interpretations ("warrants of the truth," in the coinage of philosophers of science), this is a perfect example of why prehistorians and human geographers have found Historical Ecology so appealing. The external realities of the objective world (precipitation, hydrology, shifting landforms such as levees or dunes, and so on) are, of course, an ever-present source of change. However, just as "real" are the changing perceptions of landscape. These perceptions refer in part, of course, to the character and availability, on the ground, of exploitable resources. However, they are much more than only these, for they echo deeper socially embedded ideas about causation (see Kohler and Gumerman 2000: 3). These functional perceptions will change, for example, as new plants and animals are domesticated or are introduced from afar, new uses or markets are found for minerals or exotics, or new specialists invent new art or manufacturing processes. We must not forget that every bit as important and "real" are perceptions of the occult or the supernatural (including formal religious) reasons for why things are the way they are. These three levels of causation – "objective" bio-physical reality; human exploitation strategies and perceived motivations; and the supernatural, religious, and other forms of "para-scientific" modes of explanation – should be welded together seamlessly in Historical Ecology.

Historical Ecology has been described as the "metalanguage" and framework for mutual debate amongst all the disciplines that deal with these three levels of causation (Balée 1998b: 1). In principle, this encourages a radically new undertaking to understand humans' interaction with and active effect upon the bio-physical environment, an investigation that can come from "natural" (bio-physical) scientists and "historical" scientists (social scientists, evolutionary ecologists, and historians) listening to one another. Historical Ecology encompasses the complex recursive (that is, giving and taking, back and forth) relationship between humans (individuals, their communities, and their cultures) and the biosphere. Given significant consideration are the historical events that reveal this dialectical nature of human action upon and perception of the environment (Balée 1998a: 13–14; see also Biersack 1999; Crumley 1994; Ingold 2000). At its core are several essential premises (from Balée 1998a: 14), three of which we will consider postulates to be examined "evolutionarily" in this book, using the case of emerging Middle Niger urbanism. These three are absolutely basic to understanding how the physical instabilities of the Middle Niger landscape, perceived as sources of stress and opportunity, and as requirements for action, encouraged over perhaps millennia the self-organization of communities of corporate specialists into progressively more complex congeries – with true, non-hierarchical urbanism being one of the results:

1. Much, if not all, of the non-human biosphere has been affected by human activity.
2. Human activity does not necessarily lead to degradation of the non-human biosphere and to the extinction of species, nor does it necessarily create a more habitable biosphere for humans and other life forms by increasing the abundance and species diversity of these organisms.
3. Human communities and cultures together with the landscapes and regions with which they interact over time must be understood as total phenomena. Total landscape phenomena require investigations of causation to proceed at multiple scales of analysis (representing geomorphological scales, tropic levels, scales of perception, etc.).

Clearly, the last premise recalls the point made in the preceding chapter, namely that reductionism and deterministic explanations cannot even begin to unravel the complex and emergent behaviors that we call self-organization – Middle Niger urbanism included. Clearly, Balée's first premise recalls the shift, both in archaeology and in the larger environmental movement, from the idealistic position that pristine landscapes predominated in much of the world until the global imposition of Western imperialism and market capitalism. The corollary of this earlier position has, for the longest time, been that the goal of environmental protection and health should be the restoration of these pristine landscapes. Now scholars from a multitude of disciplines have come to the realization that the long-term, deep-time footprint of humankind has been profound and ineluctable (Evans 2003; Redman 1999; Van der Leeuw and Redman 2002). Some historians and prehistorians are somewhat aggressive in their characterization of how radically regional landscapes have been transformed (and this argument is deeply implicated in the contemporary politics of indigenous peoples' rights) (Mann 2002; Roosevelt 1998). The urban hinterlands of the Middle Niger were no less thoroughly transformed, albeit apparently not by the large-scale corvée work projects that some have considered a signature of pre-industrial urbanism on an arid-lands floodplain.

This last point is critical to understanding the articulation of the Middle Niger landscape – varied and with uses shifting year by year – with the unusual form of clustered urbanism described in this book. S. McIntosh (1999b: 73–74, 77) makes the argument for a legacy, reaching back millennia, of nucleation (growth ending in the true town) without a pattern of agricultural intensification, predicated upon massed-labor earth modification projects, that forms the expectation of much archaeological literature about the rise of civilization. She makes the argument that production can be maximized just as effectively by "diversification within specialization," that is by the encouragement of specialized subsistence niches linked by exchange and interdependence. As corollaries and, again, against expectation, monocropping of domesticated crops is resisted (indeed, wild plants and animals form a major part of the diet) and farmers drift over a variety of landforms or floodplain soils – electing "low inputs to labor across a diversified portfolio of agricultural investments" (S. McIntosh 1999b: 74).

In a very real sense, then, the anthropogenic landscape produced after millennia of this strategy is one of great subtlety in the face of the enormous unpredictability of climate and environment. But that subtlety is contained within a paradox that is entirely consistent with the new focus of Historical Ecology: "The paradox is the maintenance of diversity, involving continued heavy reliance on wild plant and animal resources, despite the growth of subsistence specialization. There is no increase in commitment to domestic rice over wild cereals; nor is there evidence for increasing labor-intensive technologies for rice farming ... or for hydraulic interventions of any magnitude" (S. McIntosh 1999b: 74). Thus, the strategy of "diversification within specialization" apparently does not lead to degradation of the non-human biosphere, nor to the extinction of species, but it emphatically does create a more habitable biosphere for humans. This premise of historical ecology is the cornerstone of this book's argument for sustainability.

It is really this, the second of Balée's premises, that bridges our study in this chapter of the Middle Niger biosphere to the more theoretical understanding of self-organizing phenomena of the previous chapter. Human action transforms the landscape. Such action does not necessarily degrade it, nor does it necessarily augment it (in terms of biomass production, nutritional status, species diversity, etc.). Although, in the case of the Middle Niger cities, I think one can argue more for the latter (improvement without massive, hierarchically organized public works) than for the former (although the human hand cannot be ignored in the desertification at the floodplain's Saharan margins). Here, preeminently, is where the importance of scale comes into play.

This book is about the emergent organization of smaller, more homogeneous communities into the massive ancient cities of the Middle Niger. The process to be described is the end of a long path of self-organization upon and within a transformed landscape. That transformation takes place at several scales. Therefore, we have to study the circumstances and the internal evolutions of environment and of communities at different scales. At times, at a local (village) scale, overgrazing, over-cultivation and the other consequences of population growth cause "micro-desertification" that can be clearly seen even on satellite imagery of the dry basins of the Middle Niger (fig. 2.2). At a regional scale, human reduction of ground cover will surely have contributed to the high sediment yield of Middle Niger rivers during the rainy seasons of drought periods. This sediment load contributed not a little to the strangulation of distributary channels, to the eventual simplification of the hydrological net in this highly anastomosing floodplain (Jacobberger 1988).

Yet, at these and at other scales, the high population densities, large settlements, exaggerated occupational specializations, and efflorescence of industrial activities characterizing Middle Niger urbanism did not lead to a deterioration of the floodplain. The well-known siltation and salta-tion crises of the Mesopotamian alluvium (Pollock 1999: 37–38; T. J. Wilkinson 2003: 93, 98) were not reproduced here. Locally, high yields of rice were obtained by extensive cultivation practices that had no need for the drafts of corvée, coerced labor, that so characterize our perception of other ancient civilizations. The point to be made is that Historical Ecology encourages a multi-scalar examination of human–environment interactions. The multiple scales can be spatial, as in the examples above. Or, they may be temporal. And we need to consider different scales of human manipulation, equally. As we will see, the climate of the Middle Niger has an unmistakable role in the emergence of urbanism and special-ization, but the complex and clever human responses to climate change can only be understood by looking at variability along several temporal scales (season variability, interannual, interdecadal, century ...). The principal characteristics of evolution that we wish to plot are resilience (the ability of a system to maintain its structure in the face of disturbance and to absorb and utilize change) and sustainability (capacity to continue a desired condition). That being the case, we must be prepared to con-sider the Historical Ecology of the Middle Niger at various temporal and spatial scales. The scale of demographics and complexity increased along the path from mobile hunting and gathering to full urbanism. Scale, then is one multidimensional axis of any Historical Ecology.

A second axis, one that must similarly be examined at several focal points, is variability. Variability can be defined in three dimensions (R. McIntosh *et al.* 2000a: 15–16). The first dimension is *variation*, or changes in the status of a system (climate, settlement, political organization) that fall within a range that is tolerable, without requiring major adjustments in adaptation or causing surprise or risk. Take a system right up to the

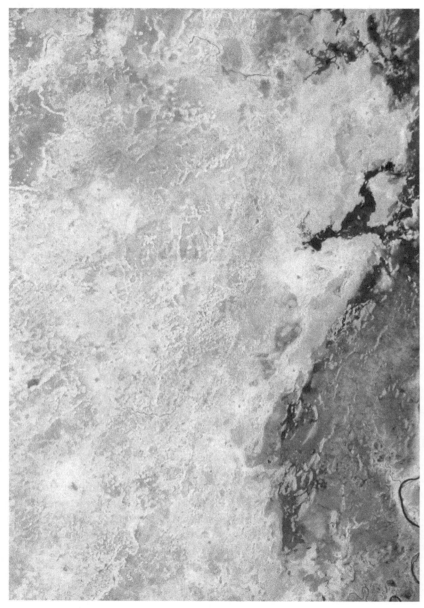

Fig. 2.2. High albedo villages at Méma–Macina border

edge of order and chaos, so beloved of complexity and self-organization theorists, palpably beyond the tolerable range of variation, and one has the potential for phase transitions. The second aspect of variability is *shape of variability*, or variability modeled geometrically or statistically as an aid to abstracting patterns from observations. What is urbanism, in all its global richness and variations, after all, but a concept useful to contrast with a developmentally pre-urban condition of landscape and with the less complex, less demographically excited village existence? And the last aspect of variability is *cumulative deviations*, a statistical method for measuring long-term trends, a measurement of a time series that is sensitive both to accumulated quantities and to changes in trend. When we speak of mode-shifts (or phase transforms) in the trajectory of the self-organizing Middle Niger landscape, we make an observation through the lens of cumulative deviations and their consequences.

But it is landscape, the last and most important dimension of Historical Ecology, that allows natural scientists and historical scientists to speak with one another about common processes. There has been an explosion, not just figurative, but very literally, in archaeological writing about landscape. This is not surprising, given the coming together of the many trends that has led to Historical Ecology. Much of the recent literature deals with the power of symbolic representations of landscape (e.g. Tilley 1994). In this book, I will emphasize several aspects of landscape, not least of which is the idea that the bio-physical and the human world is a nested, hierarchical ecosystem.

Landscape comprises all physical, biological, and cultural phenomena interacting within a region. Many aspects of the physical landscape will manifest themselves as physical residues of antecedent landscapes – a kind of cumulative deviation within a local developmental trajectory. These residues, emphatically, include evidence of human action upon the physical environment. "Hence, biophysical scientists (geomorphologists, paleobotanists, etc.) and historical scientists (archaeologists, paleoethnobotanists, etc.) can study traces of interactions at different scales among the elements of landscape ... human institutions and behaviors (which can themselves be hierarchically organized) are nested within the biophysical. The human is explicitly not superimposed on the biophysical" (R. McIntosh *et al.* 2000b: 15).

Knapp and Ashmore (1999: 10–13) speak of landscapes as constructed (the physical world transformed by human action as people project ideas and emotions onto the world), conceptualized (natural and constructed forms interpreted given meaning through localized social practices and experience), and ideational (mental constructs – the shared mental image and the eliciting of some spiritual value or ideal from the landscape). In this construction, they are reflecting a burst of archaeological enthusiasm about the newly appreciated role of *perception* of causation in the world as a prime engine in the production of action upon the world. After all, all archaeologists have ever done is to investigate and identify the fragmentary record of past human action upon the world, as those actors perceived the world. Landscapes, not least of which is the Middle Niger from the very beginning of our story here, are all cultural landscapes. Cultural landscapes reveal to the aware all the signs of the cognitive organization of environmental elements, aligned according to human functions of memory (patterned, routinized, inter-generationally transmitted memory that might be called Social Memory), of patterns of behavior, of compressed mental models of regularities that human communities employ in their conceptualization of interacting (causal) physical and social agencies. The study of landscape begins by unpacking interactions at a variety of scales. The concept of landscape derives from the idea of co-evolutionary interaction (all elements mutually influencing each other over time); the great surprise is just how often this co-evolutionary landscape throws up its own emergent, transcendent forms. Humans are not epiphenomenal to all this. We are not standing on the fringes, waiting to be washed away by physical forces beyond our control, beyond our ken. We create a socially constructed world, and the landscape is the stage upon which we strut.

Time to introduce the Middle Niger bio-physical landscape: the physical features of its six basins, the principal external agency of change (its intense, exciting, ever-exuberant climate). The chapter ends on a methodological note, with the archaeologist's tool for the reconstruction of how an evolving model of landscape might have emerged at various times (geokistics).

Mesopotamia, with a difference

The Middle Niger civilization, like that of Mesopotamia or Pharaonic Egypt, was a gift of an arid-lands river. The Middle Niger has often been compared to Mesopotamia – but with a significant difference. There is an even more striking difference between the Niger's inland floodplain and that of the Nile. It is these differences that make the concept of the self-organizing landscape so compelling a way to think about the emergence of cities here. We will track two key and intertwined landscape traits that provide the external dynamics that set the initial and continuing conditions for the peoples of the Middle Niger's historically peculiar accommodation systematics. These were: (1) a wealth of resources, but always highly changeable and set in fluid configurations; lodged in (2) an almost chaotic matrix of the bio-physical. For phenomena on the "edge of

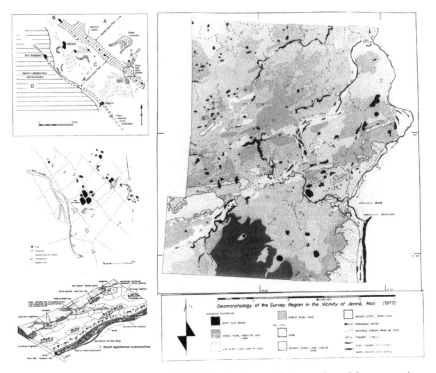

Fig. 2.3. Contrasted Middle Niger (Upper Delta), southern Mesopotamian, and Upper Nile floodplains

chaos," for all emergent phenomena, this is the almost perfect context for self-organization dynamics, as defined in chapter 1. Let us turn now to the differences (not to ignore the undoubted similarities) with the Nile and Tigris/Euphrates and to the individual personalities of the six basins that comprise the Middle Niger.

Figure 2.3 contrasts the complexity of a typical, if idealized, sector of the Mesopotamian (Sumerian, southern), Nile (Upper), and southern, live Middle Niger floodplains. The Middle Niger is expansive, like Mesopotamia and unlike the constricted Nile Valley. The Nile is more similar in the regularity of its constituent landforms to another West African floodplain that will occasionally be employed here for comparison, the Middle Senegal Valley (R. McIntosh *et al.* forthcoming). The Euphrates and the Tigris, at full flood, spread out over a far wider back-swamp than the 8–12-kilometer Nile Valley.

In Mesopotamia, however, the organization of the floodplain is organizationally rather simple (see T.J. Wilkinson 2003: 45–99). Strong single anastomosing channels, with only a moderate tendency to meander, are separated by significant sandy levees from broad backswamps acting as vast decantation basins with a predictable graduation from sandy silts to clays as one travels away from the rivers. This simplicity may have facilitated the organization of labor, whether household based (the *oikos* of Pollock 1999), or despotic and on a large scale. The great complexity of the Middle Niger (where water and wind have struggled, with uneven success, in each of the six basins) could not contrast more sharply.

Each Middle Niger basin has a distinctive landform personality, a distinctive seasonal rhythm to its hydrology and soil moisture. Each of the six Middle Niger basins is a mosaic of landforms, some sculpted by wind, some deposited by water, all modified subtly or grossly by the hand of man (fig. 2.4). Each element of the mosaic has a highly variable utility for each of the several subsistence groups occupying the Middle Niger (see Gallais 1967 and 1984; R. McIntosh 1998: 34–130). From these groups' individual perspectives, these landforms perform in often dramatically different ways from one year to the next, one season to the next. To recall Knapp and Ashmore's (1999) "ideational" landscape – each Middle Niger ethnicity has its own and distinct (and is subtly self-identified with) mental image of the same physical domain. This reflects the enormous range of variability in the floodplain regime (annual flood characteristics: height, length of the flood, date of the waters' arrival, nature and intensity of the preceding rains, etc.), of precipitation over the Middle Niger, and even of temperature and of surface winds.

Whereas some might characterize the underlying West African Sahelian climate as "chaotic" (Park 1992: 91, 97–98), the critical issue here is that each of the various ethnic and subsistence producer groups who eddy within the floodplain perceives climate's effect upon each of the landforms in significantly different ways. An ethnic group's perception of the utility and potentiality of a given landform can radically alter, from one year to the next, one season and the other. This perhaps is the greatest single contrast with both Mesopotamia and the Nile: High unpredictability in the bio-physical and highly flexible in the perceived landscape, the Middle Niger has always demanded a novel accommodation systematics. The story of self-organization here is in part about a historical accommodation of all these groups, all these potentially conflicting perceptions and desires for exploitation. Self-organization is, at the same time, the accommodation by which the variety of landform perceptions began to interact in a mutually enhancing way. When the peoples of the

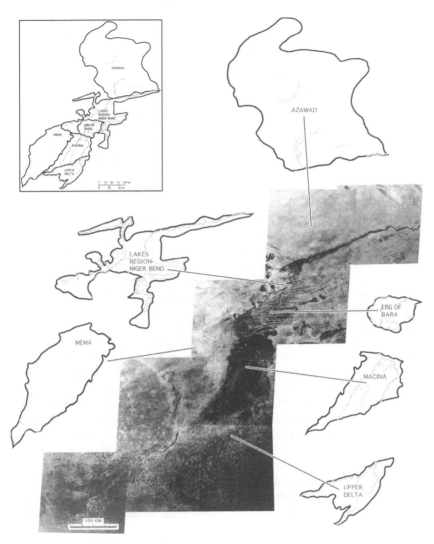

Fig. 2.4. (Exploded) Middle Niger basins, showing for each their signature geomorphological and hydrological elements

Middle Niger got it right, the accommodation systematics gave rise to even more ethnic and producer groups. With more ethnic and producer groups (or corporate belonging) one finds ever more elaborate perceptions of the landscape. In the end, one has a cityscape where a rich but chaotic bio-physical situation has been transformed from risk and surprise (too often in the worst sense of the word) to resilience, exploitation of the land without degradation, and sustainability.

Before diving into the individual wind-and-water-sculpted personalities of the six Middle Niger basins, it will help to mention the two geological/geomorphological processes that lend some unity to long-term landform evolution: faulting and subsidence and the anastomosing river.

The first is a persistent, if low-intensity, degree of faulting and subsidence, one barely perceptible to those on the ground. Faults happen, even though the Middle Niger occupies the southern edge (actually, a sub-basin called the Ségou Basin) of the extremely stable, extremely old (Precambrian) Taoudenni syncline (Buckle 1978: 11; Makaske 1998: 101 and fig. 4.2). The Taoudenni syncline (a concave-warping of basement rock now filled with younger sedimentary rock and unconsolidated sands) serves as the foundation, especially at its margins, to multiple superimposed basins and troughs, all built upon one of the world's oldest and most stable geological shields, the West African craton. Precambrian rock (mostly sandstones) outcrop to the east and south of the Middle Niger floodplain. To the north and west, the "dead delta" alluvium of the Méma and Azawad basins is framed by loosely consolidated or unconsolidated, Tertiary-date continental deposits filling the grand syncline.

Persistent warps of the basal bedrock give an overall tendency to Middle Niger rivers and streams to migrate to the east. In some cases, the uplift–downwarp planes have dramatically changed the course of rivers and, in the case of the Méma, they have virtually shut off the life-giving flow, strangling the life out of the region's cities, as we shall see below. There are two major subsidence troughs framing the Middle Niger to the northwest and east. The latter, the Gao Trough, gives the Niger River its WNW–ESE trend downstream of the Niger Bend (after the Tossaye Sill) (Makaske 1998: 101; Makaske and Terlien 1996: 4, fig. 2.2). Although outside the strict confines of the Middle Niger, this feature is important because the westernmost erosion-resistant barrier of this trough (the metamorphosed craton rock of the Tossaye Sill) gives the rest of the Middle Niger its stable, low base-level control of the Niger (Blanck 1968). The second major warping feature (the Nara Trough) frames the Méma to the north and anchors several parallel (WSW–ENE) fault-warping planes that ramify southward through this now-"dead delta" (see Makaske 1998: fig. 4.2). In principle, the alluvial Quaternary infill of the Middle Niger basins becomes younger as one travels east. The northernmost and westernmost dry basins of the Middle Niger, the Méma and the Azawad, also have a currently erecting cover of aeolian sand.

Other smaller NNE–SSW-oriented faults course through the "live deltas." These provide the local orientation of the Niger and of its major tributary, the Bani, meeting the Niger at Mopti. It is not surprising that these should have contributed to a complex local evolution of channels within the "live delta" basins, the main of which were episodes of dramatic shifts of channel position by a process of avulsion underlain by subsidence (Makaske 1998: 115–71; Makaske and Terlien 1996: 5).

The second geomorphological process underlying the landform evolution of all six basins (although the process has effectively ceased in the two driest ones) is anastomosis, the peculiar fluvial process of the anastomosing river. Such rivers present a coherent floodplain comprising multiple – often shifting – channels, separated by narrow floodbasins, "a river composed of several interconnected channels, which enclose floodbasins" (Makaske 1998: 18, 27). As Makaske goes on to explain, rivers rarely follow the shortest straight-line path, or even one route at a time. In the anastomosing river, many channels are possible and all provide information about the longer history, about changes to sediment sources, and flow strength of the river. These have, at times, been confused with braided channels. They differ from braided rivers, however, by the relatively fixed course of the channels and the low-energy conditions of their construction. Unlike braided streams (with exposed convex-up sands and gravel bars and comparatively small islands) these channels are separated by concave-up swampy floodplain basins, fringed by levees, and boasting significantly larger islands. They differ also in important ways from classic deltas, although they share with deltas the dominating presence of a slight (often negligible) gradient and a stable, low base level.

Anastomosing rivers are important for their wide, well-circulated floodplain providing, like the classic terminal delta, extensive arable and pasture land, as well as rare and diverse ecosystems. Add multiple episodes of aridity and dune erection (contributing other landforms just as important as those of fluvial and lacustrine origin for the overall environmental diversity) and one has in the anastomosing Middle Niger a classic formula for a milieu rich in resources. Sadly, one source of the urban wealth of Mesopotamia and of Egypt is lacking here. The Niger (and Bani) are relatively sediment poor. Unlike the pre-Aswan Nile, in particular, those sediments that are deposited in channels and in backswamps are nutrient depleted (Rzoska 1985).

The Niger has its origin far to the south, in the Precambrian granite and sandstone mountains of the Futa Jallon that receive well in excess of 1,400 millimeters of rain each year (fig. 2.5). These sediments are usually so fine as to be carried in suspension. There is some addition of silts and sands from the sandstone, schists, and dolerites of the Monts Mandings

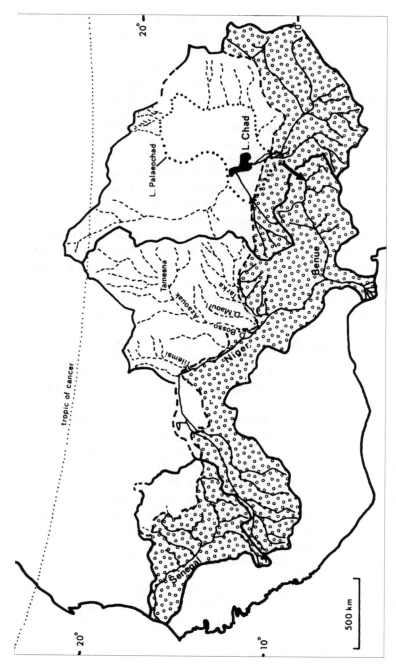

Fig. 2.5. Niger River drainage

downstream. Even closer to the Middle Niger, sands are transported into the basins with the annual floods from the sandstones and schists of the Bandiagara Plateau. Some sands and silts slip laterally into the floodplain from the loosely metamorphosed "Continental Terminal" (composed of sediments of non-marine origin, dating most likely to the late Tertiary, specifically the Oligocene to Holocene) deposits enclosing the Middle Niger on all sides (see Grove 1978: 5; Le Houérou 1989: 50–51). It is important to note that significant exposures of laterite have formed on areas of this "Continental Terminal" and even on the unconsolidated Quaternary alluvium elsewhere at the floodplain's margins. This laterite would be the ore source for one of the first and most important specialists, the blacksmiths. Paleozoic sandstones underly the Pleistocene/Holocene alluvium of the Middle Niger; they dip under and emerge to the west, especially in the Lakes Region, as low and sometimes severely deformed hills (fig. 2.6) (Hughes and Hughes 1992: 394) (for the detailed geology, see Urvoy 1942).

Within the basins, the general rule applies that fluvial sediments grade away from the rivers, from sandy loams to sandy clays constructing the near-channel levees and channel bars, to silty loams of the levees' back-swamp-side margins, to progressively purer and heavier clays as one descends into the deeper backswamp depressions. This rule glosses over the more insistent fact that local soils may differ widely, given the local history (source of sediment loan, energy characteristics, etc.) of parent streams and the proximity of other features (contributing locally) such as dunes, laterite benches – not to forget the always present, modifying hand of local communities.

Thus, rice farmers in the most fluvially active of the six Middle Niger basins, the Upper Delta, are highly attuned to the subtleties of bathy-metric progression (that is, depth of annual flooding), relative clay and sand content, water-retention potential (both open-surface ponding and soil moisture), and residual nutrients of floodplain soils. These farmers have evolved historically appropriate (that is, risk adverse), highly elaborated strategies for sowing up to forty-two varieties of indi-genously domesticated African rice (*Oryza glaberrima*) (as well as Asian rice, *Oryza sativa*, and even a few varieties of wild rice, *Oryza barthii* spp.)(Gallais 1967: 199–200, 218). As extra insurance, rice farmers plow long, thin fields that traverse several soils and bathymetric contours. Dunes vary in their sedimentology (from unconsolidated fine or coarse sands to relatively consolidated loamy sands) – each type with its own potential for millet and other rain-fed, minority grain cultivation. And levees can differ equally, differentially favoring various strategies of flood-recession (*décru*) cultivation of sorghum.

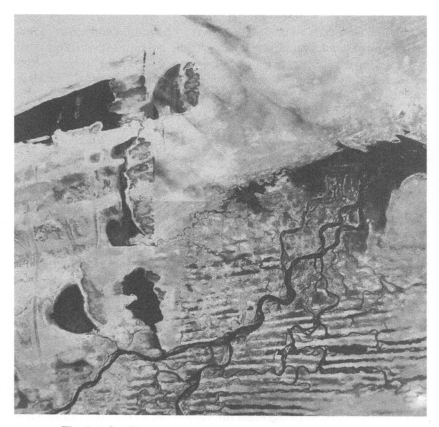

Fig. 2.6. Satellite imagery of folded ancient rocks in the Lake Faguibine area (Lakes Region)

The annual floods are most dramatic in the easternmost and most southern of the six basins, the Upper Delta (recall figs. 2.3 and 2.4). This basin encompasses roughly 6,000 square kilometers of the 55,000 square kilometers presently active (annually flooded) Middle Niger. But during the not-infrequent humid episodes of the 2,000-or-more-year duration of urbanism here, many now far drier, far more marginal basins were just as well watered annually. At times, and particularly at the Late Stone Age formative moments leading to urbanism, the Middle Niger covered fully 170,000 square kilometers. To the east of the Upper Delta are the Paleozoic sandstones of the Bandiagara Plateau. Separating the alluvium and sandstone is a narrow highland strip of Pleistocene clays and sandy-silts (Bénédougou) capped, in places, by lateritic crusts.

We will take a Historical Ecology approach to the paleoclimatic sequence in the next section of this chapter, but here we must broadly sketch the most salient moments. A late Pleistocene dry phase (the low-latitude counterpart of the high-latitude Late Glacial Ice Age) had dramatic effects. By about 20,000 BP, the Niger and Bani rivers had ceased to flow in the present region of Lake Débo and for an as-yet-undetermined distance upstream. A strong dune system formed, called the Erg of Bara, the remnants of which forms the Middle Niger basin of that name. When precipitation improved, during the early Holocene (after 10,000 or 9,000 years ago), the rejuvenated rivers were blocked, forming a massive Lake Paléo-Débo, of which Lakes Débo and Korientzé are vestiges. Lake Paléo-Débo is the counterpart of the massive Lake Mega Chad that filled the Chad Basin to maximum at around 8,500–8,000 years ago (Brunk and Gronenborn 2004: 105; Servant and Servant-Vildary 1980). The Niger eventually breached the parallel dunes of the Erg of Bara to flow northwards in channels known now as the Bara-Issa and the Sebi-Marigot.

The geomorphological mosaic of the Upper Delta has clearly been many millennia in the making (Brunet-Moret *et al.* 1986; Voute 1962; Urvoy 1942). The principal dynamic at work has been the shift of the Niger and Bani to the east, ultimately driven (as described above) by subtle subsidence and faulting. The Niger abandoned the Diaka channel in the Macina Basin before assuming its present channel. The Bani joined with the Niger, also, after the late Pleistocene dry period. In principle, wind-blown features are in the minority in the Upper Delta. There is, however, a large isolated red dune north and west of Jenne and a smattering of smaller white and yellow dunes. The smaller dunes can be dated to the early and middle Holocene's shorter dry periods. The large dune was breached several times during the early Holocene (R. McIntosh 1983; Makaske 1998: figs. 4.35a to 4.35e). Before the rivers could run free of the dune, however, a swampy depression formed upstream of the dune. This depression is the rich rice country now known as the Pondori. During this pluvial, a meandering Niger created multiple meander scars and levees, south and east of the Pondori. The Bani formed a massive levee (the Nyansanare).

The map of landforms and soils of the Jenne hinterland in figure 2.3 takes this geomorphological sketch one scalar step further. This illustrates the four floodplain soils, the four discrete levee soils, and the three or more generations of dunes as they are perceived by (some of) the several subsistence-ethnic groups who call the Upper Delta their home. Making the mix much more interesting for our purposes is the likelihood that Marka (Nono) rice farmers would subdivide those four gross floodplain soils into a kaleidoscope of what might be called "utility soils units." Likewise, the

Fulani (Peul) herders might classify a dune entirely differently from its neighbor because of proximity to ponded, permanent water with the water-plant fodder (*bourgou*), even if those two dunes are indistinguishable sedimentologically! Clearly, the utility of each of these landform units for rice farming, or dry-season cattle herding, fishing for different swamp or deep-channel species, or garden plotting will change year-by-year with differing annual precipitation, flood heights, span of full flooding before evacuation of the waters, etc. In the next section we will review the principal axes of these interannual, interdecadal, intercentury, etc. climate variations. Here it is important to fully appreciate just how "chaotically" complex is the mosaic of soils and landforms – and the fact that herders will "see" a very different reality here than will rice farmers, or sorghum farmers – or, for that matter, ancient crocodile hunters.

In overall physical organization, our second "live" basin, the Macina, is less complex than the Upper Delta. As one enters the Macina from its northwestern frontier (from the sad Méma), one first traverses high sandy floodplain, commensurate with a region locked in a struggle to hold the Sahara at bay (and seen at the center of fig. 2.4). Then, traveling east, a floodplain of middle depth dominates the basin from west of the Diaka marigot to the Niger at the Macina's frontier with the Upper Delta. North of the sandy plain (west of Lake Débo) one finds a low erg, or parallel dune system (the southwestern appendix of the Erg of Bara, to be discussed next). Deep basins flank most of the mid-axial length of the Diaka. An important deep basin south of Lakes Débo and Walado covers about 150,000 hectares. This is the Bourgou-Dialloubé (nearest the lakes) and Bourgou-Yallabé (to the southwest) (*bourgou* being the local term for the rich floodplain vegetation, dominated by *Echinocloa stagnina* and *Oryza barthii*, providing pasturage that sustains the herds during the last months of the dry season).

The density and availability of palatable, dry-season *bourgou* vegetation increase from southwest to northeast within the Macina. Visible particularly in the eastern sector, the tangle of intermingled multiple landforms (a "chaos" of exploitable microenvironments) is clearly part of an ancient – and absolutely lovely – bird-foot delta etched in clay and loamy sand as a larger Lake Débo receded to its present size (see fig. 2.7). Such bird-foot deltas are more typically erected in large bodies of water that recede slowly, but steadily, as is hypothesized to have been the case for the massive ancient Lake Paléo-Débo. However less complex than the Upper Delta, the mix of floodplain (at different depth with annual inundation, or bathymetric progression) and sandy highlands (dune and levee) provide a critical service in the Macina. This is preeminently cattle country. The Macina is occupied by the transhumant Fulani particularly during the dry season, after the annual rains, when the herds are driven here from the arid neighboring

Fig. 2.7. Satellite image of ancient delta at the distal Macina

north and south, just after the flood recession begins (Gallais 1967: 119–91). The herds move in to this refuge in enormous numbers (1.5 million cattle, 0.5 million goats, and 0.25 million sheep). Having entered this basin, the herds slowly graze their way from the Macina's southwest (first evacuated by water) to the northwest (richest in backswamp ponds and "pre-Débo" lakes, anticipating their final several months crowded together on the banks of Lake Débo). To keep the fragile health of the herds the Fulani depend absolutely on the proximity of *bourgou* pasturage and *seno* (sandy highland). Herds wander the floodplain by day, fattening on the thick mattress of vegetation. By night they are kept on the sandy highlands, high and dry, to prevent water-caused diseases of the hooves.

In some ways, the landscape organization of the Erg of Bara region is the simplest in organization of the six Middle Niger basins, dominated as it is by massive late Pleistocene (Last Glacial) dunes. A great field (erg) of these dunes blocked the Niger at the beginning of the First Holocene Pluvial. Lakes Débo, Korientzé and Walado (and others) remain as evidence of the large body of blocked water. These lakes frame the Erg of Bara region to the south and the structural trough they occupy is yet further evidence of folding and faulting. The large Lake Region lakes frame this basin to the northwest (Lakes Korarou, Tana and Kabara) and northeast (Lakes Aougoundou and Niangay).

The Erg of Bara represents a transition zone between the lush floodplains of the Upper Delta and the Macina and the active combat zone of wind versus river of the Lakes Region–Niger Bend. The dunes here are not active. They have long been stabilized by a light cover of spiney acacia trees and grass. Dunecrests average 2–3 kilometers apart. Between are interdunal ponds, approximately 1 kilometer wide, that fill to 2–3 meters with the annual flood. And on the dune crests live (principally Bambara-speaking) farmers, within easy access to highland sands (for millet), mid-dune slope recessional soils (for sorghum and garden crops), and narrow deep rice fields, long and parallel the length of the deepest interdunal ponds (Galloy et al. 1963).

When pluvial conditions returned at the end of the Pleistocene hyper-aridity, a rejuvenated Niger did eventually breach the high Late Glacial dunes of the Erg of Bara. Now the divided river snakes through the region in several parts. The Rivers Issa-Ber and Bara-Issa issue out of Lake Débo; the Koli-Koli channel emerges from Lake Korientzé. The dunes are cut by innumerable marigots, oxbows, interdunal lakes, and ponds. The river cut through the dunes at a time of significantly higher discharge, leaving behind an even more complex welter of landforms than the Niger could even dream of erecting today. Below Débo, the fluvial system remains classically anastomosing: Channels divide and reunite in a complex, web-like pattern with broad floodplain and parallel dunes between. The heavier soils of the interdunal depressions support standing water well into the dry season. There are, however, fewer of the large, deep, bourgou-filled depressions here than in the Macina (or even the Upper Delta). As one might expect, however, the dune and interdunal-depression-dominated landscape has attracted farmers, fisherfolk, and herders.

The active, "live" floodplain of the Middle Niger is capped to the far north and northeast by a basin of lakes, dune cordons, and sandstone exposures, the Lakes Region and Niger Bend. This region takes its name, in part of course, from the unexpected proliferation of Sahelian lakes. Lakes – a present-day memory of long-past millennia, when the Middle Niger was a single great sea of water, fringed with wetlands and the source, by way of channels coursing far to the north, of annual floods filling vast ponds, playas, and lakes in the present Sahara. Lake Débo to south of Lakes Region (at the Upper Delta, Macina, and Erg of Bara confluence) is the largest of these residual lakes. North of the Erg of Bara and to the west is Lake Faguibine (45,000 ha at high water) linked to swamps running to Lake Télé, near Goundam, and a series of ephemeral lakes (or daounas, as in, for example, Daouna Beri and Daouna Keino). To the east one finds Lakes Korientzé, Aougoundou, and Gaou. These three are within the still active floodplain zone; Lakes Niangay, Dô, and Haribomo are, strictly speaking, outside the Middle Niger. The peoples of these last-mentioned lakes have the occupations and the ethnicities of Middle Niger folk and so these lakes are included in our landscape summary. Lakes Niangay, Dô, and Haribomo are filled by Bandiagara Plateau runoff, by rainwater, and by highwater flood from exceptional Niger River floods (Hughes and Hughes 1992: 394). The lakes and divided Niger channels progressively funnel the annual floodwaters into the constricted floodplain of the Niger Bend near Timbuktu. Thus, at Timbuktu, the floodplain has narrowed to a width of 10–15 kilometers (reminiscent of the main Nile). The floodplain is further reduced to 6 kilometers in width at Gourma-Rharous (somewhat arbitrarily, we shall consider that town as the eastern limit of the Middle Niger). Ancient fluvial and lake deposits abound further north of the river, but there we return to the desert (to the Azawad, the first of the "dead" basins, discussed next). Today the river and desert struggle to dominate one another in the Lakes Region and Niger Bend. That was the clash won ultimately in the Azawad by wind and sand.

The Lakes Region–Niger Bend is unusual for the numbers and complexity of laterite, evaporite (calcites primarily), and rock exposures (sandstones, schists, quartzites, dolerites). More so than in the deeper, southern basins, these exposures provide much of the organization of the region's lakes and dune features. The most important geological features are the sandstone Goundam Hills and laterized tabular late Tertiary (Continental Terminal) sandstone and clays of the Niger Bend. Rock exposures illustrate the long and continuing history of tectonic warping and faulting that has had a profound effect upon the river's history. The entire Middle Niger has been subjected to deep subsidence (synclinal warping) at least from the Eocene. And the Lakes Region–Niger Bend is far from dormant (Monod and Palausi 1958; Riser et al. 1986). There has been recent uplift of the old beaches of Lake Faguibine and extrusion of volcanic material in that lake's vicinity. The result of faulting and folding, dating from at least the Eocene to the present, is a series of sandstone plateaux and hills on the left bank of the Niger and fields of less extensive hills dominating the lakes of the right bank. The same was the origin of the Daounas highlands west of Lake Faguibine.

The first of our now-dry basins, the Azawad sand plains north of the Niger Bend (and the related Taoudenni paleolake depressions further to the north), tells of the eventual triumph of wind over rain and flood. Just when that triumph occurred – deep millennia ago or perhaps only just during the last millennium BC – only future research will reveal. Just what was the rhythm of that triumph, slow and drawn out, maddening local populations with pulses of alternating wet (pluvial) and desiccating climates? Only future investigation will tell. The Azawad today still retains its personality as a mosaic of river, swamp, lake, and wind-borne deposits, as do all six Middle Niger basins. Layered transformation is perhaps the best description of the cumulative effects of alternating agencies of rain, river, and desiccation that caused the complex interweave of microenvironments throughout even this, the driest precinct of the Middle Niger. In the northernmost basin the wind appears to take perverse pleasure in savaging testaments to wetter times.

In the paleolake region of Taoudenni, dunes trail downwind from tall columns of eroded lake deposits (R. McIntosh 1998: plate 2.2). South, slightly, in the Azawad proper, ancient shallow lakes (playas), permanent streams, and once-generous rains left behind carpets of freshwater shell mixed with bones of massive perch, catfish, and crocodile. However, for perhaps five millennia, the wind has dominated; dominated but not, until the last millennium BC, did it overwhelm. There is ample evidence of lacustrine conditions: lakes (both shallow and of some depth) with a vast display of fish, osracod, diatoms, and aquatic mammals and reptiles. Many of the interdunal depressions were water filled year-round, making complex, self-contained microenvironments of lake, swampy margins, and sandy dune crests. The late Pleistocene dunes that dominate the Azawad generally trend NE–SW (related, as they are, to the parallel Erg of Bara dunes). They are intersected north–south by paleochannels, such as the El-Ahmar channel (1,200 m wide at its mouth and some 100 km long in its thrust into the desert) departing the Niger Bend just east of Timbuktu. These are the channels that brought Niger floodwaters far to the north at pluvial times of excessive floods, augmenting the rain-fed filling of the interdunal lakes and exposed playas.

And finally, with a geomorphological profile somewhere between the very dry, dune-structured Azawad and the four "live" basins is the Méma – in some ways the most interesting, most evolutionarily intriguing of the six basins (De Vries et al. 2005). The high density of many large cities on the Méma floodplain, thriving as recently as the thirteenth or fourteenth century AD (Togola 1993, 1996), attests to the recentness (and precipitousness) of the final demise of this so-called "dead delta." Here, oscillation of settlement density probably marched in step with oscillations of climate. That was the case, presumably, particularly during the Late Stone Age. In a later chapter, we shall argue that the Méma is critical to a test of a thesis, the Pulse Model, that Late Stone Age subsistence specialization – and, indeed, the major "rules" of Middle Niger accommodation systematics – arose in an environment of oscillatory, high unpredictability. Steep demographic declines during the late first and early second millennia AD probably mirror the incremental strangulation of the major paleochannels (especially the Fala de Molodo) that once kept the Méma every bit as viable as the Upper Delta or Macina today. The geomorphology of the Méma is a good illustration of the abrupt spurts and pulses of climate that swept the entire Middle Niger.

The Méma is roughly 25,000 square kilometers of delta, lacustrine, and aeolian deposits. This dry basin is framed to the northwest by sandstone outcroppings thrust up by movement of another major ENE–WSW-oriented tectonic structure (Nara graben – Makaske 1998: fig. 4.2) and by the massive dune system called the Erg de Ouagadou. The Méma is framed to the northeast by the live parallel dune system called the Aklé (separating the Azawad Basin from the low-relief Méma). To the east and south is the Macina Basin. The Méma Basin is crossed by three major paleochannels that trend roughly southwest to northeast. The first of these (from south to north) is the Fala de Molodo. Furon (1929) considered this to be a relict of a Pleistocene channel of the Niger leading north and then west of the present Méma all the way into the Hodh depression. The second is the Niakené Maoudo, separated from the Fala de Molodo by the ironpan-covered sandstone hills (recent uplift artifacts?) of the Boulel and Boundouboubou Ridges. Finally, the Bras de Nampala crosses the extreme west of the Méma. These paleochannels are defunct today. However, in the past, each encroached upon the framing dunes and erected complex systems of high levees, interspersed with seasonally flooded pans and playas. These features indicate very clearly that, periodically, they were very powerful streams that changed channel often. They all fed large backswamp regions.

We end this section with a map of the Méma landforms and hydrology (De Vries et al. 2005) (fig. 2.8). The map was compiled from air photos and satellite imagery, combined with a verifying "groundtruth" survey, in an attempt to decipher the complex geomorphological evolution of the basin in advance of archaeological survey. The map and geomorphology explication will serve us in two ways. To bridge this section of descriptive landscape and the following of dynamic paleoclimate, the map under-scores the point made above when we compared the Middle Niger to the Mesopotamian and Nile floodplains. In figure 2.8, the mosaic of fluvial, lacustrine, paludial (swamp), and aeolian features are a testimony to the

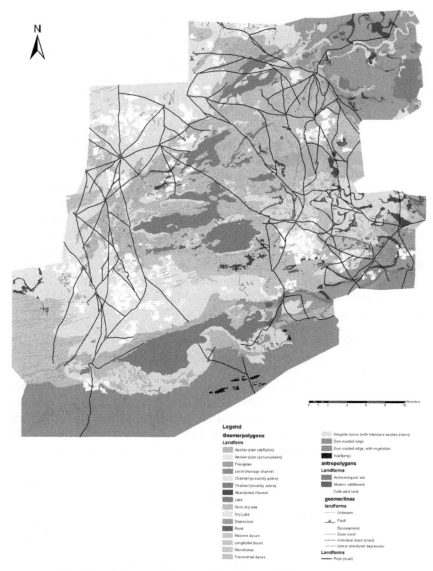

Fig. 2.8. Geomorphology and hydrology of the Méma

complex interplay of rain, wind, desiccating heat, and the active hand of human communities in a millennial ballet of highly abrupt, highly oscillatory climate change. The map helps us understand the structural (faulting and subsidence) underpinning of the movement and eventual senescence of the paleochannels. And a moving description of the land-form evolution will be the mechanism for introducing the overall paleo-climatic trends of the Middle Niger, from about 20,000 BP to the present.

Paleoclimate: phase shifts at multiple time-scales

Not without reason, the arid West African climate has been called among the world's most variable and unpredictable (Koechlin 1997: 12–18). A few quotes are in order. Shukla provides the classic description of the instrumental record: "In the recorded meteorological data for the past 100 years, there is no other region of the globe of this size for which spatial and seasonal averaged climatic anomalies have shown such persistence" (1995: 44). Taking a longer chronological and a continental-scale per-spective, Sharon Nicholson despairs: "The largely semi-arid African continent has undergone extreme climatic changes which are probably unmatched in their magnitude and spatial extent" (1994: 121). If the password of those manning the gates of self-organization studies is "at the edge of chaos," then Park allows easy egress to the peoples of the Middle Niger and the Middle Senegal by his characterization of Sahelian climate "chaos," an essential unpredictability of the past and present (1992: 91, 97–98). Park continues: "No amount of knowledge of past trends will ever enable local people to manage that variability by way of storage or trade." But the Middle Niger peoples have indeed traced a history of progressive strategies of flexibility, phase transformations in the self-organized landscape that allowed ever greater complexity, including urbanism, in the face of long-term climate rhythms that can incontestably be described as "at the edge of chaos."

In order to appreciate the effect of climate upon inhabitants of the Middle Niger, it is imperative that we understand paleoclimate as a scalar phenomenon. Scalar, that is, along two dimensions: spatial and temporal. Along both dimensions, our understanding depends on resolution (Dunbar 2000; Ruddiman 2001: 64–70). Some aspects of change can be directly identified, measured, and contrasted with adjacent phe-nomena ("resolved") at certain scales. Others can simply be suggested, indirectly reasoned, or "intuited" from various proxy measures. The continental West African climate record, frankly, is not very well resolved until the erection of the astonishingly dense (and still well maintained) colonial meteorological field observation stations, beginning in the 1890s. However, we can judiciously extrapolate to the inland Sahel from recent exciting millennial-scale and even better data gushing in from the offshore Mauritanian and Guinea coast deep-drilling projects

(ODP, Offshore Drilling Program) and even from high-resolution linked Atlantic monsoonal data from as far away as the Cariaco Basin off Venezuela. A word, first, about proxy measures, the mainstay of paleoclimate research (Bradley 1985; R. McIntosh 2003: 145–46).

Proxy measures depend for their logical power on the researcher demonstrating causative linkage between the data that can be measured and the processes or phenomena that we wish to understand, but cannot directly observe or resolve upon. For example, deep-sea sediment cores drilled off the Mauritanian coast indicate recent and abrupt changes of 2 °C or more to the temperature of the upper several meters of the eastern North Atlantic. Sea surface temperature (SST) in this case is measured by the proxy measure of changing populations of planktonic foraminifera. The foraminifera shells litter and accumulate upon the sea floor. They are short-lived and their shell can deeply litter the sea floor (DeMenocol *et al.* 2000a and 2000b). Different populations of planktonic foraminifera are highly and differentially sensitive to environmental conditions, especially water temperature, as well as salinity, turbidity, etc. Hence, it is a pretty good bet that shells of these populations, lifted in the deep-sea cores, give us a secure proxy measure of SST. Salinity is another useful thing to identify. Slight changes to the salinity of ocean water at different depth (tropic) levels can dramatically affect the working of the so-called "ocean conveyor belt," a major means of global heat transfer from the tropics to the polar regions (Bryant 1997: 58–64; Ruddiman 2001: 18–43).

We can take this further. Knowing tropical North Atlantic SST says nothing about continental Sahelian climate – without, that is, a causative link. Today, SST in that part of the eastern North Atlantic has a control-ling (or, at least, a highly correlated) effect on the desiccating winds that blow across the Sahara. Take this even further. Today, a pattern of lower SST in the eastern Atlantic between 10° N and 25° N and higher SSTs in the Gulf of Guinea are correlated with (cause?) a displacement southward of the annual monsoonal rains (Folland *et al.* 1986; Fontaine and Janicot 1996; Lamb and Peppler 1992). These rains sweep well into the southern Sahara on good years (yearning for 20° N) and barely kiss the desert's hem (at Timbuktu's latitude of 17° N) on the bad. For the first millennium AD and last millennium BC, the period critical to the rise of Middle Niger cities, the relative numbers of different planktonic foraminifera species can therefore be taken as trustworthy *first order proxy measures* of ocean surface temperature. SST is, however, a phenomenon of little direct significance for the lives of the people we are concerned about. We can only hope that, because of the causative mechanism observed today, foraminifera prove to be *for the distant past* equally trustworthy *second order proxy measures* of inland temperature, rainfall, length of dry season, etc. – all the climate effects that very much touch the lives of Middle Niger people.

However, even if the SST spikes (abrupt cooling by 3–4 °C) in the Mauritanian offshore cores (c. 20° N) at around AD 1300–1900 (DeMenocol *et al.* 2000b: 2199; see R. McIntosh 2003: 147, fig. 1) translate into dramatically dry conditions in the Sahel, chronologically they are still poorly resolved (fig. 2.9a). That means we can pity the Middle Niger folk for having to have suffered truly epical droughts during the past millennium, droughts far worse than the Sahel Drought that began in 1968. But how long did the "mega-droughts" last? Were there two long droughts (as implied by the proxy measures, at this resolution), or were there multiple episodes of varying intensities and duration? Can we extrapolate to the Middle Niger, with any more confidence, from the Lake Chad sequence further to the east? There, significant lake oscillations (lake level rises and falls of 6 meters) are documented for the last millennium (Brunk and Gronenborn 2004: 112–13, fig. 4; Maley 2000). So often, for the archaeologist and historian, poor temporal climate resolution leads to grinding frustration: Would that we knew the continental, Sahelian implications of DeMenocol *et al.*'s throw-away observation that Holocene SST and other oceanic climate measures are increasing in variability in recent millennia, with the time of the Little Ice Age (AD 1500–1850) representing the largest amplitude horizon of the last 20,000 years (2000b: 2201)! Don't leave us hanging!

Add to this problem of temporal resolution that of spatial resolution. We know from the American Southwest, among other well-researched, high-resolution arid lands, that spatial patchiness is a common attribute (Dean 2000; Rautman 1996: 202–4). Rains might fall on one valley and not on the plateau nearby. In some cases, spatial patchiness sets up a superb landscape matrix for exchange and reciprocity amongst neighbors, as has been documented for Ancestral Puebloan (Anasazi) societies (Tainter and Tainter 1996; Rautman 1996). Now, research has begun on expanding back into deep time our experience today of high patchy rainfall in arid West Africa (Janicot 1992a and 1992b). But the state of our knowledge, beyond the turn of the century, when colonial authorities established networks of remote weather stations, is primitive, to say the least.

These cautions about proxy measures, temporal resolution, and unproven spatial patchiness aside, during the past two decades we have made some strides towards reconstructing the structure of Middle Niger paleoclimate (reviewed in R. McIntosh 2000b: 144–53). We have improved data and an improved sophistication in our understanding of what those data mean. This applies not just to the reconstruction of the West African paleoclimate over the past 20,000 years, but to our appreciation of factors such as unpredictability, abrupt change, phase shifts, and variability of intensity and amplitude, factors that directly affect people on the ground. We still glance enviously at paleoclimatologists in the American Southwest, with their dense matrices of dendroclimatology data, but perhaps a bit less so than before.

Just for a moment, let's return to causation. Ultimately, climate change (at all scales) is caused by seemingly small deviations in the amount of incoming solar radiation (insolation: Ruddiman 2001: 193–209) (and to changes to the distribution of the earth's mass – a factor locally of little consequence on the stable West African craton!)(R. McIntosh 2003). Overlapping solar cycles of different periods produce a complex rhythm of solar radiation reaching the earth.

Further complicating matters, heat is transported from the equator to the poles along the ever-changing, coupled land–atmospheric–oceanic system (Bradley 1999). This can be thought of as a "conveyer belt" that links climate on all parts of the globe (hence the importance to the Sahelian climate of the neighboring eastern North Atlantic SST). Some fraction of heat is "artificially" kept from reradiating out into space by water vapor and other gasses, other factors that have affected global climate change for billions of years. Three driving mechanisms of climate change, all well researched, are the variations in insolation controlled by the so-called Milankovitch, or "orbital-beat," cycles: (1) eccentricity (changes in the shape of Earth's orbit), cycling at 100,000 years (100 ka); (2) obliquity (changes to the tilt of Earth's axis), cycling at 41 ka; and (3) precession (shifting schedule of the equinoxes), with a paired cyclicity of 23 ka and 19 ka (Bradley 1999). Unambiguously, the result of recent research into monsoonal patterns globally shows a regularity of stronger and weaker monsoons with a periodicity matching the 23,000-year rhythm of orbital precession – Kutzbach's orbital monsoon hypothesis (Kutzbach 1981; Ruddiman 2001: 195–98). An important discovery from research into these ultimate forcing causes is that thresholds and phase transitions apply equally to these orbital-scale processes and to the more human-scale meteorological processes studied by Lorenz (hence his mathematics of chaotic, nondeterministic "intransitivity" mentioned in chapter 1; Lorenz 1976 and 1990). A linear (gradual) change in precessional insolation (the causative heat) during the Holocene translates not into gradual shifts from stronger to weaker monsoons. Rather, the result is an abrupt mid-Holocene transformation (see figs. 2.9a and 2.9b [especially the last 5,000 years]) – an unambiguous phase shift (see Ruddiman 2001: 342–50 for millennial oscillations elsewhere during the last 8,000 years).

The overlap of these orbital cycles produces a complex rhythm of forcing to the earth's climate system. However, their effects can in most

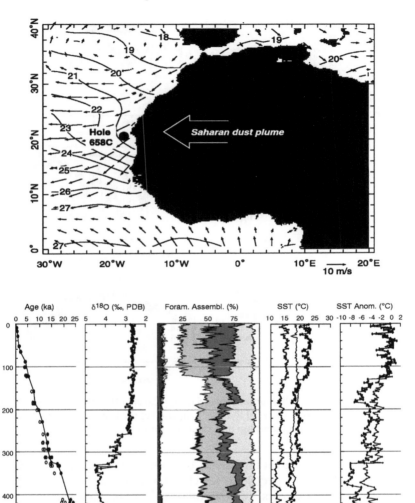

Fig. 2.9a Holocene climate proxy measures and reconstructed sea surface temperatures (SST) from deep-sea sediment cores (ODP hole 658C) drilled off the Mauritanian coast

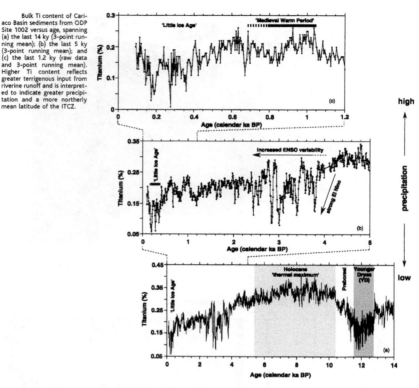

Bulk Ti content of Cariaco Basin sediments from ODP Site 1002 versus age, spanning (a) the last 14 ky (3-point running mean); (b) the last 5 ky (3-point running mean); and (c) the last 1.2 ky (raw data and 3-point running mean). Higher Ti content reflects greater terrigenous input from riverine runoff and is interpreted to indicate greater precipitation and a more northerly mean latitude of the ITCZ.

Fig. 2.9b Bulk titanium record of the Cariaco Basin sediments spanning (a) the last 14 ka; (b) the last 5 ka; and (c) the last 1.2 ka (Ti variation as proxy for precipitation and riverine runoff)

cases only be resolved at time-scales of 1,000,000 years (10^6 – that is, one has to have this perspective to see changes unrolling over a duration of 100,000 or 10,000 years) or of 100,000 (10^5) years. Middle Niger urbanism clearly appeared more recently. So, here, we need only occupy ourselves with mesoscale paleoclimate – that is, the climate effects of these larger patterns of earth-orbit eccentricities that are resolvable at a time-scale of 100,000 years (10^5 yr) and less.

Figure 2.10 presents a fair approximation of the state of our knowledge of climate change at a time-scale of 10^5. In this figure, we go back to around 20,000 years ago. This is as good a starting point as any, because all of West Africa then was in a hyperarid period and, as a consequence, we have very little evidence of human occupation anywhere within the present-day Sahara and Sahel. The Middle Niger and possibly its migration reservoirs to the north, east, and west (see below) were essentially clean slates. Hyperaridity in the African lower latitudes correlates with the maximum spread of glacial ice in the higher latitudes. Ultimately, ice ages and their recession are caused by changes to heat arriving at the earth's surface. That insolation change is due to the aforementioned Milankovitch cycles. For the past several million years, essentially, the forcing insolation cycle has been the 100 ka eccentricity, with a 41 ka obliquity "kicker" causing both the saw-tooth pattern to ice age cooling and a 400 ka eccentricity-variation complicating things even further (Droxler et al. 2003: 3–4; see also Bradley 1999; Kutzbach and Otto-Bliesner 1982; Kutzbach and Street-Perrott 1985)!

Further, more complex non-linear shifts within the land–atmospheric–oceanic "conveyer belt" that transports heat from the tropics to the polar regions may be responsible for distinct modes resolvable at the million-year time-scale, but also at more human-scale time-scales. More research is needed. However, it looks increasingly likely that it is on this "conveyer belt" that we can place the finger of blame for abrupt climate shifts (Bryant 1997: 106–11), for mode shifts (some of which are stable, some unstable) (Bradley 1985: 13–14; Dunbar 2000), and for apparently random periods of high variability (HTV: High Temporal Variability; HAV: High Amplitude Variability) (Dean 1996: fig. 3, and 2000). These are the chaotic realities of climate to which the Middle Niger peoples had to respond.

Whatever the causes, at the time-scale of 10^5 years (fig. 2.10) we can see a number of critical phase shifts. These are true climate discontinuities, Bradley's "catastrophic discontinuities" (1985: 13–14) or Hassan's "nickpoints" (1996, 1997, 2002a) that required rapid cultural change and adaptive innovation by human communities. Phase shifts separate discrete plateau-like "stable" states of "predictable variability" – and could quite easily be modeled by a three-dimensional phase transform diagram, such as figure 1.6 above. The physics of such 10^5 and 10^4 abrupt climate changes and their ecological impacts is further discussed by Alley et al. (2003).

West Africa emerged from the long, long hyperaridity of the late glacial period, not in a slow regreening, but in fits and starts. When these began in the case of the Middle Niger, we do not know. How we wish we knew how closely in time these correlate with the better-dated upper latitude deglaciation fits and starts (the meltwater pulses of 15,000 and 11,000, the "deglacial two step" of rapid sea level rise from c. 17,000, slowing from 14,000 to 12,000 and resuming a rapid pace thereafter, and the Younger Dryas recooling from c. 12,900 to 11,700: Ruddiman 2001: 302–9). Strong evidence from elsewhere in West Africa suggests

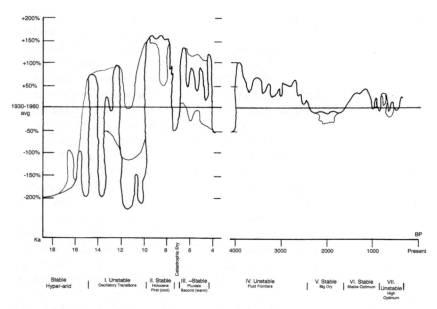

Fig. 2.10. Middle Niger paleoclimatic phases and regional variations over the past 20,000 years

spasmodic climate recovery as early as 17,000 and certainly by 15,000–13,000. This proxy evidence comes from the Saharan highlands (Jäkel 1979: 27, fig. 8; Maley 1983: 382, fig. 2) and from the recovery of the rain gauge Lake Bosumtwi in Ghana (Talbot and Delibrias 1980) and from Lake Chad (Durand 1982; Servant and Servant-Vildary 1980). West African evidence for "la charnière Pleistocene–Holocene" (the Ice Age–Holocene hinge) is amassed by Vernet (1995: 62–70) (for the off-shore picture, see DeMenocol *et al.* 2000a: 354, fig. 4). Such radical climate phase shifts are entirely consistent with better researched (and better "resolved") monumental changes occurring in the upper latitudes not long after the Late Glacial Maximum of 18,000–16,000. The abrupt climate change episodes, at which temperature rises and falls up to 10 °C within a decade, would have had devastating effects on conservative, cold-adapted (high latitudes) or dry-adapted (tropics) communities. In the end, at around 11,650 years ago, the earth warmed 5–10 °C within perhaps twenty years. This was an astonishingly sudden increase that ended the Younger Dryas and issued in a West African mode shift of quite stable, wet, and still relatively cool climate – the First Holocene Pluvial (documented in Vernet 1995: 71–99). This change in global climate at the end of the last glaciation was accompanied by a rise in sea level, from its low of −121 meters (measured from the present-day level) at around 18 ka. Archaeology records population dislocations throughout this period – and we can only imagine the effects on West African populations living along the (now deeply submerged) coast (Vernet 1998).

Is it to this period, ultimately, that we might someday tie the migrations, adaptations, and (most critically) the flexible state of mind of populations that led to later environmental accommodation – including Middle Niger urbanism? Such a day when we could construct an empirical test of that proposition seems a very long way away.

The period of rapid and high amplitude mode shifts, surely correlated in some way with deglaciation events such as the Early Dryas, each beginning and ending with a "catastrophic discontinuity," is our first climate phase of figure 2.10 (compare table 17.1, p. 322 of Hassan 2002a). This is our Phase I: Oscillatory Transition of around 13,000 to 10,000 BP. This highly unstable phase marks the transition from the (continental tropics stable?) late glacial hyperarid phase to the equally (or more?) stable and cool (First) Holocene Pluvial. Roughly 10,000 BP began a period of recharged Saharan and Sahelian lakes and a quick march northward of the wetter-climate vegetation to colonize and stabilize the vast fields of longitudinal dunes (ergs) erected up to 400 kilometers south of today's dunefields during the hyperarid period. This is best documented in the eastern Sahel: Lake Chad became Mega Chad, from 8,500 to 8,000 years ago at 45 meters above recent centuries' lake lowstands (Brunk and Gronenborn 2004: 105).

Archaeologists of the southern Sahara are noodling through a curious mystery, however. The linked paleoclimate and archaeological research of the 1980–88 Missions Paléoenvironnements du Sahara Occidental et Central, headed by Nicole Petit-Maire, found that the great northern Malian lakes, those of the Taoudenni Basin and of the northern Azawad of the Middle Niger, were full and replete with gallery vegetation, fish, aquatic mammals, reptiles, etc. by 9,500–9,000 years ago (Petit-Maire 1986a: 66 and 1986b: 11–13). But it is only at 7,000 BP that we begin to see the humans who should have been drawn to this edenic scene! This pluvial (Phase II: stable, cool [First]) Holocene Pluvial does indeed appear to have been quite low in variability (with maybe a several-century drought at c. 8,800 years ago), but it was abruptly and brutally interrupted around 7,800 years ago.

A West Africa-wide, catastrophic dry period hit as early as 7,800 (Brooks 1998: 139) and certainly from 7,500 to 7,000 years ago (Vernet 1995: 101–3 and 2002: 47–49). This dry hiatus must somehow be linked, but with a palpable time lag, to the now well-documented upper-latitude "mini-Dryas" millennium (?) of cooling of about 8,200 years ago (Alley *et al.*, 2003: 2007, fig. 3). This brief, but surely devastating, dry episode interrupted the cool (First) Holocene Pluvial phase and ushered in the next phase (stable, relatively) Phase III: warm (Second) Holocene Pluvial, dating, for argument's sake, around 7,000 years ago to perhaps 4,200 years ago. Certainly more stable than what is to follow, this Second Holocene Pluvial boasted humid peaks at 6,700 and 4,500 years ago and dry incursions at 6,400, 5,500, 4800, and (terminal) 4,200 years ago (Vernet 2002: 47). There is larger evidence of a world-wide cold spell from around 5,500 to 4,700 BP which must, at the very least, have manifested in the Sahara and Sahel as a higher incidence of droughts – if not as a long, coherent, and catastrophic dry phase. Lake Chad Basin, after a minor maximum (+20 m of today's lowstand!) at 6,500 to 6,000 years ago, went into prevailingly arid conditions from around 5,400 to 3,500 BP (Brunk and Gronenborn 2004: 105).

Overall, the warmer pluvial period had highly seasonal rains (as opposed to the more regular, even, year-round rains of the First Holocene Pluvial) and evaporation was far greater. There was probably more temporal and spatial patchiness also, although we just cannot resolve upon these variations as yet. Clastic sedimentation profiles in wadis and lakes indicate more instability of precipitation. And yet the Sahara and Sahel were now densely populated by hunters (land and aquatic), gatherers, and fisherfolk – all taking advantage of the rich abundance of plants and animals now occupying the stabilized dunes and lakes of the interdunal depressions and linked to a recharged Niger River (Petit-Maire 1986b: 13–15).

Interestingly, even for the Second Holocene Pluvial, there is no evidence for any occupation anywhere in the basins of the Middle Niger other than the Azawad. Perhaps we have just not located the evidence yet. But why would interest in this area have been any less than in comparable regions elsewhere? Unless, of course, the higher precipitation and higher floods from the proto-Niger, charged with flood water from even further to the tropical south, created untenable conditions. One might envisage large and stable lakes (even a single mega-lake) analogous to the contemporaneous transgressive water bodies of the Lake Chad Basin (Breuning and Neumann 2002: 132–35) or permanent swamps (Vernet 2002: 54 and forthcoming) with water-borne disease suites that effectively drove humans away.

I believe that it is really with the beginning of the next climate phase, beginning with another catastrophic dry incursion around 4,200–4,000 years ago, that fundamental attitudes to climatic stress and surprise had their birth. Phase IV: Fluid Frontiers of about 4,200 to 2,500 or 2,300 BP is so named to reflect, in the physical world, the rapidly changing contours of the oscillating lake and playa shores, rainfall isohyets, and vegetation zones. The Lake Chad Basin was quite arid from 4,000 years ago until around 3,500, when the lake expanded in its last transgression, declining almost by half at around 2,800 BP in its "terminal lake stage." In so doing the abundant firgi plains were opened to human occupation (Brunk and Gronenborn 2004: 107–8). (In the human world, Fluid Frontiers indicates mass migrations and massive new accommodations to change in the bio-physical sphere, including domestication, adaption of new subsistence practices and settlement patterns, and, ultimately, specialization.) When the dry episode of around 4,000 years ago ended, conditions returned to those approximating the last pluvial (Vernet 2002: 55). But not for long: Further Sahelian drought crises have been documented for between 3,800 and 3,600 and again at 3,300 and 3,000 years ago (Breuning and Neumann 2002: 125; Hassan 2002a: 323, 331). The high population densities recorded for this early part of this period in the southern Sahara and Sahel briefly enjoyed the last functioning of the hydrological networks now recorded as extensive paleochannels coursing through the desert's fringe (Gorgol, Xolimbiné, Azawad, Tilemsi, Azawagh).

Then conditions steadily deteriorated (and in a highly oscillatory fashion) – with the effect that populations were under extreme pressure to migrate or to find new solutions to "food security" if they wished to maintain some semblance of an older, familiar way of life. After a sig-nificant dry period around 3,000 BP, sedentary, non-pastoral occupation effectively ceased in the Sahara above around 18° N, even with a signifi-cant wet pulse at 2,800 (Vernet forthcoming). (Recall that 2,800 BP ended the Chad transgressive stage – our old friend spatial patchiness!) There was still a Sudanic (lion, elephant, etc.) fauna in many areas during the penultimate millennium BC (and even large fish, crocodile, and hippo in the better-situated lakes and season streams). But evidence for these fauna evaporated like the water in the once-permanent lakes, now become seasonally expanding and contracting playas, soon to be sad, salty sebkhas. Dunes remobilized. Rainfall at Tichitt in Mauritania was perhaps at 200 percent of present levels just after 4,000 BP, but by 3,000–2,600 BP it had declined to 125 percent or less (Munson 1981).

This was the period of the first *serious* occupation of the Middle Niger and of the Middle Senegal to the west (S. McIntosh 1999a; S. McIntosh and R. McIntosh 1992). We have no dates for settlements in the dry basin of the Méma before about 4,000 years ago and the four deeper, more active Middle Niger basins appear not to have been occupied until the first millennium BC. All the climate oscillations of the Fluid Frontiers phase (Phase IV of fig. 2.10; c. 4000–2,300 BP) would have made these millennia prime for pulse migrations of Late Stone Age peoples out of the desiccating Sahara and drying playas, streams, and grasslands of the Sahel into the permanent refuge of the Middle Niger floodplain. (The same principle would have applied to the Middle Senegal Valley, the Lake Chad Basin, and the wooded and forested regions far to the south.) Lake Bosumtwi was in deep regression from 2,500 to 2,000 BP. Vernet (forthcoming) speaks of an abrupt Sahelian drying and even retreat of the equatorial forest beginning at 2,600, with a finality to the Sahara's fate; as Vernet laments, "un seuil biologique est franchi" ("a biological threshold has been crossed").

By around 300 BC and until about AD 300, West Africa shared with many other tropical regions (Southeast Asia and the Amazon Basin, amongst others) a stable dry phase (R. McIntosh 2000b: 155). Precipitation was at probably somewhat or moderately below present levels for a half millennium or longer during this Phase V: Big Dry! Perhaps its very stability aided the massive influx of peoples into the still-well-watered Middle Niger. Middle Niger urbanism took root.

The Big Dry was followed, from around AD 300 to (maximum) 1100 by a relatively stable period of increasing precipitation (to perhaps +125 to 150 percent of today) to AD 700, when rainfall maintained a stable plateau until around AD 1100. Lake Bosumtwi came out of regression in about AD 200 and within a century the northern basin of Lake Chad, the Bahr el Ghazal, was fed by discharge from the northern highlands (highstand at the seventh century). By AD 500 some Saharan highlands to the west (the Tagant) even had a vestigial "Sahelian" reoccupation up to 20° N. We will call this Phase VI: Stable Optimum (stability being relative to the dynamic instability of the phase to follow). So far, the West African lowland tropics show relatively few of the deep arid interludes that interrupted this optimum in the Amazon (at AD 500, 800 and 1000). However, surely more droughts will be recognized as our resolution at the 10^4 time-scale improves.

However, it seems to have been the case in the Sahel that, in places as early as AD 900, but in others perhaps as late as 1100, there was a demonstrable "catastrophic discontinuity" between this and the following unstable Phase VII: High Unpredictability. In the Middle Niger, to date, there is little to warrant subdividing this AD 1000–1860 phase, although I suspect this will be remedied with improving resolution. It is worth recalling that Lake Chad was in transgression (minor, to be sure) for perhaps two centuries after about AD 1000 (Brunk and Gronenborn 2004: 111–14). Recall also that this unstable phase corresponds to the better-understood 10^4 time-scale climate oscillations of Europe (the Medieval Warm period of AD 1290–1522; Little Ice Age of AD

1550–1860). The middle and upper latitude record for the Medieval Warm and Little Ice Age have come under detailed scrutiny of late (Dunbar 2000; Ruddiman 2001: 356–81). And, although the tropical record is comparatively spotty, there is now an extraordinary sub-decadal resolution of the monsoon over the Cariaco Basin of the Venezuelan coast, with strong teleconnection associations with the Sahelian monsoon (fig. 2.9b). While it is too much to ask for decade-by-decade exact correlations with the Sahel, it is worth examining the overall flavor of variability in this extraordinary high-resolution record of monsoon variability from the other side of the Atlantic.

The Medieval Warm period began abruptly and with a short interval of high variation. Precipitation was high and stable. High Amplitude Variability marks the close of this and the beginning of the Little Ice Age, with particularly high amplitude characterizing the time since 1600. Indeed, Brooks (1998: 139–49) insists upon an early second millennium AD of diminishing rainfall and shifts of ecological zones several hundred kilometers to the south, and would certainly agree with Vernet's (forthcoming) diagnosis of multiple droughts and famines in the Sahel. Then, still in northern West Africa, Brooks (1998: 140, 150–52) speaks of higher precipitation (and a disastrous spread of tsetse 200 kilometers to the north) from around 1500 to 1630. Brooks then posits a dry, drought and famine period from 1630 to the end of the nineteenth century (with particularly severe droughts in the 1640s, 1670–80s, 1710–50s, 1770–80s, and especially 1790–1840; see also Webb 1995: 8). The coincidence with the rhythm of the Cariaco Basin sequence is just too suggestive! (Note also in fig. 2.9b the mode shift, "strong El Niño," at c. 4,000 BP, beginning almost a millennium and a half of HAV "Increase ENSO variability.")

Overall, these intermittent severe droughts must have put particularly severe strains on the dry basins of the Middle Niger in historical times. Indeed, we shall see that a stable urban strategy weakened at the end of the first millennium AD and toppled by AD 1400 in the Upper Delta, the Macina, and in the Méma. After about 1650, we can rely as never before on historical records of droughts, floods, famines, and pestilence for reconstructions of patterns in the climatic data. In particular, with those historical records we can begin to compare what Nicholson (1994) calls "anomaly types" tickled from twentieth-century instrumental records augmented by the historical sources (sketchy though they may be).

Ironically, when we turn from this tentative, but consensual paleoclimate reconstruction at the 10^4 time-scale, to look at patterns unrolling at the 1,000 (10^3) time-scale, our resolution decreases. We know historically that significant oscillations of West African lake levels of a few

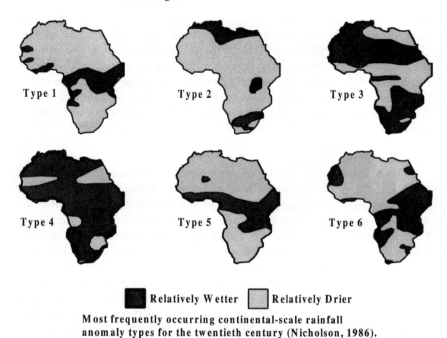

Relatively Wetter ▢ Relatively Drier

Most frequently occurring continental-scale rainfall
anomaly types for the twentieth century (Nicholson, 1986).

Fig 2.11. Nicholson Sahelian climate modes ("anomaly types")

decades in length occurred at 1680–90, 1740–60, and 1800–40, to take
the example of Lake Chad declines – but did the lake oscillate as often and
as deeply in the millennia before? However, it is spectacularly at the next
shortest time-scale, that of events resolvable at the century scale, that
most advances have been made.

In a masterful, extensive study of historical, instrumental weather data
from all over the African continent, using colonial records of really quite
surprising coverage going back into the late nineteenth century, Sharon
Nicholson has posited phase-like regularities in continental-wide rainfall
variability (Nicholson 1986, 1994, 1995). Nicholson has published six
reccurring precipitation patterns, or "anomaly types" (fig. 2.11), through
which African climate has recycled repeatedly well into the nineteenth
century. For example, Mode (or type) 1 describes the dry conditions over
virtually all of West Africa that characterized the infamous Sahel
Drought, beginning in 1968. Mode 1 also describes drought conditions
in the last decade of the nineteenth century, lasting until 1917, and also
conditions from around 1828 to 1839. Mode 3, on the other hand,
describes the unusually wet conditions over the Sahel and southern

Sahara of the 1950s and into the early 1960s. Disastrously, these were the anomalously wet conditions that encouraged the expansion of herds, leading to severe overgrazing, livestock losses, and landscape damage when the Sahel Drought hit at the end of that decade. As our historical and archaeological deep-time climate data become higher in resolution, we will test just how far back in time these "anomaly types," or precipitation modes, can be extrapolated. But, for the moment, it is a reasonable working hypothesis that, at the centennial time-scale, the Middle Niger climate leapt in a virtually random, unpredictable manner from one mode (one statistical range of variability) to the next.

There are two take-away lessons for us to derive from Nicholson's six modes. (1) In terms of human response, farmers, herders, fisherfolk, each in their own way, have had to deal not with smooth and gradual changes in the on-the-ground realities of climate variability, but with surprise. Nicholson analyzes the leaps from "anomaly type" to "anomaly type" in terms very familiar to us by now: phase transitions and the mathematics of Lorenz's intransitivity (Lorenz 1970, 1990; Nicholson, pers. comm. 2001). At this centennial and inter-decadal time-scale, change is not just abrupt and unpredictable, it is radical as well. (2) If one is to be confronted during one's lifetime with three or more radical departures from "normal" climate, would it not make perfect sense for one's society to have developed mechanisms to record, archive, and transmit to following generations past experience with those recycling modes? This, we will see, is one of the geniuses of the peoples of the Middle Niger.

Up to this point, we have looked at abruptness and phase shifts as characterizing much of the Middle Niger climate change at various time-scales, including of course, Nicholson's gems, her six inter-decadal modes. The northern West African climate is no less full of surprises on the last time-scale, the interannual. Figure 2.12 shows at a glance the astonishing year-by-year amplitude of rainfall variability at the northernmost and southernmost extremes of the Middle Niger. This amply supports Koechlin's (1997: 12–18) statement that the (northern) West African climate is perhaps the world's most variable. And the degree, or coefficient, of variation in interannual rainfall increases as one progresses from the dry savanna, on the way north to the Sahel, and into the southern Sahara (fig. 2.12, bottom). As if this high interannual variability (read: unpredictability, surprise, and risk!) were not enough, there is yet more.

We have some initial reason to believe that some of the Nicholson mode shifts were preceded by short (a few years or more) but intense periods of very rapid, very high-amplitude yearly rainfall variability. These would be the equivalent of Dean's (1996: fig. 3) HTV (High Temporal Variability) and HAV (High Amplitude Variability) episodes

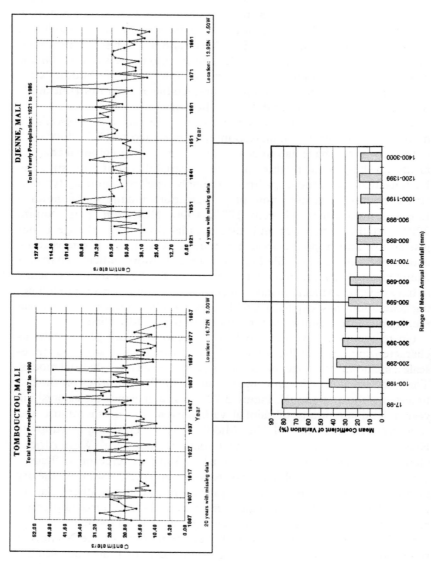

Fig. 2.12. Total yearly precipitation during the twentieth century: Timbuktu and Jenne

so well documented from the dendroclimatological data from the American Southwest (DeMenocol *et al.*, 1993: 225; R. McIntosh 2000b: 148–49). I believe we are seeing the effect of just such an HTV episode in the devastating effects for farmers and herders in Mali during the decade after 1985. That high unpredictability may mark the end of Mode 1 and a transition to new mode (?). In the event, such periods of flooding one year, followed by negligible rains the next, are the most difficult conditions to respond to, particularly if their onset cannot be predicted. Such has been the lot of the peoples of the Middle Niger for millennia. And yet they created a thriving, stable (sustainable) urban civilization.

Take-away lessons: (1) The Middle Niger climate, today and long into the past, has been characterized, not by stability and "generosity," but by intermingled periodicities and random excursions at different time-scales, as well as by alternating tempos and strengths of climatic pulses. There has also been a fair smattering of God's random acts of unique surprise. (2) These pulses and excursions (and the surprise and risks for humans left in their path) are the on-the-ground realities to which populations have to respond. Having the tools to adapt is a matter of survival. And those tools are not just material or territorial (domestic animals, technology, or appropriate water holes within a transhumance territory), but they are mental as well. Knowing what resources can be exploited under radically changed climatic conditions, knowing where the famine foods are and how to process them, knowing how to adjust group size, knowing when to pull up stakes and move to better land – all of these strategies are as a matter of perception of change in the landscape, perception of risk, and perception of those radically new events that trigger a Social Memory (an archived repository of the communities past experiences – useful or to be avoided!). We turn now to perception of landscape as key to subsistence security and perception of risk.

Geokistics: risk, surprise, and subsistence security

Some might read with surprise the characterization of the Middle Niger as an environment of riches. Equally disconsonant with expectations would be Vernet's (forthcoming) (an old Sahara hand) statement that West Africa from 16° to 12° N represents an "opulence sahélienne"!

Just as the Sahel is cursed with poor, dune-based soils, the particular hydromorphic soils of the Middle Niger, compared to other world flood-plains, are rather poor. The Niger and Bani Rivers bring in 1.2×10^6 tons of dissolved load, generally poor in phosphorus and nitrates and other agriculturally useful nutrients (compared to the Nile and eastern African lakes, with their headwaters in regions of younger volcanic rock) (Rzoska 1985: 87 and table 9). The Middle Niger lacks any immediate sources of mineral wealth: gold, silver, or copper, for example. And the urban civilization the floodplain supported certainly lacked the classic indicators of state wealth: lavish monumental architecture, resplendent art, and kingly treasuries locked deep in the bowels of the citadel. Yet the word "wealth," as used here, has a different orientation altogether.

Remember the formula of those who theorize about the best conditions for the emergence of self-organizing landscapes (chapter 1): Search for a context of a surplus of energy (dissipative structures), a diversity of co-symbolitic (co-evolving) entities that are "sandwiched between the dangerous uniformity of equilibrium and the dangerous chaos of turbulence" (Prigogine and Allen 1982: 14). Wealth: a landscape supporting any number of possible, non-deterministic paths to the resolution of tension between monotonous monocultural homogeneity, on the one hand, and being overwhelmed by the fates, on the other. And the Middle Niger landscape provides all the elements of energy surplus (in the form of high productive potential) – only to those who know what they're about – and (as we have seen in the preceding section on the high-variability, low-predictability climate) potential for chaos!

The key to the wealth of the Middle Niger landscape is encapsulated by a rather fusty, technical term: edaphic conditions (Koechlin 1997: 19–20; Le Houérou 1989: 50–60). How do soils perform in relation to water (surface water, water infiltration, water storage, and evapotranspiration)? In arid-lands situations such as these, is it any wonder that farmers and agronomists, pastoralists – and, needless to say, fisherfolk – give more importance to soil moisture than, necessarily, to fertility. Slowly, ever so slowly, born of ancient Precambrian bedrock, the soils of West Africa are notoriously low in nutrients. Founded upon recent (Last Glacial) sand dunes, the soils of much of the northern West African savanna and the Sahel are monotonous and, frankly, depauperate. (I once asked a discouraged Western agronomist what, if he had all the fertilizer, all the mechanized help, and any choice of seed, would he grow on, actually, a rather fine spot in the Malian Sahel. His answer: Sports fields!). Hence the special destiny of the Middle Niger floodplain.

The Middle Niger today comprises some 55,000 square kilometers, of which in a good year an area of 3,200,000 hectares will flood annually. By the end of the dry season, only 1,600,000 hectares of standing water will be left. That means that this landscape, 425 kilometers long, oriented SW–NE, with a mean width of 87 kilometers (a mean width that constructs to ≤ 10 kilometers after Timbuktu and to around 1 km near Gourma-Rharous) is virtually unique in lowland, arid West Africa. The key to that uniqueness is the diversity of soils and landforms (described above individually for each of the six Middle Niger basins) – in the context of an assured (if variable) external source of water. Positive edaphic conditions!

The flood is dramatic. The Middle Niger has a negligible gradient of about 1:50,000; the overall elevation drops only 8 meters over 425 kilometers (Hughes and Hughes 1992: 393). The 3,200,000-hectare flood begins at Ke-Macina in August–September and its flood crest only reaches Timbuktu in December. The Niger contributes some 50 billion cubic meters (with a mean discharge at Ségou of 1,585 m^3/sec., a maximum 5,000 m^3/sec. in August and a minumum of 70 m^3/sec. in October). The second river source, the Bani, contributes 20 billion square meters. There is a minor discharge from the Bandiagara Plateau into the south-western lakes of the Lakes Region and Niger Bend. The flood crest goes northward at an average rate of 5 kilometers per day – taking a full month to go from from Ke-Macina to Mopti, another month to Goundam, and yet another to arrive at Timbuktu (Hughes and Hughes 1992: 395).

At Timbuktu, the outflow from Middle Niger is 35 billion cubic meters per year, at a mean flow rate of 1,110 cubic meters per second. Dry-season outflow can be as low as 60 cubic meters per second. Thus, something in excess of half of the riverine influx is lost each year to evaporation and infiltration. Compared to the Nile, for example, the Niger water is low in minerals, high in fine particles, and moderately turbid. But the appropriate comparison is not with the distant Nile, or Tigris and Euphrates, but with neighboring regions within the subcontinental context of the Sahel. And here the issue of key ecological conditions, edaphic conditions, is all-important: What is the possibility of exploiting rainwater, that fundamental limiting factor for primary production (Koechlin 1997: 12)?

Critically important is length of time allowed for active vegetation growth – that is, the period during which the available moisture exceeds or is equal to half of the potential evaporation (Koechlin 1997: 14). At a typical southern Sahelian site of 698 millimeters rainfall, this is five months, and at 304 millimeters, this decreases to two-and-a-half months. (Jenne in the southern Middle Niger averages 589 millimeters.) The northern Middle Niger is embedded within the sub-desert of <200–250 millimeters (Timbuktu receives 150 mm, the official boundary between Sahel and Sahara). Sub-desert suffers a dry season of more than ten months. The Sahel of 200–550 millimeters has a dry season of eight to ten months; the steppe vegetation sub-Sahelian zone receives 550–750 millimeters (for a seven- to eight-month dry season); and the southern frontier of the Middle Niger boasts the transition steppe-to-savanna vegetation of the northern Sudanese zone of 750–1,000 millimeters (dry season of six to seven months).

Koechlin (1997: 17) elaborates for us the reality of Sahelian aridity. Because of high average temperatures (maximum regularly of 45 °C), with low atmospheric humidity most of year, and with high potential evaporation values, the water balance (actual evapotranspiration [AET]/ potential evapotranspiration [PET]) is in the negative for much, if not all, of the year. For example, Mopti receives 552 millimeters of rain. The town has a PET of 1,984 millimeters, giving it a positive balance of only one month per year. Gao, with 261 millimeters of precipitation and a PET of 2,255 millimeters enjoys not a single month of positive balance (Koechlin 1997: 17). But Mopti is within the Middle Niger. It enjoys not only the short rains of (March, if lucky) April to July (August, on the outside), but also the four to five months of the flood! Gao is all by its lonesome out there in the northern Sahel, with only a constricted river valley as consolation.

So the issue becomes, how do the varied landforms – the mingled, convoluted products of millennia of struggle of wind and river – perform with the flood? Dry phases have left their signature on the manuscript of the Middle Niger in the form of a great variety of dunes and sandy levees (where the river scooped up sand, only to deposit it during a later flood on its banks). In general, sandy soils make better use of moisture. They are permeable and so retain moisture at a certain depth for deep-rooted plants. Thus protected, there tends to be lower evaporation. But sandy soils are chemically impoverished and there is a quick drop in fertility with cultivation.

Compact soils, those ranging from light (sandy) loams to heavy clays also run the gamut from reasonable permeability to less good runoff (that is, escape of water before it can be absorbed at appropriate depths for utilization) and relative difficulty of root penetration. The heavier and more compact the soils, the greater the problem of water retention at shallow depth, where moisture can be evaporated away. All these soils have their own risks of degradation. Arid tropical soils are extremely fragile soils. Damage can come about because of wood removal for firewood, overgrazing of grasses, and can even be effectively "sterilized" by the production of hardpans (iron laterites or calcite calcretes) (Centre de Suivi Ecologique 1996; Koechlin 1997: 23–24; Le Houérou 1989: 90–94). Although the Middle Niger boasts a high diversity of the slightly higher fertility hydromorphic vertisols (tropical black), these can be extremely compact in the backswamps and can become deoxygenated. As with any arid land floodplain, there is the ever-present danger of salination.

A major component of the wealth of the Middle Niger is the floodplain's natural flora (for identifications, Berhaut 1967; Gallager 1999; Shawn Murray, pers. comm. 2004; and Neumann et al. 2001). The Middle Niger flora is officially classified as *Typha* swamp (Hughes and

Hughes 1992: 395; Le Houérou 1989: 80–81), which understandably emphasizes the hydrophilic grasses: acroceras (*Acroceras amplectens*), the *bourgous* (aka shamma millet) (important graze, flooded two months or more) (*Echinochloa pyramidalis* and *E. stagnina*), lovegrass (*Eragrostis atrovirens* and *E. barteri*), wild rice (*Oryza barthii*), the annual wild panic grass (*Panicum anabaptisum* and *P. laetum*), and a groundcover at the basins' uppermost margin, vetiver (*Vetiveria nigritana*).

However, this floodplain is, preeminently, a mosaic. And as in any ecological mosaic, one finds interdigitated microenvironments, each with their own suites of plants and animals. On recessional fringes (low levee, low dune and upper, usually sandier, floodplain soils) is gamba grass (*Andropogon gayanus*), Bermuda grass (or common stargrass or chiendent) (*Cynodon dactylon*), and *Hyparrhenia dissoluta*. Along the levee-lined channels one finds important gallery forest trees and shrubs of mimos (*Mimosa asperata*), kélélé willow (*Salix chevalieri*), with spiney sedge (*Cyperus maculatus*), with, in the better-watered southern Sudanic Sahel, the African ebony (*Diospyros mespiliformis* and spp.) and sausage tree (*Kigelia africana*). Levee woodlands are colonized by jun or dyum (*Mitragyna inermis*), various acacias (*Acacia nilotica, A. polycantha,* and *A. sieberana*), desert date or soapberry or thorn tree (*Balanites aegyptiaca*), nettle tree (African micocoulier) (*Celtis integrifolia*), and African locust bean tree (*Parkia biglobosa*), *inter alia*.

In the heavy loam and clayey backswamps one finds permanent or long-seasonal pools with coontail (*Ceratophyllum demersum*) (a recent New World introduction) and lily pads (*Nymphaea* spp.) and recessional parts of pools and channels are fringed with *bourgou* (*E. stagnina*), knotweed (*Polygonum senegalense*), and cattail (*Typha australis*). In the dune-dominated landscapes of the northern basins we find palms (*Hyphaene thebaïca* and *Borassus aethiopum*) and trees such as *Acacia nilotica*, nguère (*Guiera senegalensis*), mimos (*Mimosa asperata*), and jujube (*Ziziphus mauritana*) (Hughes and Hughes 1992: 396).

Grasses of hydromorphic soils are critically important to the story of local domestication of cereals. In the deep basin one finds wild rices (*Oryza barthii* and *Oryza longistaminata*). Next in progression is *bourgou* (*Echinochloa pyramidalis*) and, on the depression margins, thatching grass (*Hyparrhenia rufa*) and vetiver (*Vertiveria nigritana*). Others on margins are gamba grass (*Andropogon gayanus*), Guinea millet (*Brachiaria deflexa* and *B. mutica*), fingergrasses (*Chloris* spp.), sedge (*Cyperus* spp.), crab grass (*Digitaria* spp.), shama millet (*Echinochloa* spp.), panic grass (*Panicum* spp.), paspalum (*Paspalum* spp.), wild millet (*Pennisetum ramosum*), and wild sorghum (*Sorghum arundinaceum* and *S. bipennatum*), *inter alia* (Hughes and Hughes 1992: 293). The importance of these grasses cannot be overstated. In addition to providing the wild species (*O. barthii*) most likely to have been the parent stock for local domestication of (red) African rice (*Oryza glaberrima*), these wild grasses are still actively collected in a mixed wild and domesticated diet. Thus, although *Oryza glaberrima* (African red rice) and *Pennisetum americanum* (millet, aka *P. glaucum* or *P. typhoides*) and sorghum (*Sorghum bicolor*) rank as the staple crops, there is also a large spectrum of minority domesticated plants (some of which play a pivotal role in the ceremonial life of various ethnic groups) such as fonio (*Digitaria exilis* and *D. iburua*), Guinea millet (*Brachiaria deflexa*) and Bambara groundnut (*Vigna subterranea*), *inter alia* (National Research Council 1996). Beyond these are wild cereals gathered by preference (and not just as famine foods): wild fonio (*Digitaria exilis*), shama millet (*Echinochloa colona*), "desert panic" (*Panicum laetum*), kram-kram (*Cenchrus biflorus*), wild rice (*Oryza barthii*), and bara or kodomillet (*Paspalum scrobiculatum*), as well as collected wild Sahelian fruits, jujube (*Ziziphus* spp.), nettle tree (*Celtis integrifolia*), and West Africna plum (*Vitex doniana*). The fleshy herb portulaca or pourpier (*Portulaca quadrifida* and *Portulaca oleracea*) of open sandy soils and sandbars is gathered and cultivated as a cure for headaches, asthma, and as a poultice.

Today the Middle Niger provides 90 percent of the national fish catch (c. 100,000 tons) and the 55,000 specialized fisherfolk can choose among more than one hundred species (Hughes and Hughes 1992: 294–95, 396–97). The fishes of the Middle Niger are part of an extraordinary population of the roughly 190 species common throughout the West African "Niger–Chad Sudanian" ichthyological province, seventy of which also occur in the Nile (Lowe-McConnell 1985: 101–2). Could there be any more eloquent testimony to the ubiquity of the fluvial world during the early and middle Holocene pluvials? Living in the deeper, well-oxygenated waters are the enormous Nile perch (*Lates niloticus*). In the swamps one finds catfishes (*Clarias* spp., *Synodontis* spp., *Bagrus* sp.), *Gymnarchus niloticus*, the osteoglossid detritus-eating *Heterotis niloticus*, the electric-fish (*Mormyrus runae*, *Polypterus ansorgei*, and *P. senegalensis*), and lungfish (*Protopterus annectens*). Not so welcome are the rice-eating fish the alestes (*Alestes baremose* and *A. nurse*) (itself the basis of a large oil-rendering industry), citharinidae (*Distichodus brevipinnis*) and tilapia (*Tilapia zillii*). (For fishing, see Quensière 1994.) There are more than 350 bird species. The middle Niger is a breeding ground for pelicans, cormorants, herons, and pratincoles; it is also a major southern flyway for European migratory species. (Doing a walking survey of the floodplain in winter can be truly breathtaking!)

Today there are few wild mammals found (Le Houérou 1989: 122–23). Those present in the archaeological profiles (e.g. S. McIntosh and R. McIntosh 1980, I and S. McIntosh 1995) are those endemic for almost all Sudanian–Sahelian wetlands (Hughes and Hughes 1992: 297–98). Particularly important to the story of Late Stone Age specialization were the aquatic mammals (hippopotamus and manatee [*Trichechus senegalensis*]) and crocodile. Hunting these formed the basis of one of the earliest specialized corporate activities in the Middle Niger and, although no longer widely practiced, large reptile and mammal hunting persists as the ethnic signature of the Sorko Bozo.

This is not the place for a full review of the beginnings of food production in West Africa (see Harlan 1993; R. McIntosh 1997; S. McIntosh 1994: 169–73). Suffice it to say that the coming of herds of cattle, small stock (sheep, goats), and (in the north) camel, as well as the domestication of the West African staple crops rice, millet, and sorghum, adds to the wealth of the Middle Niger – and to the variety of possible responses to ecological change. This last point is critical. In other places in the world, archaeologists are accustomed to thinking of food production as swamping a previous, more mixed, exploitation strategy. In the Middle Niger, as in many other parts of West Africa, domesticated species are simply added to a table groaning in diversity (S. McIntosh 1995: 352–53, 377–79).

Cattle came into the Sahel from the north (and ultimately from the eastern Sahara) as early as 5,000 years ago (MacDonald and MacDonald 2000; S. McIntosh 2001: 324–25; Van Neer 2002: 251–53) and by 4,000 BP were in the Niger Bend paleochannel of the Tilemsi (A. Smith 1980). With them came an underappreciated following of sheep and goats. Although the data are poor, it does appear that the local, West African domestication and the spread of indigenous crops was genuinely late and adapted in a patchy fashion (R. McIntosh 1997; S. McIntosh 1994: 169–73). African rice, *Oryza glaberrima*, was most probably domesticated in the Middle Niger itself and presents a classic case of a local, high-yield crop well adapted with many varieties to the changing conditions of the floodplain (National Research Council 1996: 17–37). Sorghum (*Sorghum bicolor*) (possibly originating in the eastern part of northern "central Africa": Harlan 1971, 1993) and (originating further to the west) millet (*Pennisetum americanum*) are the other two main Middle Niger crops. There is no good evidence of sorghum in West or Central Africa before the last millennium BC (the first, to date, is from the Middle Niger city of Jenne-jeno), but Breuning and Neumann (2002: 148–49) give their reasons for supposing that the process of domestication began sometime between 4,500 and 2,000 years ago. Compared to the Near Eastern domesticates, millet appeared late as well. The oldest millet (determined from seed impressions in pottery) is from Tichitt in Mauritania (an important potential source of the early migrants into the Méma), at 3,500 BP (Amblard 1996). By the time millet appeared in the well-dated Chad Basin and Burkina Faso wetland archaeological sequences, by around 1200–1000 BC, it was fully domesticated (Breuning and Neumann 2002; Neumann 1996).

Food production spread unevenly throughout West Africa; many peoples apparently were quite content to remain hunters and gatherers well into the Present Era. Given the enormous risks of the agrarian life in the Sahel (Delville 1997: 149–51), it is little wonder that prehistoric peoples wanted to keep open as many subsistence options as possible! And if the adoption of pastoralism and farming was patchy in West Africa, I suspect it was especially so on the patchy landscape of the Middle Niger. This, I suspect, is because diversity of economy would play out as a major strategy of food security. Hassan (2002a, 2002c) inventories the prehistoric and historic African strategies to deal with the kinds of frequent droughts, abrupt climate changes, and unpredictable mode shifts that we have documented above. Of course, we have not even mentioned many other sources of great stress and surprise, such as infestations (of biblical proportions) of desert locust (*Schistocerca gregaria*), that cruelly visit the Sahel under drought-driven conditions (Desert Locust Information Service n.d.; Launois 1996). Among the risk-reduction and stress-relieving strategies are settlement abandonment, migration, temporary displacement to less-afflicted regions, community fissioning, demographic "adjustments" (infanticide, senilicide, banishing marginal members), collecting weeds and famine foods, harvesting premature crops, selling parts of herds (including breeding stock), perennial storage of cereal beyond the needs of one year, planting different crops (including drought-resistant crops), paying for rain makers, praying, and asking help from friends and relatives. This list is surely not exhaustive.

The important point for thinking about the Middle Niger is the wealth (that is, diversity) of the bio-physical landscape, juxtaposed against virtually "chaotic" flood and rainfall conditions. How, then, did it come to pass that specialization in subsistence pursuits became the watchword of the various ethnic groups of the Middle Niger? How, then, did a settlement pattern of towns (and villages) of specialized, physically discrete components develop? In the words of Raynaut *et al.* (1997: 199), "The situation is particularly complex, however, in that the specialization of modes of resource exploitation along ethnic lines is quite marked." Specialization, one might think, is rigid and inflexible. Specialization, one might think, is the very last strategy that should be developed in such a risk-filled, surprise-packed environment. The next chapter proposes a hypothesis (and report upon a preliminary test) of how this overall strategy of specialization might have emerged in the later part of the Late Stone Age and might have led to a clustering of settlements of specialized communities. Such clustered Late Stone Age

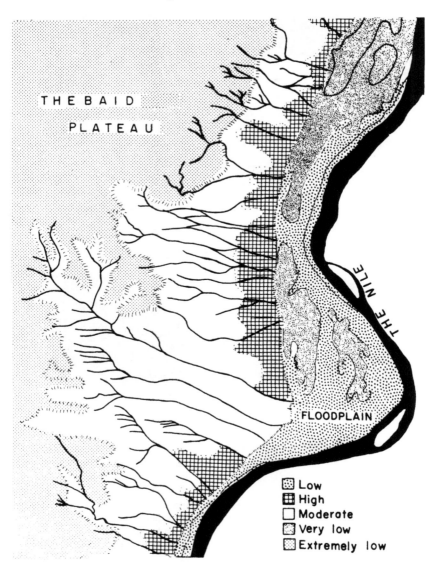

THE BAID

PLATEAU

THE NILE

FLOODPLAIN

☒ Low
⊞ High
☐ Moderate
▨ Very low
▨ Extremely low

Fig 2.13. Geokistics map of the Nile Valley

hamlets and villages are thought to be the origin of the highly clustered first cities of the Middle Niger.

However, before turning to the Pulse Model hypothesis of early specialization and clustering, we will end here with an exercise to bring home the

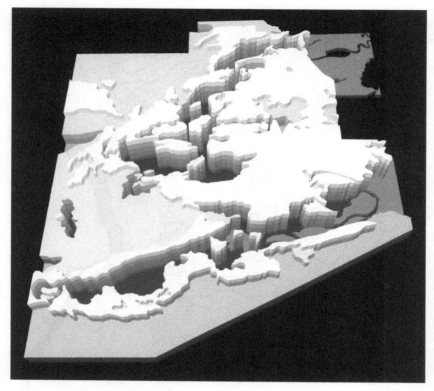

Fig. 2.14. Simplified geokistic map of the Méma (compare to fig. 2.8)

wealth of the Middle Niger landscape. The exercise is called geokistics (Hassan 1985: 95–97). Hassan (pers. comm. 2003) describes the origin of the concept:

I coined the term geokistics to describe the suitability of an area for settlement, taking into account various geomorphological aspects (e.g., protection from floods, vista, slope [as controller of movements and access], aspect, relief, geological hazards [torrents, earthquakes, volcanic eruptions, etc.], topographic controllers of access to vital resources, terrain and its suitability for subsistence or other activities, geological [rocks and minerals], etc.). Various grid cells in the landscape are evaluated ... The key variables and their weighing depends on the type of settlement under consideration (a seasonal encampment, a permanent village, a shrine, a fort, etc.). The geoekistic map can be used as a predictive model for settlement location (and, thus, an aid for surveying) or could explain the reason for placing certain settlements where they have been found (after consideration for post-depositional processes).

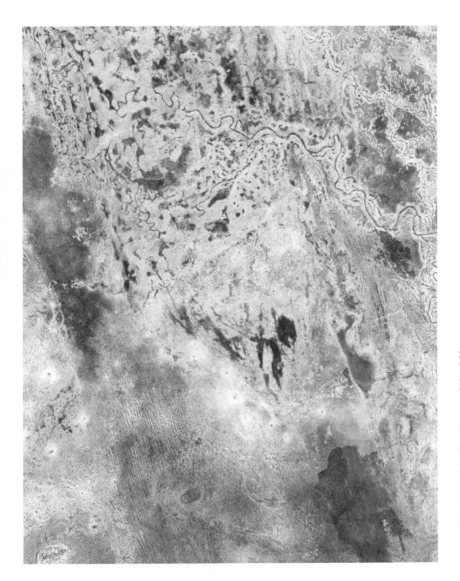

Fig. 2.15. Satellite image of the Méma

Geokistics describes a scale of desirability of the various elements of the landscape for past (and present) populations. Let us use the example of Hassan's own geokistics of an idealized sector of the main course Nile River valley during the Predynastic (1985: fig 4.4)(fig 2.13). The desirability can be assessed for subsistence/resource exploitation or for settlement, or for both. Here the complications begin. What parts of the population are to be considered? Different subsistence-based ethnic groups? Urban versus country dwellers? The potential for subdivisions can be endless – with a resultingly richly nuanced tableau of landform desirability. This picture of competing and overlapping perceptions of desirability can, in a multi-ethnic situation such as the Middle Niger, help us to understand various accommodation strategies that will be discussed in the following chapter. As a further complication, one has to factor in significant shifts of landform perception, as interdecadal, inter-century, and longer paleoclimate patterns change. As the topography and geomorphological situation becomes modified by all the agencies mentioned above, the landform framework for regional geokistics changes also. Thus, in a wealthy region at the edge of environmental "chaos" such as the Middle Niger, each subsistence group has its own geokistic map of the landscape and these maps shift flexibly as climate dictates.

What happens, also, at those points of tension, on those landforms at certain seasons when the exploitation desires of one specialized group overlaps and conflicts with those of another? Even today, a major source of homicide in the live basins of the Middle Niger is the receding flood season – in those years when the Fulani cattle herders are forced to move their herds onto the recently evacuated soils, to graze on *bourgou* vegetation, before the rice, sorghum, or millet harvests have been completed.

I end this chapter with an idealized geokistic map of the Méma, the Middle Niger basin to which we next turn our attention when thinking about the long-ago circumstances that might have led to persistent specialization and emergence of ever-more-elaborate corporate belonging. Figure 2.14 is presented with a caveat, however. To be true to the themes of this chapter, one should juxtapose multiple geokistics – one for every subsistence-defined ethnic group, with multiple iterations for the variety of climatic modes to which these groups are required to adapt! Imagine this project for, say, three specialists, then ten, then an urban score or more – projected on the true landform complexity of the Méma (fig. 2.15). Chaos!

3   Accommodation

Pulse Model

Who most elaborately employs native "geokistics," as presented in the last chapter, to think about their landscape? Specialists. When describing the specialized, Cushitic-speaking Waso Boran of northern Kenya (to take pastoralists as an example), Andy Smith reminds us that, while the need for pasturage and water are paramount in the strategy of seasonal movement (transhumance) over the landscape, other considerations are never far from mind. Other considerations may be slope of terrain, salubrity of locale and availability of construction materials for temporary dwellings, soil color and texture (indicating drainage, cooling at night, etc.) (1992: 170–71, 182). Smith quotes Dahl (1979: 43) about the Boran's specialized knowledge of landscape:

When talking about different pasture areas, the Boran herdowners express themselves in terms of soil; soil texture and colour provide the points of reference for their classification of the district into ecological units. Each soil concept also has connotations concerning the availability of salt licks, the mineral content of water and vegetation, the presence of insects and other parasites.

A perfect example of native geokistics.

The Boran, like any specialists, are not like the rest of us! They know things we do not. They see the world through very different eyes and incoming information about change in the physical world is filtered through their specialized mental construct of historical ecological causality. Specialists, be they subsistence specialists (rice farmers, herders) or artisans (potters, blacksmiths), generate specialized knowledge. They traffick in that knowledge amongst themselves but, very often, they are paragons of secrecy towards outsiders. If successful, the knowledge needed becomes ever more specialized – crowding out, as it were, the wider corpus of "whole landscape" awareness and knowledge that characterize generalized hunters and gatherers (previous or contemporary) or mixed-strategy agro-pastoral fisher–gatherer–hunters!

Big problem: The more specialized one's knowledge, the more difficult it might become to survive the landscape surprises of massive, abrupt, phase transform shifts of climate or resource availability. That being the case, why was the Middle Niger (a landscape, preeminently, of high variability, at many temporal and spatial scales, and of classic stress) the arena of a brand of urbanism supremely celebratory of specialization? How did this ever get started from a Late Stone Age generalized foundation? The Pulse Model is an empirically testable hypothesis about the conditions of the self-organizing landscape that allowed the horizontally complex cluster of specialists that we recognize as Middle Niger urbanism.

How can the dynamic, nearly "chaotic" landscape of the Middle Niger just described be linked causally to the elaborate specialization and clustering of settlements that characterize urbanism here, apparently from its origins? How can the concept of the self-organized landscape, describing a progressive series of phase transformations of human–land relationships, aid our thinking about this issue? The "Pulse" of this section derives from the ecological and climatic patterns of the millennia preceding the mid-first millennium BC emergence of the earliest true cities on the Middle Niger alluvium. But the Pulse Model (R. McIntosh 1993) is primarily about the mental and symbolic circumstances of emergence and maintenance of occupational specialization. It gives a prehistoric slant to current thinking by historians and anthropologists as to what lies behind the creation of individual and corporate identity – and, hence, to the mechanisms by which multiple, each quite discrete, corporate groups shared the mosaic Middle Niger landscape.

Proceeding from the landscape dynamics of the last chapter to the rules of accommodation systematics at work, even today, amongst the Middle Niger peoples – that is the task for the present chapter. Accommodation. That is our operative word. So, let us make all this a bit more concrete by looking at a series of, admittedly idealized, illustrations of the transformations this accommodation might have entailed.

In truth, the first great self-organizational transformation of the landscape may have taken place outside the Middle Niger. So little archaeology has been done that we just do not know about transformational processes in the Azawad. But, when pastoralists and, perhaps, fisherfolk and aquatic hunters first appeared in the Méma and, certainly, in the four live basins, they were perhaps already well on their way to incipient specialization (Jousse and Chenal-Velarde 2001–2002; MacDonald and Van Neer 1994; see also R. McIntosh 1998: 55–66). The Pulse Model deals primarily with accommodation of multiple – and potentially conflicting – regional exploitation and settlement strategies. Hence,

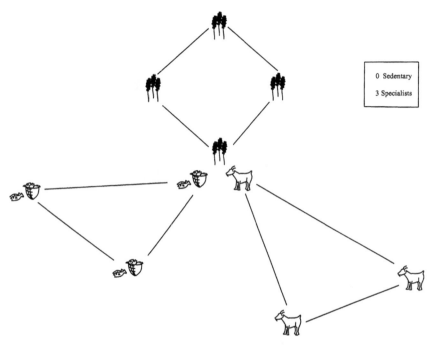

Fig. 3.1. Self-organizing landscape I: three specialists, all fully non-sedentary

figure 3.1 represents the hypothetical situation in which three specialists, farmers (millet stalks), fisherfolk (fish and basket), and herders reach an initial accommodation. (Let's represent the herders by the mythological animal the "ovicaprid," because faunal paleo-osteologists can rarely distinguish between sheep and goats!). Compare this figure to figure 1.8a, where this is appropriately situated on the idealized Lorenz phase transform diagram (fig. 1.6). Each enters the scene with a three-stage or four-stage mobile seasonal round. As such, each echoes an earlier landscape strategy of moving through their annual territory, on a predictable seasonal round, to take advantage of resources – water, nutrient-necessary minerals, etc. – as they come available seasonally (see R. McIntosh 1998: 53–55; for the pastoralists' transhumance and seasonality, see A. Smith 1992: 11–19).

However, the self-organized landscape I of figure 3.1 has an interesting twist. The twist is radical enough, I would argue, to be termed a phase transform. Something has happened to change all three specialists'

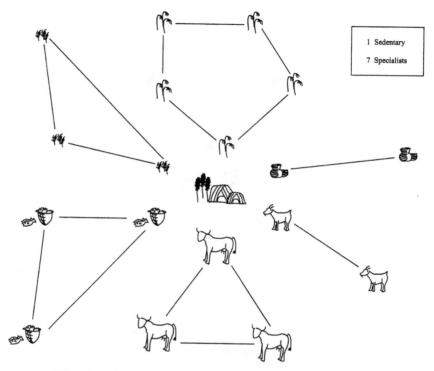

Fig. 3.2. Self-organizing landscape II: seven specialists; one full sedentary

conception of landscape, such that a season of gathering together, however briefly, in one locality is now part of their exploitation strategies. In an earlier time, on a less complex landscape, the millet growers, fisher-folk, and herders would have met only by happenstance, if at all, perhaps briefly for limited exchange, but perhaps as often with unhappy conflicts the result. By the self-organized landscape state depicted in figure 3.1, however, their exploitation strategies, their conception of the landscape, has begun to co-evolve in a way that will be a critical first step towards clustered urbanism. Several more transforms to go, each a phase of self-organization as revolutionary (and abrupt?) as transformations from water vapor to liquid H_2O to ice.

Now consider figure 3.2 (and compare this to fig. 1.8b). Two radical distinctions appear now between our simpler, previous landscape (fig. 3.1) and this; a true phase transform has occurred. The landscape is more crowded, if not in absolute population numbers, then clearly in terms of specialists. Keep in mind that every new specialist represents, potentially, a new nexus of conflict with another specialist. Yet in figure 3.2 we have further specialized cattle pastoralists forging seasonal alliances with the "ovicaprid" herders. (Cut to the range wars of the late nineteenth-century American West, violently pitting cowboys against sheep herders...) The fisherfolk have not changed much. Now the millet farmers have spawned off specialized rice and sorghum farming. And, radically, the farmers now have abandoned their seasonal round. They are the first truly sedentaries. And, radically, demand is such that specialized potters have emerged – ceramic production is not just within individual households now. They are the first true artisan specialists. And, radically, a new code of interaction, a new contract for peaceful access to the goods and services of non-kin and effective strangers, must now be evolving somewhere from the experimental to the operational. Another phase transform to the exploitative and settlement landform.

The Pulse Model purports to deal with all three aspects of this phase transform: true sedentarism, emergent complexity of specialism (including artisanship), and new contractual rules ensuring peace across this ever more complex landscape.

The next transform is one of scale, but still radical enough. In figure 3.3 (compare to fig. 1.8c), the three artisans (leatherworker – awl; potter – ceramics; weavers – cloth) are all fully sedentary. Village life is now the norm. The fisherfolk persist traditionally, as do the rice growers, whereas the millet and the sorghum farmers and "ovicaprid" herders live year-round *in the same settlement*. The cattle transhumance is looking a bit attenuated. Maybe the cattle-herding community goes on its round only some, but not all, years. Or maybe only the young men go on trek, and the majority stay behind with their many and varied neighbors, making transhumance a minority strategy. But the houses show that this is not a monotonous, fully assimilated community; different dwellings symbolize identity differences in this truly clustered, multi-group community. Yet another phase transform to the exploitative and settlement landform.

And finally, consider figure 3.4 (to compare to fig. 1.8d). At what point is a heterogeneous settlement no longer a village but rather, instead, a town? As we saw in chapter 1, to ask the question is in one sense pointless, unless one has information about the "servicing" relationship of the settlement with its larger hinterland. Yet, here for the sake of argument, we can imagine that the phase transformation from the figure 3.3 situation to the one here is one of "more of the same," a linear increase in sedentarism and in numbers of specialists, leading to a "radical difference," a non-linear shift to (incipient?) urbanism. New specialists appear (camel herders, blacksmiths – knife). Eight specialists, new and old, are

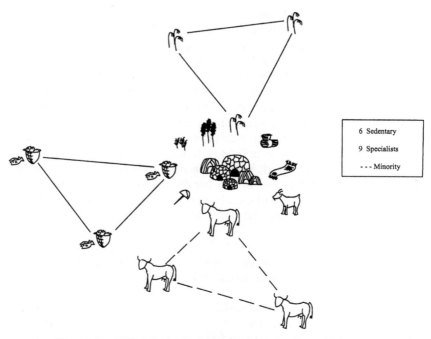

Fig. 3.3. Self-organizing landscape III: nine specialists; six fully sedentary

fully committed to year-round life in the settlement. And even those with a seasonal round (cattle pastoralists, rice farmers, fisherfolk) practice those rounds in a very minority fashion – now even the fisherfolk! Now we need some mechanism to help us think about the evolutionary potential and the developmental circumstances that might have led to this drama of pluri-specialist emergence and of clustered settlement accommodation.

Can processes of communal identity and of pluri-ethnic accommodation be identified in the very distant past? This is the problem for archaeologists that we will turn to in chapters 4 (excavation) and 5 (surveying the hinterland). Are there testable implications of the Pulse Model that will increase our confidence that this is not just a story spun, conveniently but out of thin air, to fit troubling archaeological settlement data? Consider the myths and legends used historically, and even today, by the many, many happily coexisting ethnic groups of the Middle Niger to define the boundaries between them (R. McIntosh 2000b). I argue that many of these can be characterized as abstractions of their ecological places in a highly unpredictable, stressful environment ("on the edge of

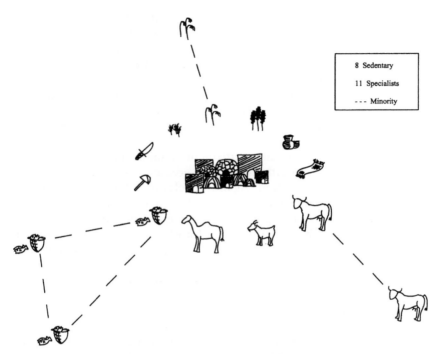

Fig. 3.4. Self-organizing landscape IV: eleven specialists; eight fully sedentary, living in a town (by Tera Pruitt)

chaos"). So, too, are the rules for dealing with one another. Here, clearly, we will be mixing a functional argument (occupational specialists accommodating each other in a generalized regional economy) with a symbolic one (identity based upon abstractions of one's place in the environment, using landscape terms of reference).

Does this (indeed, do *any* arguments of symbolic motivation) go beyond the archaeological data? After all, we cannot interview these Late Stone Age peoples about how they saw themselves, or what they intended! Yet, archaeologists increasingly understand a fundamental fact about their data and inferences: *All archaeologists have ever done is to interpret the (incomplete, often poorly preserved) remains left behind after a prehistoric peoples' complex responses to the world as socially constructed.* Communities acted upon the world in accordance with their view of reality – and such actions left their imprint upon the physical remains later unearthed by archaeologists.

The Pulse Model attempts to go to the deep-time roots of the process of clustering that is at the core of urbanism, from the very beginning. I believe that Middle Niger clustering represents a solution to the dilemma of how to maintain boundaries between specialized sub-groups under conditions of growing population and of proliferating occupational corporations – but, apparently, without a coercive centralized authority. Physical clustering allows these corporate groups to remain socially separate and yet to enjoy proximity to clients and availability of the services of many other corporations. By this model, clustered settlements serve several purposes. Satellite settlements maintain physical boundaries between specialist corporations and also serve as the spiritual or symbolic property of each corporation. Again, the classic definition of corporate groups requires that belonging be reinforced by a right of common possession or access to corporate property, including land or "ancestral topographies" (Cochrane 1971; R. McIntosh 1993: 188). The common property also serves as the signature, or ensignia, of the group, a code communicating identity. The code satisfactorily represents belonging and thereby constrains social ambiguity, one of the fundamental curses of city life.

Time called for an example. The purpose and mechanics of urban regional survey will be explained below (chapter 5). During an initial survey of the Jenne-jeno hinterland (again, a bit ahead of our story), the survey crew was very perplexed by certain characteristics of a site about 4 kilometers from the present-day town of Jenne. While part of the cluster of satellites around Jenne-jeno, this site, Kangousa, had abundant evidence of two specializations. One could interpret deep-channel net fishing from the abundance of large net-weights and lots of relatively large fishbone and, additionally, iron smelting in the form of slag heaps and furnaces. Now, there is no particular reason the two should not have coexisted. None, except that most other satellites of Jenne were showing a strong tendency towards occupational *exclusivity*. One might find fishing on one satellite within a cluster; blacksmithing on another; but rarely both occupations together. Even more peculiar was the fact that passersby looked at the survey crew almost as if seeing creatures half ghosts and half demons. Everywhere else we were greeted with warm handshakes and curiosity. At Kangousa, the passersby averted their eyes and moved on in great haste! And those passersby never, never set foot upon the site.

Only months later, during interviews of corporate groups in the town, was all revealed. Kangousa, it appears, is the universally recognized "ancestral site" of three lineages of Somono living in Jenne. Somono are the specialized deep-river-channel fishermen and boatmen of the Niger (Conrad 2002; N'Diaye 1970: 439–41). Unusually, these three lineages also were ironworkers! And local legend holds that anyone not of these three Somono lineages, who walks over the site without permission, would be smitten by a silver hammer flying through the air (a prohibition we presume that predates Maxwell!). Our good intentions must have been recognized by the protector spirit; *post hoc* permission was granted by the lineage heads, amid much hilarity on all sides!

What (from an urbanism perspective) was going on at Kangousa? If each group is provided with unambiguous insignia of belonging and if the roles and complementarity of groups are agreed upon and reinforced by myths, metaphors, and legends, then society can accommodate, over long periods of time, a process by which specialists become ever more specialized. Why? Because specialists can invest the time to develop and curate the intricate knowledge needed successfully to pursue their occupation in this highly variable, essentially unpredictable environment. The importance of this is paramount, yet the particular drive to elaborate specialization creates the fundamental paradox of life on the Middle Niger.

Without specialization, no one can master the complexities of this rich but highly unpredictable landscape. But, if too specialized, too dependent exclusively on the products and services of one specialization, odds are good that one will perish during those not infrequent years that overwhelm even the most knowledgeable, the most skillful of specialists. The best rice farmer can enjoy good crops, and even some spectacular surpluses, during many if not most years. But it is a certainty that, two years out of each decade, two decades out of each century, that rice farmer will survive only on the exchanged milk and meat from neighboring pastoralists (mixed with some millet from specialized millet farmers). Yet, if the rice farmer tries to become, himself, a generalized farmer–herder–fisher–gatherer–hunter, he will possess neither the knowledge nor the skill in any of those pursuits to make it. The Pulse Model attempts to generate, functionally, the landscape conditions for resolving this paradox and, symbolically, the clues (our old friends "proxy measures," really) by which the process of resolving the paradox might be recognized archaeologically in the deep time of the Middle Niger.

This interpretation appears to satisfy the twin requirements of explaining clustering *physically* as a field of boundaries between emerging corporate groups and *symbolically* as space coded to encourage peace and cooperation within a regional population newly or increasingly confronted with greater scope for conflict. Ambiguity of identity will inevitably be a source of conflict in the early town. Kinship and other rules of identity adequate for simpler societies will increasingly fail to keep pace with the increasing scale of social space between participants. Clustering can be a way to address that ambiguity. And the Pulse Model gives the mechanisms by which this clever tool of accommodation comes to be.

The Pulse Model posits the existence of segmented but articulated Late Stone Age "pre-urban" communities in the southern Sahara and in the "driest" of the Middle Niger basins, the Méma and the Azawad. In fact, following the landscape transforms of figures 3.1 to 3.4, there should have been a serial evolution of accommodation, as the settlement dynamics became more complex. These communities would live part of the year, each year, in small clustered hamlets. Relations of complementary reciprocity between these communities encourage occupational specialization. Over a long period of time we see the evolution of ever larger clusters that, in time, take on the function of true cities.

The Pulse Model predicts the locations where archaeologists may find the earliest or most emphatic expressions of early clustering. Many north–south-trending paleochannels of the southern Sahara and Sahel are composed of tightly spaced microenvironments, where increasingly specialized groups would be in close contact. These, also, are precisely the landform characteristics of the mosaic landscapes of the Middle Niger. Climate oscillations, those documented in the previous chapter, create a "pulse" north and south of population movements or shifts of ecological adaptations for some distance along these long, longitudinal fossil corridors and within the alluvial basins. This would be a scene of particularly dynamic interactions among groups and of dynamic human adaptation to changing environment.

The Pulse Model predicts greater intensification of specialization as the response to the ecological dynamism and, at the same time, a strengthening of reciprocal relations among specialists as a way to smooth over the stresses and surprises of a semi-arid tropical climate of high unpredictability. In the Saharan paleochannels and Méma and Azawad basins we would see the emergence of those settlement and subsistence strategies that were later carried into the deep basins of the Middle Niger during the first millennium BC. And as these arid environments have had little occupation during the past two millennia, we should find excellent preservation of sites and of organic remains within the sites. For the success of the model there must be a social dynamic that evolves ways to establish identity, resulting in the successful accommodation of increasing numbers of specialists.

The Pulse Model requires an approach to ethnicity and to "corporateness" in general that emphasizes the fluidity of the representation of self and of symbolic codes for communal mobilization. Happily for the prehistorian, traditions from the past and material items can be powerful symbolic resources.

Things or places serving as codes to expected behavior and insignia of identity are rarely rigid corpuses ready-made for the ethnographer to pluck and preserve behind museum glass. They are, rather, symbolic fragments that can lead to change by focusing ideas and mobilizing group support. Material culture, Vansina's "crystallizer of metaphors in tangible form" (Vansina 1984: 158), can be as powerful in this regard as myths, ideologies, or traditions. And as a system of active symbolic representation, the past need not be seen as exerting a dead hand. The past can provide criteria of which symbols are relevant to the reinvention of future identity. The historical ties of people and their traditions can provide an enormous, but selectively appropriated, reservoir of symbols sending collective messages within the group (props for claims of common identity) and to those outside. Thus, the task for the archaeologist is not just to identify those stylistic attributes or artifact insignia that might, in the past, have communicated information about ethnicity, lineage affiliation, residence groups, or other corporate belonging.

We appreciate better than ever before that among the various purposes of these social networks was the distribution of environmental (natural and social) risks and benefits among the participants (e.g. Braun and Plog 1982: 505–7, 518; Halstead and O'Shea 1989; Rautman 1996). In this view, as environmental unpredictability rose, so would the integration of the non-hierarchical regional social networks comprised of kinship crosscutting, pan-residential corporations that characterize many pre-state societies (M. Smith 2003). The historical and prehistoric evidence shows the dominating effect of social approval and perception of environmental stresses on the decisions taken in response to climatic change and surprise. Indeed, if we wish to understand the ways in which the environment is socially, rather than externally, known, we must understand how a society's traditional perceptions of environmental constraints are a part of that community's social construction of reality.

Because people act upon those perceptions, social views of the environment may be obscured, but are never entirely out of the prehistorian's realm. If one of the core values is the distribution of environmental risks, then archaeological materials will be created as people act upon that core value. These materials can direct the archaeologist to networks of interactions maintained by the different corporate subdivisions as part of that adaptive strategy. And, from symbolic representations of belonging among contemporary Middle Niger groups we can derive clues about how belonging and identity was constructed in the distant past. These representations are framed in terms of ecological abstractions. The ecological abstractions can be thought of as the Middle Niger population's "mental technology" (social construction of reality) by which climatic change (objective reality) is mediated, environmental risks are reduced, and specialization encouraged as a consequence (R. McIntosh *et al.* 2000b).

In this context of potential (but here, infrequently realized) land-use conflicts, intensive contact between corporations, and memories of past abuses of ethnic frontiers, there is a need to articulate ambiguity of belonging. That is, there have to be some vehicles of articulation that resolve questions of identity in increasingly pluralistic situations. Accommodation! The symbolic repertoire of ecological abstractions that invoke idealized dangers in the climate and hydrology is highly developed. In many cases, these ecological abstractions form the central myths of the group (although ecological themes are not the exclusive core of myths). These are not context specific in that they apply over the whole of the Middle Niger floodplain and provide the general narrative for inter-ethnic conflict reduction. The rules are metaphorized in lore and myth internalized from childhood. They serve as extensive regional expectations concerning cross-cultural behavior. However far from home, one has the security of knowing that certain peaceful behavior can be expected of others.

These constellations of myths, tales, and stories are the agents by which the peoples of the Middle Niger negotiate their contemporary sense of ethnicity, but they are in essence synchronic. Just as we probably will never know how deeply in the past to place the origins of a specific people named the Marka or Bozo (R. McIntosh 1998: 96–105), the specific myths that define relations between these two self-proclaimed "original peoples" are constantly being reinvented, retold, and, frankly, manipulated. However, the general process of elaboration of ecological abstraction carries lessons for population-wide manipulation of the symbolic universe in the deeper past.

Today in the Middle Niger, the rules of accommodation can be divided into three generic types. The first refers to the eponymous privileges of those groups traditionally always in place or the most ancient migrants to unoccupied territory, the *nés du sol*. Although later conquering groups claimed *de jure* title to the Middle Niger, none secured ritual authority for certain critical decisions. Almost exclusively, these are the privilege of the Bozo, the *maîtres de l'eau* (Gallais 1967: 78, 108, 158, 423; Sundström 1972: 50–53, 66–68). They entered the floodplain first and made the first enduring agreements with the local water spirits (the *yégu* and the *ba-faro*). The Bozo preserve the taboos of water (and land) use, undertake sacrifices to the spirits, and have the absolute right to scheduling fishing everywhere, to initiate the rites before sowing and harvest in Marka rice fields, and even to be called *Dougou tigi* or "Master of the Land" by the late-arriving, hegemonic, warlike Bambara. The well-being of all depends upon the attention with which they attend to the water spirits, who cause ruinous floods, migrations of distributary channels and, especially, visitations of water-spread epidemics (onchocerciasis, guinea worm, cholera, shistosomiasis, etc.).

Bonds of fictive kinship, the second category of rules, demonstrate that integrative codes need not claim ecological inspiration exclusively. Two groups may claim a mythological common origin. The Bozo and Marka assert that they once were a single group, hence explaining their shared institutions and identical totems. The Bozo and Dogon claim descent from an ancestral twin pair. Secondly, familiar kinship rules are metaphors that codify inter-ethnic behavior. Dogon and Bozo intermarriage is strictly forbidden (a prohibition shared also by the Somono). Nono–Bozo marriage is very negatively sanctioned. In cases of intermarriage (or where blood is spilled between villages), the breach of custom is beyond purification and, ideally, the entire community must be dissolved. Endogamy keeps clear the frontiers between groups and prevents the obscuring, by real kin obligations, of the formalized if fictive obligations of these inter-ethnic accommodations. Fictive kinship cements the exchange of Marka work at the low-water Bozo barrages for Bozo labor at high-flood rice harvest and other obligations of reciprocity in goods and services (Sundström 1972: 54–55, 162–67).

Lastly, salutary and undischargeable debts represent integrative rules reinforced by a large lore of extraordinary sacrifice by one group for another under conditions of ecological stress. This is debt above and beyond obligations owed to kin. Two examples will suffice. When the Marka arrived at the site of the future Jenne-jeno, they asked permission of the autochthonous Bozo to settle. Their mud houses, however, collapsed with a regularity which, to an archaeologist, suggests episodic high flooding (entirely consistent with our reconstruction of last-millennium BC precipitation and fluvial High Amplitude Variability). The Marka appealed to the Bozo, who offered a young virgin (Tapama, "la fille du fleuve," the "young girl of the river") to be immured at the settlement (Gallais 1967: 556–57; Monteil 1971: 285). To this day, young Bozo girls are kept indoors during seasons of particularly high flood!

The Dogon and Bozo share a myth of a time of severe famine (Griaule 1948: 242–52). The Bozo left their children with a Dogon chief in order to fish. No fish could be found, and the days passed without food. Before their return, the Dogon chief fed the children his own flesh, rather than see their suffering. (In a variation, Dogon adopt children of the river spirits, breastfeeding and feeding them parts of their own bodies. The children become the Bozo.) The Bozo were so moved that they entered into a formal *mangu* alliance. *Mangu* allies recognize a blood-tie of gratitude. They may not shed the blood of their ally. They are obliged to provide food, hospitality, and ritual aid, and to perform purification rituals for the other community.

These examples are illustrative of a large constellation of ecological abstractions ensuring exchange of information, peaceful travel, and access to rituals and subsistence from others without an obligation of exchange of marriage partners or expectation of immediate, equal compensation. The myths that illustrate climatic potential and unpredictability are incorporated into social systems of belief. These examples will, I hope, explain my assertion in chapter 1 that the classic Tragedy of the Commons dilemma (Millinski *et al.* 2002) just does not make much sense in the (ideal) Mande world. All these legends and myths are reinforcements of the pervasive Mande core rules of "reputation." Recall from chapter 1 that the recently discovered "solution" to the Tragedy of the Commons is as simple as "reputation," the indirect template for reciprocity, the "give and you shall receive," that can sustain a high level of cooperation and, indeed, can generate new canons of reciprocity. As explained by Millinski *et al.* (2002: 426), when reputation (however socially defined) was abused and indirect reciprocity not sustained in practice, then "contributions to the public good drop quickly to zero." Any Mande child could teach these Tragedy of the Commons theorists a thing or two!

It is time now to take the process to a more generalized plane. These contemporary ecological abstractions serve as the intellectual and spiritual property of the various ethnic groups. They provide the very stuff of continuous negotiations of corporateness in the Middle Niger. They specify the boundaries between different groups. Their claim to great antiquity, although unverifiable empirically, nevertheless possesses the power of enormous moral compulsion. This set of myths set expectations for behavior within a wide range of situations and within an enormous area.

The myths provide for positive individual and group action. Corporate relations here are balanced. The ethnic mosaic of the Middle Niger does appear a good candidate for the argument that some symbolic constellations really do do a good job of allowing multi-groups proximity and interaction in highly ambiguous contexts, without necessarily surrendering their group identity.

The Pulse Model (fig. 3.5) is a hypothetical alternative to the usual model of linear migrations of Late Stone Age peoples south (and east) out of the Sahara due to late Holocene desiccation (e.g. Davies 1967; Flight 1976).

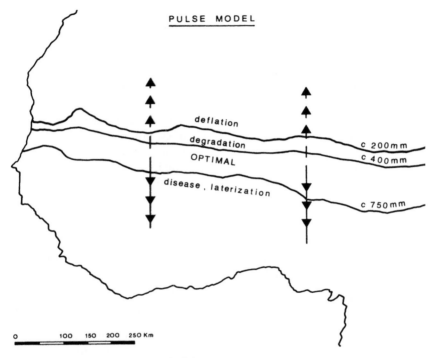

Fig. 3.5. The Pulse Model

The model is inspired by reconstructions of the inter-latitudinal ripple effect resulting in the (eventual) advance south of the Sahara and the replacement by drier ecologies of savanna and forest to the south. As we have seen in chapter 2, 10^4 and 10^3 time-scale climatic variation can be conceptualized as wave phenomena, expressed in the Sahel–Sahara as north–south oscillations of zones of ecological potential. (The pulse must necessarily be primarily north–south, of course, because of the dominance of the monsoonal climatic system.) With improving climate, for example, more northerly latitudes received more precipitation (hence building savanna soils and enjoying permanent surface water). But this advantage was lost at the end of the mini-pluvial with the weakening of the annual rains.

One might find a slow migration of peoples with economies already adapted to a particular precipitation–vegetation profile, or more entrenched communities may make forced adjustments to their subsistence and settlement patterns.

Over many thousands of years, but certainly since around 4,500 years ago, the latitudinal migrations of rainfall zones, vegetation populations, and human economies (i.e. zones of ecological and social potential) would have had the effect of forcing human populations to be flexible in their adaptations or willingness to undertake short- or medium-distance migrations. These are precisely the conditions expected to encourage the concentration of experience and knowledge about wild foods (and newly domesticated plants and animals) that help people survive a chaotic climatic regime. But the Pulse Model does not predict an infinitely repeating cycle. This is because (1) the fragility of the dune-based northern soils imposes a critical check; and (2) the hydrological and landform mosaics of certain wide-channel and interior floodplain landscapes such as the Middle Niger provide the potential for the formation of radically new social and settlement forms. These are precisely the forms illustrated, in idealized version, in figures 3.1 to 3.4.

During the many northern swings of the pulse, anthropogenic and fluvial–aeolian agencies will have inevitably begun damage to skeletal dune soils of the Saharan–Sahel frontier. At the commencement of the next arid cycle, irreparable damage is done. These thin soils (often a simple weathering of the ancient dunes) are directly subjected to the severe NE trade winds, resulting in the massive aeolian soil losses (Mainguet et al. 1980). Soil structure is disturbed, topsoil losses worsen, and the integrity of protective soil crusts is reduced. Increasingly episodic but still violent rains cause deep gullying, especially at the 250–350 millimeter zones (Jacobberger 1988; Talbot 1980). After a lengthening dry season (reducing grass cover), torrential sheet wash eliminates soil clays and loams, leaving only sterile sand or reg surface. At the next northern pulse, moving populations confront a boundary to further northward penetration analogous to that existing today at the Saharan frontier of the Middle Niger. There, an abrupt boundary separates rich Macina and Upper Delta floodplain from the Azawad and, to a lesser extent, from the seasonal transhumance plain of the Méma. Recent work confirms that the southward degradation of the Méma worked in precisely these ways (channel strangulation, soil deflation, loss of inundation basins) during the first millennium AD (Togola 1993; see De Vries et al. 2005).

The scene is set: A zone of active soil degradation (corresponding roughly to the 100–400 mm rainfall isohyet zone) forms a ceiling over an optimal zone. Humid pulses occur at the time-scale perspective of 10^4, 10^3, and 10^2 years. Ideally, the Pulse Model would combine local exploitation shifts with northward migrations as the human response to mini-pluvials. But, because of the Sahara-side soil and stream degradation, the northern shift is constrained. Without the release of migration, ever-denser populations are forced to adapt under conditions of *improving* rainfall. The importance of this confluence of factors cannot be stressed enough. More people crammed into local optimalizing conditions, which in the Middle Niger and along the Saharan paleo-channels means an explosion of mosaic landforms with quality resources – but with nowhere else to go! (Or, at least, with options for migration constrained significantly.) And out of this cauldron of possibilities, time and inherent environmental unpredictability and the self-organizing "calculus" of these landscapes ladled out those key ingredients of Middle Niger urbanism – *specialization* and the *accommodation systematics* of exuberant pluri-corporateness!

However, this still occurs within the semi-arid belt of Sahel–northern savanna most sensitive to drastic unpredictability – indeed, to chaotic climate, with a (10^2) wavelength of 10–30 (or fewer) years. Most prehistoric Sahelian populations would have had limited options under these circumstances. Experiments in cereal domestication throughout an extensive zone may have been one response (Harlan *et al.* 1976; R. McIntosh 1997; Neumann 1996). Full-time devotion to camel or cattle pastoralism was another (A. Smith 1980, 1992). However, although these adaptive pressures would have been felt along the whole of the Sahel, certain conditions of tightly packed microenvironments in the north–south-trending paleochannels and in the mosaical, now dry basins of the Middle Niger allowed special potential for novel and plural responses to climatic variability.

Among the regions most interesting as a test of the Pulse Model, one can mention the Méma, Wadi El-Ahmar (Azawad), and Xolimbiné Valley of Mali (fig. 3.6) and (in Senegal) the Ferlo Valley, as well as the Gorgol (White and Black Valleys) in Mauritania (see fig. 2.1b). These regions very tightly conform to the physical requirements of the best field locales for the investigation of early occupational or corporate differentiation of the Saharan–Sahelian Late Stone Age societies. This is not to say that specialization could not have appeared elsewhere. But these would be my best bet as to the first places such specialization would be recognized by archaeologists working within expectations of the Pulse Model. All have the following attributes: (1) A field of tightly spaced microenvironments. Groups increasingly specialized in the exploitation of one microenvironment would unavoidably be in close contact with other similarly specialized groups. Close contact requires a (functional) will to interact and exchange, as well as (symbolic) rules of accommodation. (2) Each area is "serviced" by a long, longitudinal fossil fluvial or flood corridor, allowing a "pulse" north and south of some distance. (3) Despite conditions for occupation locally better than the surrounding

Fig. 3.6. Vestigial corridor into the Sahara: the Xolimbiné paleochannel

desert, the whole of the corridor lay roughly astride zones of recurrent rainfall scarcity and unpredictability during most of the later Holocene climatic oscillations. (4) These are areas not fluvially scoured or heavily disturbed by later settlement after the first millennium BC. Remains of more ancient or of more ephemeral seasonal occupation are likely to be found here, as opposed to the live, actively alluviating parts of the Middle Niger. And, (5) Each empties into or abuts upon present-day topographic mosaic floodplains where many inhabitants are subsistence and occupation specialists. The rules for inter-corporation interaction in place today among these specialists may provide clues to the ways in which archaeologists can look for the codes arbitrating inter-specialist interactions in the more distant past.

These conditions of tightly spaced microenvironments, enough water from runoff accumulation or piezometric ponding to attract settlement from the increasingly dry surrounding regions, and long corridors cross-cutting major bio-geographical zones would have been met during the first and second millennia BC. With an active hydrology in place during the pluvial northern climatic pulses, one could expect multiple, shifting channels for communication and the creation and dynamic remodeling of a mosaic of soils and landforms. The mosaic of microenvironments would have been a likely locale for subsistence experimentation with eventual crops such as rice, sorghum, and millet and with variations of pastoralism. But those doing the experimentation still must have responded to significant climatic variability at the 10^2 and 10^3 time-scales.

The landform diversity of the Middle Niger and these paleochannels offers opportunities for plural response to climatic unpredictability. The Pulse Model predicts in these locales the gradual appearance of settlements in regular association, occupied by groups increasingly specialized in their food-production activities. These locales would have evolved into a cultural landscape of articulated, segmented communities: groups of specialists regarding themselves as different in identity, yet maintaining frequent and complementary exchange relations with the other communities. If non-coercive, this flexible articulation of communities electing to live near each other (at least for predictable seasons of the year) would allow increasing scope for even more concentration by each group of the particular potentials of one or two of the many microenvironments, i.e. specialized responses to climatic change. By maintaining generous relations with neighbors, environmental stress and benefits would be shared. This hypothesis can resolve a major contradiction, or paradox, in the strategies of food production in any situation of high historical unpredictability of climate.

When reconstructing the origins of the remarkably stable subsistence system of the Middle Niger, one needs to resolve this paradox of a push to a specialized subsistence strategy versus the pull to a generalizing economy (S. McIntosh 1995: 377–79; S. McIntosh and R. McIntosh 1979: 240–41). On the one hand, studies of the present-day *crue/décrue* system (mixed agricultural strategies that take advantage of the flood rise and flood recession for the soil moisture requirements of different species) of crops and of pastoral strategies shows that only intense, highly particularistic knowledge of soils, rainfall patterns, flood cycles, and varieties of domesticates will ensure long-term adaptive success (Gallais 1967, 1984; Galloy *et al.* 1963). However, as in any context of unpredictable climate, any monocultural, too-specialized subsistence is enormously dangerous. Diversity (a generalized strategy) is the best response. The paradoxical pull of specialization versus the generalizing obligation has been resolved in the Middle Niger by the special relations that evolved between specialists (be they subsistence-defined ethnic groups or artisan associations). These relations allow each to pursue, in ever more particularistic ways, their individual occupations, while together sharing mutual obligations and accommodation. I believe these relations are of great antiquity (R. McIntosh 2000b: 167–71).

The perspective of Historical Ecology, then, is an important key to understanding the emergence of specialization in the Middle Niger, not solely in the functionalist terms of adaptive decisions, but equally in terms of how representation of identity is framed in terms of social strategy. Inter-ethnic social strategies are very often, but not exclusively, verbally presented or symbolically coded as ecological abstraction. In the creation of social identities, a key dynamic is the conceptualization of one's relations with another, mediated by stylized representations of ecological promise and disaster. These conceptualizations of identity are canonized in widely propagated myths, ideologies, and material expressions, and just a tiny fraction of these were presented above as illustration.

Once these codes to inter-specialist behavior are in place, relationships develop between corporations (ethnic groups, artisan associations), which allow each to pursue, in ever more specialized ways, occupations concentrated upon the production of a narrow range of foods or manufactures. Specialists are thus allowed a deeper development of knowledge about and practical experience with a narrower range of pursuits, while at the same time enjoying the peace of mind of expectations of obligation and mutual accommodation.

This situation has best been studied in the Erg of Bara Basin (Galloy *et al.* 1963) and the hinterland of Jenne (R. McIntosh 1998: 89–105). Occupying the crazy-quilt geomorphology of the latter are fishermen (Bozo) and rice farmers (Nono [Marka]). These two claim to have been established in place in deep prehistoric times. Pastoralists (Fulani) and dry-crop farmers (Bambara) immigrated in, perhaps sometime after the thirteenth century. The fishing–transport group (Somono) and merchants (Songhai) were absent before the mid-second millennium AD. The Arma are legacies of the Moroccan invasion of 1591. And an agricultural client group (Rimaibe), Moorish artisans, and intrusive pastoralists (Tuaregs) are of relatively recent date. The Dogon of the floodplain's eastern periphery boast ancient relations with the Bozo and Marka (Dieterlen 1941; Griaule 1948; Sundström 1972).

Let us look in a bit more detail at the sophisticated decision making required today of the rice-cultivation specialists, the Marka (Bourgeon and Bertrand 1984; Gallais 1967: 109–11 and 1984: 23–30, 95–97; R. McIntosh 1998: 99–101; S. McIntosh and R. McIntosh 1979; National Research Council 1996: 17–37). Domesticated African rice (*Oryza glaberrima*) has somewhat successfully held off the diffusion of the higher-yield Asian variety, *O. sativa*, because of its genetic plasticity. Varieties of African rice will survive variations in water depth of between 1 and 3 meters (versus a less-than-1-meter requirement for paddy rice, *O. sativa*). Marka will sow in the same field a mixture of the over forty-one varieties, with differing vegetative periods (from 90 to 210 days), a wide range of tolerances to different soil porosity or pH, bathymetric profile (flood depth in any given year) and forgiveness of date of flood arrival, and variable sensitivity to weak or torrential rains after planting and before the floods arrive, or to the interval between the first rains (field preparation and planting) and the later sustained rains (germinative), or to predations of rizophagous fish (Gallais 1967: 199–200, 218). Clearly, a great deal of cumulative, specialist knowledge goes into getting the rice planting just right!

Marka farmers habitually sow a mixture of seeds with different adaptive characteristics; they plant in long, narrow fields cross-cutting several soil units along a bathymetric progression. They keep intervals between multiple sowings of several days or weeks. Intricate cosmological observations are used to predict climate (Monteil 1971: 35). This recondite knowledge is not possessed by all. Most tellingly, it is not freely shared.

Monographs on the Middle Niger document similar secret knowledge and subtleties of environmental response by the Bozo and the Somono; the Bambara; and the Fulani and Tuareg (see, esp., Gallais 1967 and 1984; Galloy et al. 1963; Imperato 1972; R. McIntosh 1998; Sundström 1972). In part because of the subtlety of ecological responses, in part because of the close proximity of groups occupying different microenvironments and shifting occupation seasonally, there has developed a near infinity of conflicting conceptions of landform utility. Hence, there is enormous potential for inter-ethnic conflict. Recall our concept of geokistics, developed in the last chapter (e.g. figs 2.13 and 2.14). Each subsistence-defined ethnic group has its own geokistic map of the Middle Niger; that of the pastoral Fulani will differ radically from that of the dune-dwelling, millet-growing Bambara. When it is time for the Fulani herds to move into the floodplain on their annual transhumant rounds, the cattle absolutely must be kraaled at night on the dunes to keep their hooves from rotting. If, that year, the millet harvest is late, there may be conflict – leading not infrequently to homicide – between farmer and "cowboy"!

Marka and Bozo have come into conflict in the (mythological) past. These and other inter-ethnic clashes form the pedagogical lore about corporate belonging. Conflict lore recalls appropriation of functions, privileges, or identities. Conflict lore reiterates the consequences of tampering with expected inter-ethnic behavior. The oral traditions tell of times when pagan Bozo had to flee further into the swamps to avoid Marka impression to service a flotilla during the Mali Empire (Gallais 1967: 107). Those captives forced into Niger transport service of the later Bambara kingdom became Somono. Bozo and Somono vie for privileges of river transport (once the exclusive privilege of the Bozo). Fishing conflicts are avoided by the Somono restriction to net fishing in the deep channels. Remember the story about survey at Kaniana, the mythical ancestral satellite site near Jenne? Kaniana is claimed by the Somono and the fishnet weights give deep-time credence to that claim. Other satellite sites yield only the slighter net weights, now associated with the shallow-water, swamp-fishing techniques of the Bozo. Alienation of privilege became a theme of Bozo–Fulani lore when, in the nineteenth century, the empire-builder Sékou Amadou gave the Rimaibe rights over Bozo streams and fishing grounds (Sundström 1972: 56–57, 166).

The list of *potential* conflicts goes on. Marka and Fulani were often at odds. The sedentary Marka, particularly those occupying dunes, were frequently captured and incorporated into the Rimaibe serf caste of the Fulani. Dunes in the floodplain made attractive highland locations near paddies for farm villages but, as mentioned above, were desired by Fulani as high, sandy land (*seno*) to protect their cattle's feet against the afflictions of cold clays, near the lush dry-season pasturage (*bourgou*) of the deeper floodplain.

The intrusive Bambara came into immediate conflict with the Marka, especially on the high sand plain south of Jenne, where Marka villages formed a pre-Dyula chain of trader specialists (Brasseur 1968: 466). Ideally, Bambara sorghum and millet harvest is completed in October, when the Fulani herds are driven from the last Saharan pastures to their dry-season *bourgou* reserves. The herds feed on the sorghum stubble at the Delta periphery or on the Erg of Bara dunes until the flood has receded to a level safe for penetration of the floodplain itself. But if the crop matures slowly due to a low or slow flood, the *décrue* crops will not yet be harvested when the herds arrive. If the rains in the desert are feeble, the herds will return early. Lastly, the Tuareg have always been a law unto themselves in the Niger Bend area and more recently down to the Lake Débo region, where competition with Fulani is intense (Galloy *et al.* 1963: 11–19).

Sundström (1972: 133–36) uses a deterministic symbiosis model to describe Middle Niger inter-ethnic relations. The history of conflict between the groups and the fact that conflict is expressed (at least in lore) in terms of the victor appropriating the vanquished's identity implies that traditional ethnographers' models of ethnic accommodation are inadequate. By anthropologists' classic definition of ethnic symbiosis as most appropriate to a field of distinct ecological niches (Barth 1956: 1088), the Middle Niger should be a morass of inter-ethnic hostility. And yet, it is not.

The reality is otherwise because the ambiguities and tensions of the Middle Niger ecology are successfully appropriated and transformed by the agencies of mythologies, reinforced by material cues, into expectations for appropriate behavior during inter-ethnic contact. (As the judge of the Jenne "palais de justice" once told me on a long, long drive back to Bamako, "The Bambara are the Bambara and the Peul [Fulani] are the Peul." In other words, when all know their place in the cosmos, accommodation can follow!) In other words, the Tragedy of the Commons – the Middle Niger as a whole being the Commons – has been successfully resolved. And the march of the self-organized landscape – through a progression of ever more complex phase transforms – continues on the pathway to urbanism!

Ground truthing the Pulse Model

In the world of remote sensing, "ground truthing" means physically to verify the features identified or the patterns interpreted from aerial photographs or satellite images. Ground truthing is always a hard slog and is rarely as cerebral as hypothesizing from the images. Two distinguished archaeologists have begun the long, laborious slog to ground truth the Pulse Model.

Now, the Pulse Model should apply particularly well to any of the many paleochannel and playa situations throughout the southern Sahara and Sahel. The Méma, however, cried out for urgent attention. Early surface surveys had suggested a fantastic (and unexplained) degree of clustering of Late Stone Age and Iron Age sites (Haaland 1980; photo survey and identification of some 700 putative sites by M. Haywood, in CIPEA 1981; Szumowski 1957; Togola and Raimbault 1991). These sites displayed an obvious degree of variability in their surface material. Some, like the classic site of Kobadi (Jousse and Chenal-Velarde 2001–2002; Monod and Mauny 1957; Raimbault 1986; Raimbault and Dutour 1989), were rich in fish bones and those of large aquatic mammals. Kobadi long ago became the eponymous site for the so-called "aqualithic" (Sutton 1974; discussed in R. McIntosh 1998: 49–51). Others were mounds of freshwater oyster (*Etheria elliptica*) shell (Tiabel Goudiodié) or were dominated by cattle bones (MacDonald and Van Neer 1994). Unfortunately, previous research was not conducted in a way that would allow regional diversity and variability to be identified. And so, the Méma remained an unrealized promise of great things to come, until 1989–90, when Téréba Togola and Kevin MacDonald arrived on the scene.

Together the two conducted the first archaeological landscape analysis (fig. 3.7). Together they conducted the first scientific sampling survey of the Méma. They excavated a series of Late Stone Age and Iron Age sites, but divided up the analysis, MacDonald taking the 29 Late Stone Age

Fig. 3.7. Late Stone Age and Iron Age sites of the Méma

sites and Togola the 108 Iron Age sites. Togola was interested in urbanism, and in the clustering of urban sites in the Méma – we will return to his results below. It was MacDonald who took an explicit test ("ground truthing") of the Pulse Model as the principal goal of his research. MacDonald (1994: 4) lists his objectives and questions: (1) Is there great time depth (going back into the last millennia BC) to the modern Middle Niger cultural mosaic? (2) Does the modern symbiotic, multi-ethnic specialization of the Middle Niger peoples have roots going back into the Late Stone Age? (3) If so, were environmental instabilities responsible?

MacDonald collected and analyzed the Méma Late Stone Age settlement pattern and artifactual material in a way allowing at least a preliminary identification of a grid of subsistence strategies. Were these people generalists (coherent ethnicities incorporating significant agricultural, pastoral, and/or hunting/gathering aspects within their subsistence: 1994: 17)? That is, were they hunting/gathering/fishing generalists or mixed-food-producing generalists? If generalists, were they exclusively concerned with wild resources or did they mix in aspects of farming and pastoralism as well? Were they sedentary or were they semi-sedentary (more-or-less mobile) generalists? Or were they specialists (coherent ethnicities exploiting one resource to the near exclusion of all others; 1994: 21)? Were they specialized farmers? Pastoralists? Or even fisherfolk or hunters? And if specialized, were they isolated or did they establish (as predicted by the Pulse Model) a "mutually advantageous economic association of two or more entities, resulting in the acquisition of otherwise unavailable commodities through reciprocal exchange" (1994: 21)? In other words, were there multiple ethnic groups, defined by their specialized subsistence tasks (farmers, fisherfolk, herders), but living an existence apart from all others? Or had Late Stone Age specialists already developed regular, expected, and peaceful exchange relationships with other specialists? If so, how did the requirements of exchange and contact affect the settlement pattern and seasonal movements of these specialists?

In other words, once one recognizes variability in the lithics, in the ceramics, and, especially in the food debris left behind at these pre-urban sites, what does it all mean? How does one demonstrate exchange and regularity of relations between two specialist groups? After all, a certain low level of contact and exchange (think of it as background noise) might be expected between two or more (generalist) groups whose annual round territories overlap (R. McIntosh 1998: 53–55). The trick is to differentiate between these infrequent, informal, and haphazard exchanges and the incipient specializations linked with scheduled, seasonal cohabitation of a predetermined locale, as depicted in figure 3.1.

Put this way, it should be clear that the leap from haphazard contact of generalists to the transformed landscape of the seasonally cohabiting incipient specialists really does represent a radical, self-organized landscape transition. And at what point, empirically, can one go beyond description – recognition of diversity and evidence of exchange – to explanation of why this incipient specialization (or the generalists' resistance to same) and symbiosis came about?

Although surely more work is needed to firm up the identification of MacDonald's ethnicities (the "corporations" of the Pulse Model), he convincingly shows that different groups co-occupied the Méma and regularly exchanged. Their co-evolution has elements of migration from the outside and of local transformations (MacDonald 1994: 70–118, 1996). In a nutshell, the following is the story the archaeological data tell to MacDonald.

The first peoples into the Méma, perhaps as the pulsing desiccation of the southern Sahara opens up to occupation former lakes and swamps, were mixed aquatically oriented hunters/gatherers/fisherfolk. Members of this cultural tradition ("Kobadi," c. 2000–200 BC) are responsible for the large mounds of shellfish (Tiabel Goudiodié) and, especially, for the "fisher-hunter" sites of fish bone mixed with aquatic mammals and crocodile (e.g. Kobadi: Raimbault and Dutour 1989; Raimbault et al. 1987; more broadly, MacDonald and Van Neer 1994). As introduced previously in this chapter, we must find a way to answer this question: Can the differences in these sites be explained because the sites are seasonal way stations along an annual round of exploitation by the same community? Or do they represent sub-specializations within a larger, generalized tradition? Where the Kobadi people came from is still somewhat a mystery. The best candidate to date are Saharan sites far to the north, from the (drying) playas of northern Mali (Hassi-el-Aboid) (Petit-Maire and Riser 1983). The Kobadi tradition in some senses represents a conservative carryover of an older non-food-producing economy. But these folk were no slouches! They slew and ate impressive numbers of elephant, crocodile, hippos, and Nile perch (*Lates niloticus*) and various catfish that reached up to 2.5 meters in length!

Some of the fisher-hunters of the Kobadi tradition altered their material culture after a few hundred years in the Méma to become a separate identity, the Bérétouma (1300–800 BC). But while this local fissioning (?) was taking place, there appears to have been an infusion of pastoralists (perhaps from the Mauritanian cliffs of Tichitt to the west – overlooking yet another distressed lake environment: Munson 1981). MacDonald calls these the Ndondi Tossokel (1300–800 BC), after sites of that name with an abundance of cattle remains. These sites have remains of sheep and goat as well, and even have terracotta statuettes of cattle. Sites of this tradition tend to be small and ephemeral, not at all like the vast middens left behind by the fisher-hunters. Kobadi-type sites begin to show a smattering of cattle bones and, presumably, the Ndondi Tossokel herders were eating fish and other aquatic delicacies from their new friends! There appears to have been an exchange of polished stone bracelets and of tiny groundstone axes. Later (850–300 BC) there is yet another cultural manifestation (Faita) – agriculturalists who were on the cusp of the Iron Age – as seen by the first signs of iron production at these sites.

Although nothing like the extreme proliferation of specialists we shall see in the later times, this is certainly not a homogeneous landscape of generalists. Is it really so far from our idealized state represented by figure 3.1? Much needs to be done to sort out remains of seasonal exploitation of local resources by mobile, economically flexible communities. (In a clear analog to the proxy measure problem in paleoclimatic research, of chapter 2, are artifacts and fish or faunal remains at a particular site proxy measures of a seasonal component of a generalized, non-specialized economy, or of a specialist's near-sedentary existence?) Yet, the fact that Togola and MacDonald's systematic survey demonstrated clusters of different Late Stone Age sites, close together on the same landform, certainly suggests some degree of symbiotic relationship between specialists. That is, of course, just as long as those communities were contemporaneous. Some clusters are of the same tradition (two Ndondi Tossokel at Barkérou; three Faita at Akumbu; even the one Faita mixed with seven Ndondi Tossokel at Ndondi Tossokel itself) – and so may simply represent successive occupations of the same locale by the same corporation. But what of the others? The Bérétouma cluster is composed of five sites, of which one is classic Kobadi in appearance and two have a mixed Bérétouma/Ndondi Tossokel assemblage. Kolima is composed of at least six sites, three Iron Age, and a mixed fishing with later pastoral component to one (Kolima Sud) and an agricultural (and transitional Late Stone Age–Iron Age) aspect to another (Kolima Sud-Ouest).

What does MacDonald say about these results? Despite the unfortunate lack of extensive excavation (because of unrest and banditry in the Méma during their field season) and despite the lack of paleobotanical evidence, he feels he has sufficient cause to speak of "evidence that multiple groups co-existed regionally," that "these groups were driven into each other's proximity by the desiccation of more northernly watercourses," and that "in the Méma there is evidence for interaction between a pastoral society (the Ndondi Tossokel tradition) and a fishing society (the Kobadi tradition)" (MacDonald 1994: 274).

"Thus, it would appear overall that the 'Pulse Theory' has many aspects which are beginning to be supported by archaeological evidence. Still, our initial investigations have shown that the same amplitude of ethnic diversity which exists in the Inland Niger Delta today [that is, our Upper Delta and Macina of the Middle Niger] is unlikely to have occurred in any one region during prehistory" (MacDonald 1994: 275). A qualified "Yes" to the question: "Does ground truthing support the hypothesis that the mechanisms of the Pulse Model can be traced back into the second and first millennia BC, amongst the first Late Stone Age colonists of the Méma?"

As archaeologists of a scientific bent, all we can do is to generate hypotheses and then try to disprove them. With this tentative "non-falsification" of the Pulse Model by MacDonald for the sites dating to the last two millennia BC of the Méma, what does the transition into the Iron Age in the same region contribute? Togola (1993, 1996) analyzes the settlement data for the 109 Iron Age sites found during the 1989–90 survey, as well as from limited test excavations at several of the mounds comprising the Late Stone Age transition and Iron Age cluster of Akumbu. Most Méma Iron Age sites are more deeply stratified than the Late Stone Age sites and the ceramics on their surface give a greater impression of homogeneity. (Recall that homogeneity is not disallowed by the Pulse Model, once the mechanisms of accommodation are in place and mature.) Much more excavation will have to take place, similar to those at the Jenne-jeno cluster, to be discussed in the next chapter, in order to know whether we are dealing here with a low level of specialization or with the kind of elaboration of specialization we will see in the Upper Delta. Sadly, these Méma site surfaces have already been heavily looted by local Fulani and Moorish populations, as opposed to the surfaces of sites around Jenne that were able to be recorded by archaeologists in relatively pristine condition before the looting explosion of the late 1980s and early 1990s. Fifteen sites have primary evidence of iron production (slag heaps, tuyères, and smelting furnaces) and two have urnfields.

However, as Togola explains,

The phenomenon of site clustering appears to be prevalent in many regions in the Middle Niger ... In the Méma, clustering was a notable aspect of site distribution. Over 3/4 or 88 of the IA [Iron Age] sites encountered during the survey occurred within 13 clusters of groups of sites, compared to 20 isolated IA sites. This phenomenon of site clustering in the Méma was already in expression during the Late Stone Age. Within clusters, each component was spatially separated from the other members. (Togola 1993: 42)

Some of Togola's clusters are impressive, indeed: Akumbu with eight constituents, Niessouma with nine, Boundou Boubou South with ten, and Boundou Boubou North with twenty-one! Further testing of these clusters will be required to determine whether all members were occupied simultaneously. Abandonment evidence, however, indicates a broad rule that large "focus" mounds of the more complex clusters were abandoned later, but that smaller "satellites," broadly, have an equivalent date of last occupation (1993: 44, and table 3.2). May of the satellite sites were abandoned during the earliest phase of the Iron Age.

Togola makes the following conclusions about settlement pattern change during the Iron Age (1993: 56):

1. Densely clustered small settlements flanking the banks of water corridors during the period of Early Assemblage (mid-first millennium AD).
2. Large settlements (often surrounded by smaller and satellite settlements) distributed both along water corridors and within the degraded dunes during the Middle Assemblage (seventh century AD to twelfth to fourteenth century AD).
3. A handful of small settlements with shallow deposits (indicating an ephemeral occupation) mostly distributed within the longitudinal dunes during the period of Late Assemblage (second half of the second millennium AD).
4. During [the mid-first millennium AD and the seventh century AD to twelfth to fourteenth centuries AD] the density and sizes of sites in the Méma are comparable to those in the Jenne and Dia hinterlands.

Clustering exploded in the Méma in the first millennium AD ... and then occupation was aborted with ferocity. But what is this connection between clustering and the burgeoning of population concentrations – cities – in the Middle Niger? The key to this question is – specialization.

Specialists and the deep-time core rules of Mande

Whereas theorists of urbanization have despaired of composing one standard, single-model-fits-all trait-list definition of the city, they have reached consensus on the co-occurrence of the emergence of specialists with that of urban life. Typical of expressions of this consensus come from a Near Eastern scholar, Melinda Zeder (2003: 158):

What distinguishes the urban economy from other economic forms is the degree to which different stages of production and product distribution become increasingly specialized and segregated ... Under such a system, various sets of activities related to the production and distribution of goods may be conducted by unrelated groups of people who bring different skill sets to bear on different components of the productive process, working in separate locales, over extended periods of time. Of course the success of such an economy rests of [sic] the ability of the system to bring together these disparate activities in a way that ensures a smooth progression from production to consumption. These mechanisms may be centrally coordinated by urban elites, or by more diffuse market principles through a web of entrepreneurial activities. More likely, a complex interplay of both more centralized and more broadly based forces are responsible for bringing coherence to economic relations even in the earliest urban societies.

Cities spontaneously serve as the loci of social differentiation by the simple expediency that urban dwellers live lives of prolonged, close interaction with far more, far more varied and socially distant peoples than is the case in the rural setting (Emberling 2003: 256; R. Wright 2002: 4). In the characteristically evocative words of Spiro Kostof, more activities take place, more potential tension is spawned, and more mechanics to resolve those tensions through clever social construction of new identities take place because of the urban "energized crowding" (1991: 37–38)!

"Energized crowding" is the perfect term to evoke the dissipative (excess) social energy to complement the food and material surpluses that the newly emergent subsistence specialists gleaned by their newly formulated recondite knowledge about this highly varied, highly packed physical landscape. In a sense, the archaeological record suggests not just a linear increase in the numbers of specialists to be integrated into the emerging Middle Niger villages, proto-town, and – eventually – cities. We see the complementary non-linear, emergent forms to the authority and socio-political structures of integration. Self-organization of states of accommodation!

Fortunately or unfortunately, most research on the processes by which new specializations – and with them, novel social identities – are generated in the urban arena has concentrated on ancient cities with documents. "Prehistoric" scarcely describes these situations. Ancient and literate Mesopotamia boasts cuneiform administrative records of the produce, volume, and taxation of specialists, and archaeologists have begun to look for the evidence of these specialists in the neighborhoods of these Near Eastern towns (Emberling 2003; Keith 2003: 67–75; Stone 1991; Zeder 2003). From the New World, we have early historic contact sources about the immediate pre-contact Aztec and Inca social orders. These (admittedly) outsider sources have provided some of our best information on organization and self-definition of specialist groups, on ethnogenesis broadly. Such records speak also of the production and display of "ethnic markers" (group rituals or display symbols for ethnic identity: Brunfiel 1994: 96). Similar document-informed insights into Mayan group identity and specialist identity are emerging with the cracking of the glyphs in the context of a densely excavated archaeological field (see Houston et al. 2003). (Those of us working in the Middle Niger are not a little envious, both of the ethno-historical documents available in these areas and, especially, of the long duration and high density of dirt investigation.)

Three general conclusions can be drawn from these text-rich situations:

1. The documentary sources (that is, some segment of the society's own view or image of itself) always speak of an order of magnitude or more specialist groups than can be identified directly in the dirt archaeology. The implications for those of us without a documentary back-up to our excavation and survey is obvious. Just as we have long recognized that a part of the subsistence-specialized population (*mobile* herders, fisherfolk, etc.) is perversely invisible in the archaeological record, so too will archaeologists have to struggle to identify many, if not most, artisan specialists.

2. Craft and specialization is only exceptionally organized within discrete, segregated quarters within the ancient city. Specialist production is usually small scale (although lots of these workshops, in aggregate, can result in impressive volumes of manufactures) and lots of different workshops are mixed together in the same neighborhoods (Emberling 2003: 261; Keith 2003: 67–75).

3. Mixing together of small-scale production further occludes the separateness of specialists from *direct archaeological recognition*.

Of all the present-day specialists of the contemporary town of Jenne, such as one finds documented in *Djenné. Une ville millénaire au Mali* (Bedaux and Van der Waals 1994; and esp. LaViolette 1994), for example, many simply do not leave material remains. The archaeologists would be hard pressed to prove, just from the dirt evidence, that other tasks were in the hands of specialists, rather than the responsibility of each household. Indeed, our excavations in Jenne itself (see next chapter) touched upon perhaps two hundred years of a distinguished Koranic school. Had local historical memory not identified the locale, we would probably never have recognized the clerical and didactic specialization that infused the place (Mommersteeg 1994).

All is not lost. As was the case with paleoclimate, we have developed a series of useful *proxy measures* of specialization that allow us to extrapolate the scale of specialist differentiation, if not the details of each individual specialization. Acceptance of these proxy measures by the community of urban archaeologists is predicated on the widely accepted principle that all cities – modern and pre-modern, New World and Old World, pre-industrial and Western, traditional industrial and "global" – share certain universals about how people deal with the organizational exigencies of life in large concentrations. The exigencies are universal (although the details and the scale may be very different). They include production for economies of scale (rather than to satisfy just the household), the problem of "anomie," having to maintain rules of peaceful interactions with many peoples of many different identities outside one's own kinship reckoning, new advantages, and also complications, created by the new infrastructure of information transfer, etc.

These general principles allow one (judiciously) to extrapolate about the scales of specialization likely to have been supported by this or that ancient population concentration (at the level of the city itself) and degree of regional integration (at the level of the city's hinterland):

People developed cities in many parts of the world independently, yet the resulting urban form exhibits similarities in the organization of space (broad avenues and open plazas), the placement of symbolic architecture in prominent locations, and the development of neighborhoods around occupational specialties. Even more striking, cities in the Old World and the New World without contact between them, developed into the most complex and densely occupied type of human population center, with remarkably similar configurations ... the physical similarities noted above are only a manifestation of underlying principles that prove fundamental to the organization of concentrated populations. (M. Smith 2003: 6–7)

And one of the facets of this consensus of particular pertinence for the heterarchical kinds of cities that developed on the Middle Niger alluvium is the assertion that long-term (that is, sustainable) cohesion in the city is best attained when all segments of the community share a set of long-term goals. Decision making can, of course, be top-down and coercive. But the newly emerging consensus, following Colombijn (1994: 18), is that more sustainable, more cost-effective decision making comes from "the least expensive decision [which is] consensual, but attaining such a consensus is a long process" (see M. Smith 2003: 7). In other words, perceived long-term self-interest is a better motivator of the urbanite than is coercion.

Theory of urban social organization now emphasizes a processs of urban ethnogenesis in which the city as social arena creates unprecedented, novel potential for social categories. Attarian (2003: 188–89), for example, makes the useful point that movement from the village to the town creates unprecedented alienation (an aspect of Durkheim's "anomie"). Particularly wounding is alienation from what will be called corporate property – loss of connection with an ancestral dwelling, separation from family lands, from symbolically charged landmarks. The alienated soul, now in a "chaotic" situation of radically increased interdependence (that is, not as generalized as the household-based production of the village), is especially susceptible to recruitment into and even invention of new social contracts, new memberships constructed around new economic (and other) roles. Attarian illustrates this (2003: fig. 8.3, table 8.1, and pp. 197–98) with hypotheses of four paths of identity change (rural newcomers may create completely novel categories; new identities including some based upon wealth; they may maintain older identities in the new locale; or add personnel to a new, pan-urban [monolithic] identity). Perhaps an elaboration of corporateness more in keeping with the ethno-historical evidence from non-industrial cities would be the retention by some newcomers from the country-side of familiar categories of identity, the creation of completely new categories by others, all added to the morass of corporate belonging already generated by the emergent cityscape!

Much of our thinking about invention of novel social identities in the city has dealt with craft and occupational specialization (Brunfiel 1998; Costin 1998). The new economic opportunities, the new economies of scale of the city, as well as the desires of the politically dominant or the otherwise elite for new forms of luxury items, sumptuary goods, and prestige markers, of course, can cause the elaboration of new craft specialization. But so too, in the context of non-elite life, can the increased networks of contacts through the new social forms of self-selected institutions in other realms.

In the urban context, individuals and households can increase their network of contacts through a variety of groups whose organizing principle is based on self-selection of members acting on shared criteria such as religion, occupation, or ethnicity. Such associations allow a restructuring or re-creation of power relations within a city, whether created as a guild, cooperative, neighborhood association, religious groups, or other voluntary association ... Once formed, an association can wield more influence than individual members, allowing it to act on behalf of members who seek to maintain or expand their ability to appropriate resources. (M. Smith 2003: 17)

When we speak of Middle Niger cities as heterarchies, it matters not whether the associations, or corporations, are craft associations, other occupational associations, religious or otherwise ritual, residential, lineage or kinship (including fictive), or any number of secular sodalities, self-help groups, or "power" (occult and social control) organizations. What matters is that each corporation is vested with roughly commensurate overlapping, competing, and often cooperating authority.

The previous obsession with craft guilds and associations has tended to make us less aware of these other sources of self-identity. Zeder (2003) is quite correct to complain that provisioning of food to the city can also be as powerful a source of self-differentiation as is membership in a craft organization.

Indeed, one of the most remarkable transformations of the urban economy is the way in which basic activities related to the production of food, its distribution, and consumption become increasingly separated from household units and transformed into distinct sets of activities conducted by segregated groups of specialists, provisioning a network of people engaged in the production of goods and services totally unrelated to subsistence. The degree to which urban households can afford to abandon direct involvement in food production may, in fact, be a marker of the ability of the system to ensure that the basic needs of the specialist producers will be provided for. (Zeder 2003: 157)

So, to craft specialization add subsistence specialization, trade and exchange specialization, and any number of other potential avenues of specialization (ritual and religious, information and literacy, etc.) – compounding the astonishingly expanding grid of self-identity and self-selection. Remember, also, that one individual can elect to self-identify by membership in multiple associations – and you see the potential for Kostof's "energized crowding" that makes city life so radically different from life on the pre-urban landscape.

And when cities appear on the scene, that "energized crowding" becomes a regional phenomenon. In Mande, heroes and heroines (those who elect to manipulate the occult forces of landscape – see below) travel widely and collect new identities like souvenirs in their suitcases! David Conrad *tell*s the story of Laminigbé Bayo, a blacksmith from a lineage of famous circumcisers, goldsmith, lute (*ngoni*, a national instrument of great power) player and *jeli* (griot, bard) as well as popular storyteller (and thorn in the side of the despotic Guinean government) (2002: 31–40). Bayo traveled widely in Mali, Guinea, and Côte d'Ivoire, plying his various trades, known in different places by his different identities. Identity in Mande is, indeed, a portmanteau concept – however, "reputation" is elaborately preserved. Here is yet another one of those paradoxes that make Mande so rich. An individual is not prohibited from assuming multiple identities. Yet corporateness increasingly implies possession of recondite knowledge that must be kept secret. How the individual balances him- or herself on the two horns of this dilemma defines their Heroine or Hero status! All Mande would recognize Laminigbé Bayo as one.

It is precisely because of the common confusion that comes with the exclusive use of specialization (occupation implied) that we need a new term that emphasizes both the networks of contacts and the multiple sources of authority of the city. For this reason, when speaking of Middle Niger cities, I emphasize corporate belonging. Classically, belonging to corporate groups is reinforced by a right of common possession or access to corporate property such as myths, shrines, ritual objects, or land (R. McIntosh 1993: 188; see Cochrane 1971). It matters not what the corporate property is. It matters not (within situationally defined limits?) to how many corporate groups the urban dweller ascribes. It matters not if the basis of corporate definition is residential, occupational (craft or food provisioning), kinship, ritual, or secular. The beauty of speaking of corporate groups is that some of that common property may be identifiable archaeologically. And in many cases there will be an effort by members of the corporate group to signal belonging – often in material culture. Why limit our prehistoric scope to the archaeologically discernable "ethnic markers" (group rituals or display symbols) (Brunfiel 1994: 96)? Why not open up our field of vision to encompass all sources of corporate belonging, all sources of authority that can be produced by the urban arena?

Let us now bring the discussion home to the peoples of the Middle Niger: The code [physical ensignia of groups, a form of code communicating identity] satis-factorily represents belonging and thereby constrains social ambiguity, one of the fundamental curses of city life. Once widely recognized and participated in, such systems of codes allow ever more complex social interactions among persons of increasing social distance. The process allows new scales of acceptable social ambiguity ... These developments are an important expression of a larger prin-ciple of how ambiguity of belonging is constrained as these societies became more complex. We can state that principle in a nutshell: If each group is provided with unambiguous insignia and if the roles and complementarity of groups are agreed upon and reinforced by myths, metaphors and other appeals to tradition, then society can accommodate over long periods of time a process by which specialists can become ever more specialized. (R. McIntosh 1993: 188)

And, in fact, the argument is made persistently by the Mande peoples of the Middle Niger themselves that their own deeper history contains within it core rules of corporate elaboration (B. Daiby and T. Togola, pers. comm. 1997).

Core rules of corporate elaboration: A major thrust of this book is the assertion that the peoples of the Middle Niger achieved their non-despotic urbanism and sustained that urbanism well over a millennium and a half, because of the Mande complex of core rules. As mentioned above, these are the rules that resolve the Tragedy of the Commons. With these rules, we have the classic self-organization conditions for amplifying (indeed, rampant) mutual enhancement instead of the dominating self-enhancement of, on the one hand, a classically acephalous, chaotic, and formless situation and, on the other, of the fused hierarchy. In the first extreme, all individuals are on their own. In the second, the powerful at the apex use force to carry their will over the rest of society. In Mande, these simple core rules are ways of looking at rightness and of causality in the world. In a very real sense, they allow the freedom of action as well as the ubiquitous systemic interconnectedness (Jantsch 1982: 347) of every urban dweller. And they allow the system to stay in that condition of creative non-equilibrium that allows (self-spontaneously) ever-greater intensities of corporate diversity and corporate co-evolution to take place.

In the end, the idea of the *Self-Organizing Landscape* provides all the essential elements of emerging urbanism along the Middle Niger – as a pathway of radically emergent state, of phase transform. The pathway is anything but deterministic or inevitable, but nor is it derived (as earlier Africanist archaeologists pessimistically assumed) from outside sources (the failed Arab Stimulus or "light shining from across the Sahara" thesis, so beloved of poor Raymond Mauny! – see R. McIntosh and S. McIntosh 1988). To date, the Middle Niger archaeological evidence frustrates our academic, analytical tendency to look for "Pacemakers" (top-down, hierarchically embedded decision makers, such as Weber's charismatic prince) (Johnson 2001: 14–16), working with powerful and coercive command structures. Instead, let us take it on faith that cities, like other complex, emergent systems, might emerge spontaneously out of simpler, often apparently chaotic landscapes. What is needed is a trajectory in which a few repeating patterns and a few simple core rules of interaction come together.

The city emerges (along the Middle Niger, out of an immediate anterior, "incipient-town" state illustrated by fig. 3.4?) as a pattern-amplifying machine: Here we have higher densities of patterns of behavior and movement and individuals' decision making that feed back, ever altering the participants' subsequent behavior and decisions. In this landscape of stability and change, individuals are encouraged in their corporate capacity for open-ended learning – as long as the many subscribe (not absolutely and rigidly, but "on the whole") to a constellation of a relatively few simple rules. Following these rules over time, there emerge distinct macrobehaviors with specific shape and pattern over time – a coherent phase personality that self-organizes out of many individual decisions and many local interactions.

Reputation, innovation and specialist entrepreneurship, deep-time core values, and a very ancient vision of the landscape as a natural (physical), symbolic (spiritual), and occult phenomenon – all these are intimately tied into the Middle Niger peoples' vision of their landscape: physical, social, and occult (R. McIntosh 2000b: 157–71). The core rules integrate, into a comprehensive whole, a view of landscape that enables all its aspects (the bio-physical landforms, the human actors traveling over and modifying the landscape, and the occult power elements – spirits and sacred elements) to be understood as a self-organizing whole. The three core rules concern the Middle Niger and, indeed, the entire Mande world. (1) Action upon the landscape is upon a three-dimensional map (*onomasticon*) of a power grid. (2) Mande specialists (Adepts) travel (*dalimasigi*) over that power grid for the purpose of harvesting and transforming power (*nyama*). And (3) moral and cosmic order is maintained by the *entrepreneurial* interplay of different specialists as they interact. These rules apply today and they are recognizable for centuries by investigators from fields as diverse as history (especially oral tradition), art history, and even archaeology. Just how far back?

A central concept to all this is *nyama*, the vital force that permeates the entire Middle Niger (and the larger Mande) landscape (McNaughton 1988). *Nyama* permeates places; it can be harvested, but it can also be augmented by the (entrepreneurial) acts of leaders and specialists. Indeed, to be a blacksmith is only 20 percent about making iron and fully 80 percent about generating new volumes of *nyama* by the highly skilled, dangerous, and transformative act of setting earth to fire and extracting metal. Just how ancient is this vision of landscape permeated with a vital force? Just how ancient is the role of secret power societies (sodalities such as the Komo and Poro societies of Mande today) and occupation associations (*nyamakalaw* = "handles of *nyama*": Conrad and Frank 1995) in teaching to younger generations the dangers of improperly handling *nyama*? Intricate and voluminous indeed is the knowledge required of how humans may tap the power of the earth's *nyama* and how humans may navigate over a symbol-charged, perilous landscape, traveling from highly charged node to node. I have argued elsewhere that these fundamental concepts may date back well into the Late Stone Age, but that they are now highly transformed (R. McIntosh 2000b: 159, 167–71). The essential point for us here is that *nyama* continues to be conceived of as if operating within a grid of high-power wires strung out over the landscape. To quote McNaughton (1988: 16): "*Nyama* is a little like electricity unconstrained by insulated wires but rather set neatly into a vast matrix of deeply interfaced social and natural laws." It is dangerous. It is the source of all action (again to McNaughton 1988: 16); *nyama* is the source of all moral reciprocity (human to human; human to all earth forces).

Immediate tension: If some can manipulate and augment *nyama* and others are less skilled or less inclined to do so, might we have an arena for the asymmetrical assumption of power? Read on!

To be human in Mande means to gain knowledge about the unequal flow and curation of *nyama* across this highly charged landscape. Some elect never to tempt the dangerous forces – they live lives of quiet mediocrity. Others, however, accept the role of authority that is to gather or manipulate *nyama* for the purpose of maintaining social and occult harmony in the world. These are the Mande Heroes and Heroines, Men and Women of Crises, of the vast Mande epics (Dinga of the Soninké; Fanta Maa of the Bozo; Sunjata or Fakoli; or the lithesome *sabu* of the Mali epics) (Cissé 1964; Conrad 1992 and 1995; R. McIntosh

2000b: 156–67). And all specialists, to one degree or another, share this vision of a highly charged landscape, a terrifying landscape very much at the "edge of chaos."

A useful term to describe this mapping of the power of place in Mande is *onomasticon*. In biblical exegesis, *onomasticon* can simply mean a listing of contemporaneous places mentioned in the Bible. However, biblical scholarship has increasingly evolved to make the term imply a relative ranking of those places in terms of the authority and real power wielded by the persons or lineages associated with those places (Matthews and Benjamin 1993; R. Wilson 1977). Extrapolated to Mande (where there is no analogous, convenient term), *onomasticon* refers to the landscape as a network of power localities. The network is never static. Some locations have a better potential for high intensity of *nyama*. These would certainly include certain mountains or curious rock formations; the "wilderness" because of the presence there of occult guardian-spirit beasts; and certain waterways with high concentrations of *baa-faaro* – water spirits. But it is preeminently the extractive or transformative action of Mande people of knowledge (*nyamakalaw* = Adepts = specialists = Heroes and Heroines) that allows for new power localities to emerge upon the landscape. And new knowledge, innovative skills, allows new generative sources of *nyama* to appear as well. I believe we witness this when iron smelting begins sometime in the first millennium BC and the new Adepts, the blacksmiths, TRANSFORM and not just EXTRACT *nyama* as had the older Adepts, the hunters, before them. Smiths are masters of "*nyama* ardent" – active, fiery *nyama*, not the more passive, extractive (if still highly dangerous) *nyama* of the (older) hunters before them (Cissé 1964: 201, 207).

Recall the story, in chapter 2, of the snake Bida and the local explanation for the apparent long-term prehistoric avoidance of the Vallée du Serpent. The entire lore and the "avoidance action" is part and parcel of the Mande conception of *onomasticon*. Bida's underground circuit plots a pathway of raw *nyama* just too dangerous for most mere humans to navigate. It would be unthinkable to situate one's village along Bida's path!

Further, from the most elemental (and earliest?) lore of the hunters and aquatic specialists, to the post-Islamic epics of the grand empires of Ghana, Mali, and Songhai, this is a landscape traced by knowledge quests. Questing is a very Western term and the Mande equivalent, *dalimasigi*, has few of the Christian, medieval overtones of searches for Holy Grails or dragon slayings. The knowledge quest is more basic (and more pervasive) here in Mande. *Dalimasigi* is a navigation of a sacred or symbolic landscape that may have more in common with travel along the Mayan *sacbeob* roadway (sacred pathways through the rainforest replicating a cosmological map) or the "white roads" of the North American

Hopewell peoples (Freidel *et al.* 1993: 76–78; Lepper 1995). The nodes upon the landscape may be physical landforms (as when Sundjata is rolled in the dust of powerful caves); they may be persons (particularly powerful or knowledgeable) to be visited; or they may be local cells or sodalities of Adepts (hunters' lodges, for example). The knowledge to be gathered may be esoteric information, or energy-laden objects, or trophies taken at the killing of avatars of dangerous places, etc. But the overall process is that of an Adept, in apprenticeship (which lasts all one's life, after all), being sent with the blessing and sanction of the home occupation association, into the dank, dangerous, symbolic landscape to learn new skills. Back home, these new packets of information may be shared within the home closed-membership, secret corporation, the *naame*, or the knowledge may remain private and personal.

Conrad (1995: 2) best describes the sum of centuries (millennia?) of *dalimasigi* upon the Mande landscape as "charismatic figures moving through a dangerous symbolic landscape harvesting power, authority and knowledge." What comes next is particularly pertinent to thinking about how and why Middle Niger cities came to have their distinctively clustered form. We can speak now of a distinctively Mande view of landscape: relationship of acts of nature and human acts that create a three-dimensional hierarchy of places, an uneven distribution of the vitalizing forces of the world made even more potent by complementary, componential-yet-linked, human acts of transformation.

Note, this is decidedly NOT the Western hierarchical concept of ecosystem (including the idea of cityscapes as ecosystems and as information systems) (e.g. O'Neill *et al.* 1986). In the hierarchical concept, flexibility (ability of the system to respond to change and crises) and information flow (especially from the bottom, the primary producers, up to the decision makers) is reduced. One can see that illustrated in "Attenuation of an input signal" (O'Neill *et al.* 1986: 77, fig. 5.1), in which information (input) from lower levels in a classic hierarchy are dampened by black boxes or "gatekeepers" in order not to overwhelm those at the apex. Compare that with a Mande view of specialist Adepts or corporations as sources of *signal amplification* (fig. 3.8).

In the Mande take on landscape, the role, ultimately, of the Adept or of the occupation corporation is to augment occult power by transforming the "ecological signal" of the landscape for the good of the community. Critically, one's reputation depends upon the faith of all that one is working for the good of the community, and not just to garner power. We have seen in the conception of *onomasticon* that human actions work in concert with occult actors of nature to create a sacred landscape. This sacred landscape can be thought of as a 3-D spatial blueprint of

Hierarchical Concept of Ecosystems   **Mande Landscape Amplification**

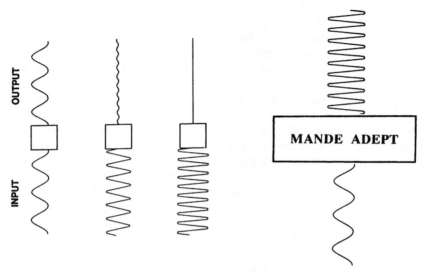

Fig. 3.8. Comparison of the Mande view of landscape amplification with the hierarchical concept of ecosystem and information flow

covenantial augmentation of power. That power, or *nyama*, that portmanteau concept of the vitalizing force of the world that can be packaged and made even more potent, is the potentially dangerous energy flowing through all things. When McNaughton (1988, 1991) speaks of the entrepreneurial role of Mande corporations and Adepts, he is referring to a special potential of *clustered* specialists and complementary corporations *together* to create augmented landscapes.

This is rather in the realm of speculation, but a classic story of the founding of a power-charged locale might go something like the following. High-*nyama* places are searched out by Mande Adepts, the vanguard of a community on the move. Guides to the unequal distribution of power over the landscapes come from a general knowledge of the Mande *onomasticon*, but each entrepreneurial Adept must carry out an individual *dalimasigi*. Why are some places selected and others passed by? Some may already have had a high ecological diversity (how defined? As having naturally a high-*nyama* potential and many natural resources?). Some may be recognized as special locations for transformation acts (especially, iron smelting).

Yet, for whatever reasons selected, no locality should ever be mono-polized! For this process of componential-yet-linked signal amplification, it is necessary to invite the collaboration of multiple corporations (fig. 3.9). Remember that each association jealously retains its own corporate secrets (and dangerous activities are thus avoided by the uninitiated of alien occupations). Sometimes the secrets are kept by confining their perform-ance to separate locations (satellite occupation locales). Blacksmiths can do their transformative acts alone, to be sure. But, by this vision of the landscape, their activities are augmented if they can also tap the services (functional and occult) of other corporations (woodworkers, potters, etc.). And this complementarity may be so formalized that the productive and ritual calendars of one group have to be actualized by members of another. The result: a radical interpretation of ecological diversity!

Within the Middle Niger (as a very traditional Mande landscape), what are the functions of the clustered settlements (cities and earlier villages)? They can be seen to function on three levels. Firstly, they represent a highly successful *functional* amplification of the ecosystem. Here, produc-tion specialists self-organize into a landscape of factions functioning as a network of complementary production. Purely on this functional level, such multi-corporate, complementary networks of relations translate into ecosystem complementarity (a poor year for one group is offset by the promise of exchange with a neighboring group having a better year), and this equates with ecological resilience. Economic Reciprocity = Long-Term Sustainability! In this way, the corporate complementarity is not so different from the exchange and reciprocity landscape posited, for example, for areas of the prehistoric American Ancestral Pueblo world (e.g. Dean 1996; Rautman 1996).

Secondly, the multi-corporate, clustered settlement reinforces a vener-able logic of sacred or occult landscape. (In Mande historical explanation ...) Such settlements can represent a highly successful signal amplification of the occult power-grid that resonates within the bio-physical world. Here, specialists self-organize into a landscape of factions for the task of elevating their locality to an extraordinary position on the 3-D spatial blueprint of power. Consequently, this topographic amplification equates with ever-increasing scales of social complexity (population size and density; occupational segmentation; integration spatially). And not to forget that this social complexity equates also with symbolic complexity and reciprocity.

Thirdly, and finally, clustering is reinforced by and, in turn, symbolically reinforces a logic of heterarchy (that is, authority distributed horizontally and able to resist centralization). These settlements repre-sent a highly successful amplification of horizontal authority: Specialists

Mande Landscape Amplification

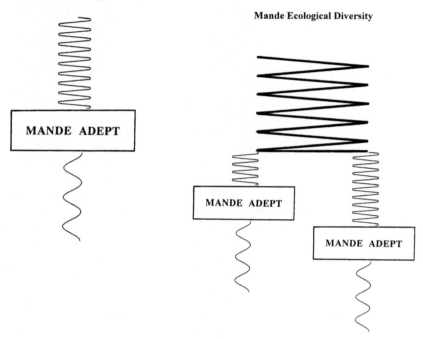

Fig. 3.9. Complementary landscape amplification when multiple, clustered corporations act together: Mande Ecological Diversity

self-organize into a landscape of factions that share overlapping, counter-poised, and competing interests and expressions of decision making (Crumley 1995: 3, 1998). The understood complementarity of the system dampens the (otherwise natural?) desire of individuals and groups to gather unto themselves more and more authority. Certainly, this centralizing, monopolizing tendency is in check whenever one group is in the position to frustrate the production of another – simply, in the case of the Middle Niger groups, by refusing to activate critical stages in the functional, manufacturing, or ritual calendar of the offending group. Check and balances. Reputation! Heterarchy equates with resistance to a monopoly of authority and power by any one constituent (successful, apparently, at least for some 1,600 years at Jenne-jeno).

Done correctly, heterarchy and complementary corporate clustering can be at least as successful as hierarchy (the state) in encouraging a stable, highly segmented, urban society. Put another way, we have seen yet another phase transition to a densely populated, multiple-corporate landscape – in which authority need not rest upon the despotic power of our old friend, *ex astra*! In the final chapters of this book, we return to the city as a network of complementary production. Here, let us end this chapter by simply recalling the problem with state-driven ancient cities. They are fragile. Their society is prone to collapse because their hierarchical infrastructure is rigid. They lack the flexibility to deal with the unexpected (revolts of the underclasses; undermining by disaffected factions within the elite; cheeky climate; or those impertinent neighbors). Cities characterized by a state apparatus lack that essential element of sustainability we have called "over-engineering" and the Middle Niger peoples would call "Mande Ecological Diversity."

And perhaps most importantly, because few but the privileged minority benefit from the despotic state system, few feel a "responsibility" to the whole. Lacking flexibility; rigidly engineered; not self-generating an "enlarging responsibility" – this is a template for an ancient city very different from that presented here. But the Middle Niger, by sharing the Mande view of the self-organizing landscape, solves this essential, core, and fundamental problem of maintaining trust and reputation as society becomes more complex, as city populations become engorged. The Mande Adepts, the Middle Niger corporations, if their behavior is consistent with the core rules, build upon a bedrock of deep-time complementarity that allows for ever greater scales of complexity, without exploitation. The Tragedy of the Commons turns into the Mutual Harvest and, indeed, Augmentation of the Commons!

4 Excavation

Recognizing heterogeneity

The present chapter, and that to follow, are about the nitty-gritty of how archaeologists recognize cities in the field, through the veil of dust, the sting of sweat in the eyes, the sheer tedium that is likely to be the archaeologist's more insistent experience. These chapters are not in the least intended to be cookbooks of excavation (this chapter) and regional survey (chapter 5). However, the time has come to demonstrate just how all the preceding theory and hypothesizing about urbanism meshes with what remains in the earth. All we, as archaeologists, have to work with are the (incompletely preserved) material expressions of past urban dwellers' actions upon the world. What to make of it all? We turn to the Middle Niger city we know best, after just shy of thirty years of investigations, Jenne-jeno.

The dilemma is that some actions of ancient peoples leave behind material expressions (grinding stones used for food preparation, say) that could have been used in the households of any number of *different* specialist families, families attached to *different* corporate groups. Let us look more closely at those lowly, utilitarian grinding stones, ubiquitous in all levels at the ancient *tell* of Jenne-jeno – hundreds peppering the meters and meters of strata made of mud wall-melt, mixed with tossings from long-ago meals (fig. 4.1) – and still used in the contemporary town of Jenne. And then we will examine a sample of other archaeological features, each of which illustrates a different theme of archaeological reasoning.

At the Middle Niger city of Jenne-jeno, grinding stones are among the most common of artifacts (lagging far behind the hundreds of thousands of potsherds, of course) (S. McIntosh 1995: 246–47). Grinding stones are intrinsically interesting, as they all have had to have been imported from outside the floodplain. And it is all the more interesting that the greatest density of grinding stones per square meter comes from the lowest – the earliest – levels, implying that a sustained and voluminous

Fig. 4.1. The *mille-feuille* strata of Jenne-jeno; Mr. Sulaiman stands on
the original floodplain surface, over 6 meters below *tell* surface

trade in these low-value-added, non-luxury, and bulky items existed even in the last centuries BC and early centuries AD. That this trade was somewhat organized, if not quite systematically, is further implied by the fact that the several hundred grinding stones came into the site in a limited spectrum of eleven shapes (S. McIntosh 1995: 261, fig. 5.5).

And so you see how a chain of archaeological inference is constructed: [High volume of bulky, low-value-added stone (especially prevalent in the earliest levels)(absolutely exotic to the alluvium) = > early organized trade/exchange (long-distance/medium-distance?)] + [Imported in standardized shapes (with no subsequent chipping of cores or rough-outs on site) = > purposeful (market-intended) production (by specialists?)].

Does this equation, this chain of inference, further imply the presence, from the foundation of Jenne-jeno, of *specialized* traders, self-identifying themselves by membership in a *discrete corporate group*?

Certainly, from the first moment that Jenne-jeno's successor site, Jenne, enters historical documentation (later in the second millennium AD), the city is intimately associated with *specialist* traders. (Recall the words of Imam al-Sa'di [1900: 22–23]: "Everyone conducting business in Jenne is blessed by God with great profit and, indeed, only God Himself [may His name be blessed!] keeps a true accounting of the fortunes that have been made there. It is because this blessed city that caravans flow towards Timbuktu from all points on the horizon, from the east, from the west, from south and from north.") These traders were self-organized into a discrete corporate body renowned throughout West Africa, the Dyula (or Wangara) (S. McIntosh 1981).

Can we extrapolate backwards from the ethno-historic Dyula and anchor our inference to the early grinding stones in order to say that the Dyula or a predecessor group existed over a millennium before their first historical mention? Obviously not. Can we, nevertheless, say that some flavor of long-distance transport and commercial corporate group existed at the founding of the town? Not even that – transport of these objects could always have been in the hands of farmers or herders, just visiting the "market" settlement on the floodplain, the exchange just being an *ad hoc* affair. The archaeologist (as in this case) may have a "gut feeling" that the volume of stone and the standardization of shapes being imported in do imply some supra-individual organization of the trade. But there is no preponderance of evidence to that effect.

That having been said, we cannot dismiss, entirely out of hand, even an early date for the presence of individual traders and, perhaps, of commercial corporations. (Indeed, Perinbaum [1974], working purely from historical sources, hypothesized a very early antecedent to the Dyula/ Wangara amongst the chain of Marka settlements at the Bénédougou, the eastern highland fringe of the Middle Niger. That highland played an interesting role, as we will soon see, in the manufactures of earliest Jenne-jeno.) We can suggest a corrective, however imperfect, deriving from larger ethnographic and historical, cross-cultural experience.

Let us review the evidence, from excavations, for the import into deep-alluvium cities, such as Jenne-jeno, of iron ore (and, later, copper). In brief, bulky iron ore and/or bulky partially smelted blooms were shipped into earliest Jenne-jeno (third century BC) from somewhere on the peri-phery of the alluvium (and most probably from the aforementioned Bénédougou, near San, not closer than 75 km distant: R. McIntosh 1998: 214). By around the fifth century AD, copper (in this case, ore is less likely than ingots or already cast and refined pieces) appears from distant Saharan sources, hundreds of kilometers away. These (and other) data lead us to the conclusion that, "in an extremely fragmentary way, then, the archaeological evidence from Jenne-jeno does document the development of trade networks involving Jenne-jeno: from inter-regional Sahel–savanna exchange in Phase I to external trade with the Islamic world by late Phase IV" (S. McIntosh and R. McIntosh 1980, II: 445).

(A brief note about the Jenne-jeno region ceramic sequence, the dating for which will frame much of the following discussion. The sequence is based on the intricate analysis of literally hundreds of thousands of potsherds, excavated in tight stratigraphical context, and dated by what is arguably the largest [coherent] corpus of radiocarbon dates for all of West Africa [S. McIntosh 1995: 360–72]. The sequence begins around 250 BC with the founding of Jenne-jeno. The first phase, "Upper IND [Inland Niger Delta] Fineware phase," or Phase I/II, has a number of time-sensitive ceramic decorations or shapes, especially the very-fine walled ware that gives the phase its name. This phase lasts until about AD 400. The following "Painted Ware phase," or Phase III, continues until about AD 900 and is followed, until around AD 1400, when the site was abandoned, by the "Fine Channeled and Impressed Ware phase" [or Phase IV]. Phase V ware is known from the deep deposits underlying the present-day successor town of Jenne.)

To return to "exotic" artifacts found at Jenne-jeno: The question is, do the earliest represent gathering and transport, on an *ad hoc* basis, by enterprising but unorganized individuals, or something more formalized, more corporate? Can we ignore cross-cultural experience? Hopkins (1973: 53), looking at the Africa-wide experience, argues that institutio-nalized trade over distances greater than 10 kilometers has implications for the corporate organization of the traders. Institutionalized: There is the rub. The volume and bulk of the iron ore and/or blooms coming into Jenne-jeno and, certainly, the difficulties and dangers of the desert crossing for those bringing copper and bronze would, to some, argue for some degree of institutionalization. Certainly the distances involved satisfy Hopkins' criteria. If so:

The classification adapted here is a simple one based on distinction between local and long-distance trade. Local trade refers to transactions that took place within a radius of up to about ten miles of the area of production. This was the range that could be covered in one day by foot or by donkey, while still allowing time to exchange products and return home. Beyond this radius it was necessary to make arrangements for overnight stops, to reallocate work in the household, and sometimes to make use of professional carriers and commercial intermediaries ... The distinction between local and long-distance commerce becomes useful because it draws attention to differences in degrees of specialization, in types of commercial institution, in the composition of goods traded, and in the nature of consumer demand. (Hopkins 1973: 53)

Commercial families with distinct ethnic affiliation (Dyula and trading Marka), specialized shops catering to different clientele, professional carriers and boatmen – all of these existed (and had done for a long time) when Jenne emerges into historical documentation. Do we assume the same simply because items of distant origin are found also at the ancestral archaeological site? And then there is the frustrating case of Saharan salt, one of the pillars of the later, Arab-documented formalized trans-Saharan camel trade (Bovill 1970; Lovejoy 1985). It is hard to imagine that an agglomeration of people the size of early Jenne-jeno, baking in the Sahelian dry-season heat, could have done without this basic requirement of the human body. Salt must, in tropical parts of the world, be taken in mineral form (here, most likely from the rock-salt deposits of northern Mali) (S. McIntosh and R. McIntosh 1980, II: 446). However, do we have any *primary* evidence of salt or of caravan organization? Sadly, again ...

This is just another example of the frustrating fact that many corporate groups are archaeologically invisible. (And of the reason why archaeologists argue from negative evidence only at their peril.) This was amply demonstrated in the last chapter in the case of those Mesopotamian or Mesoamerican settlements for which we have the literate people's own testimony as to how many specialists existed, compared to the (independent) identification of specialist groups purely from the nitty-gritty archaeological evidence. Sadly, there will always be an undercount by archaeologists of specialists, as perceived by the community itself. Heterogeneity in the emerging city will most likely be underestimated – and this is a serious impediment to our ability, adequately, to assess the date, the rate, and the pattern of urbanism's change from relative village homogeneity to one of the hallmarks of the city – heterogeneity of its internal population.

Consider this problem of undercounted diversity in light of the implications of the Pulse Model and of the Mande (Middle Niger) core rules of reciprocal reputation. Let us recall that, with over a dozen subsistence-defined ethnic groups in the Middle Niger, some conflicts are inevitable. But why is the floodplain not a morass of bloodshed and conquest? What was the local concept of landscape that positively encouraged ethnic differentiation, elaborate niche specialization, and a shared commitment to a regional, generalized economy? *Not only* are fisherfolk divided ethnically into hand-net, shallow-swamp fishermen (Bozo, with several variations), deep-channel collective-net fishermen (Somono), and the hunters of aquatic fauna such as crocodile, hippos, and giant Nile perch (Sorko); *not only* can the fisherfolk absolutely count on the labor of rice farming Nono, Marka, and Rimaibe during the season of fish migrations; *but also*, the critical rituals of appeasement of the water spirits that obligatorily begin the deep-swamp fishing calendar of the Bozo are initiated by their Nono farmer neighbors. Over deep time, there has developed an ethos of Ecological Resilience, absolutely grounded in a resistance to any one group's monopoly *perception* of landscape that encourages both niche specialization and a highly contractual web of surplus and labor-exchange obligation (but not necessarily exchange of marriage partners). Given that *diversification* (broadening the subsistence system) and *exchange* (playing off temporal variability against spatial variability) are classic tools of risk buffering (Halstead and O'Shea 1989: 1–5), it becomes critical that we are able to recognize emergent corporate belonging. Identification of emergent corporate elaboration is vital for our understanding of how the Late Stone Age emergent subsistence specialists evolved into the elaborately heterogeneous city populations of historical Middle Niger towns. Pity ... in all too many cases ... no such luck. Sadly, the best we can do is to establish a typology, a rough template of recognizability of specialization.

Before going on, why the bother? Recall our working definition of a city from chapter 1: "Whatever else the city may be, it is a unit of settlement which performs specialized functions in relation to a broader hinterland" (Trigger 1972: 577). The first part of that definition ("a unit of settlement") really does not help us to think about how to identify the city, especially its diverse, multi-corporate population, *as it emerges*. Let us modify Trigger's first-part definition by considering two recent musings about the non-elite elements of the community: In both ancient and modern cities, the vast majority of urban dwellers are not elites, but members of ordinary households (a point that takes on enormous importance when we put on our Middle Niger lenses to look anew at Mesopotamian and Chinese cities in chapter 6). Households' production and consumption patterns form the basis of the city's economy. Their participation in ceremonies affirms the effectiveness of an organizing authority. Their labor permits the manifestation of an urban ethos, as constructed through both fanciful monuments and through the practical infrastructure. From the perspective, also, as members of discrete households, of corporate production and non-manufacturing groups, residents actively view cities as places of community and opportunity. Where, in all this, has Durkheim's anomie disappeared to? In urban environments (including those with households as nodal to the web of belonging), kinship ties are reaffirmed and augmented, rather than destroyed; social contacts are diversified; and neighborhoods become the principal geographical anchor of social interaction (Keith 2003; LaViolette 1987; M. Smith 2003). Kinship, corporate group, and now households: The city becomes an interaction multiplier (in other words, the exuberant, self-organizing *Emergence: The Connected Lives ...* of Johnson [2001]).

[Cities'] significance lies in their role as centres of *authority*, as places that are able to generate and disseminate discourses and collective beliefs, that are able to develop, test, and track innovations, and that offer "sociable" settings for the gathering of high-level information (economic, political, cultural) and for establishing coalitions and monitoring implicit contracts. (Knox 1995: 8–9)

This is certainly a more optimistic view of the city than the dismal *ex astra*. Common to Monica Smith, Johnson, and Knox (and to the multitude of new urban theorists, untainted by the Yahwist vision of city as dark moral exemplar) is the affirmation of heterogeneity, both on the vertical social scale and, most importantly, of the horizontal connections of everyday life, everyday people! A simple tweaking of Trigger's classic definition allows us to think more constructively about the positive, the generative potential of ever-elaborating corporate belonging in the emerging urban arena: "Whatever else the city may be, it is a settlement with a qualitatively more heterogeneous population, which performs specialized functions in relation to a broader hinterland."

A qualitatively more heterogeneous population ... Mind you, nothing is said about absolute population size, or about relative population size vis-à-vis that of hinterland villages, or about the presence or absence of elites, literati, lords, or other varieties of social parasites! If ancient fisherfolk cannot easily be discriminated as to specialization – shallow-swamp, deep-channel, aquatic mammal harpooning – in the town, neither can that fine discrimination be made at the ruins of any contemporaneous village. In other words, archaeologists must console themselves with the belief that, at least, a judgment can be made as to whether fisherfolk (as a generic specialized sub-population) may have existed at a site (whereas,

in reality, the people would have recognized many more fishing specializations, organized along the lines of discrete corporations). Reconciled to
only such generic ascription, archaeologists can be happy when, as at the
deep-channel fishing/iron-smelting site of Kangousa (chapter 3), the
preponderance of the evidence allows for the exceptionally finer resolution
on the corporate heterogeneity (i.e. identification of deep-channel net
fishermen).

Preponderance of the evidence ... to satisfy what jury? The jury of
one's peers, obviously ... other field archaeologists who struggle with
the same difficulty of recognizing specialization at their own Near
Eastern, or Californian, or southern African field locales. Now, in the
case of some specializations – and the implied corporate basis of belonging packaged with those specialized occupations – the argument of preponderance of the evidence is tightly constrained by technical or labor
considerations. In others, the argument for acceptance is constrained by
knowledge. I would argue that, in the case of the iron production visible in
the lowest levels of Jenne-jeno, the argument of preponderance of the
evidence for corporate specialists can be made both in terms of technology and of (occult) knowledge. By the nature of the pyrotechnic beast,
these early smiths were both fine chemical engineers (after Rehder 2000
or Woodhouse 1998) and (extrapolating from later practice) awesome
ritual practitioners (McNaughton 1988).

Let us look at the metallurgical sequence from, at present, the fullest
and best dated iron-manufacturing sequence from the Middle Niger.
Iron appears, with a vengeance, with the first inhabitants of Jenne-jeno.
Clearly, iron production was not invented at the site (whatever and
whenever the highly debated origins of iron in sub-Saharan Africa may
be: R. McIntosh 1998: 145–50; Deme and S. McIntosh forthcoming;
Rehder 2000; Woodhouse 1998). At Jenne-jeno, iron and slag first
appear in the lowest levels (dating to the last centuries BC), and in
appreciable quantities, although not yet in the volume they would assume
by the later first millennium AD. Furnace parts, blow pipes (tuyères),
and the morphology and chemistry of the slag itself show that primary
reduction of ore was the order of the day from the earliest times. The fact
that that early iron was smelted *in situ* does speak of specialists, of
corporate organization, and (inferentially) of interlinked constellations
of sophisticated technical knowledge and of high occult prowess. Early
Middle Niger blacksmiths were Adepts, most probably, in both spheres.

This point is so important that we should look at the evolution of iron
production in greater detail. Iron (S. McIntosh and R. McIntosh 1980,
I: 167–69, tables 9.38 and 9.39; S. McIntosh 1995: 269–72, table 6.3), and
slag (S. McIntosh and R. McIntosh 1980, I: 166, fig. 9.2; S. McIntosh

1995: table D2), and ore (S. McIntosh 1995: 273–74) are present from the beginning of the sequence. Metal was produced at the site during the entirety of the 1,600-year occupation (S. McIntosh and R. McIntosh 1980, I: 165). However, the flavor and location of smelting (primary reduction of metal from its oxide ore, an act highly charged with *nyama*) and smithing (reworking and purifying iron – less occult charged, but still highly dangerous) activities changes through time. From the beginning, ores are a carefully selected, high-grade laterite hematite with 54 percent reducible iron content (Tylecote in S. McIntosh 1995: 273). The iron turns out to be an astonishing medium – high-carbon steel (S. McIntosh 1995: 268) – a continuous-phase pearlite, assuredly not made by mistake, but purposefully crafted by specialists for its great durability and hardness. And the localities excavated in 1981 by units CRT and HAMB (see below) appear to have been concentrated centers of production, yielding furnace parts, blow pipes (tuyères), waste iron (?), and smelting and smithing slag (S. McIntosh 1995: 273, 275, 278).

These data are remarkable at an early West African Iron Age site for several reasons:

- In the first place, the iron produced was of exceptionally high quality. These were no amateurs. Purposeful production of steel under bloomery conditions implies high-quality knowledge and much experience.
- In the second place, perhaps some bloom, already smelted, was imported from the periphery of the Middle Niger. However, ore was being imported in and was smelted in place – far from the ore sources.
- Equally important, smelting took place on the denuded alluvium, far from easy access to large numbers of the trees needed for the obligatory charcoal. (Does that imply a specialist corporation of charcoal burners?) From a Galbraithian, rational economic point of view, this makes no sense! What other motivations might the smiths have had for incurring such high transport and procurement costs?

This was no static industry. Smelting (primary reduction of ore into a bloom) and smithing (subsequent refining of the bloom, including removal of slag inclusions, into useful iron) apparently took place together in these Phase I/II (250 BC to AD 400) localities. Later, the primary reduction and the secondary refining tasks would be separated. Smelting apparently dispersed to selected satellite sites, at least by Phase III (AD 400–900) and Phase IV (AD 900–1400) (Clark 2003). (We know from the unit HAMB, testing the adjacent satellite site of Hambarketolo [linked to Jenne-jeno in later centuries by a causeway, but probably quite separate, although less than one hundred meters distant], that satellites of Jenne-jeno appeared by Phase I/II. Were they from the beginning the homes of specialists, in some cases exclusively, as several appear to have been later?) Smelting went off-site and the less-polluting smithing appears to have remained at the principal settlement. We have an intact *smithing* workshop (House 10, below) from Jenne-jeno, dating to the earliest centuries of the second millennium AD, yielding no evidence for smelting activities.

Admittedly speculatively, I have made the argument (R. McIntosh 1998: 179, 188) that the specialist technical knowledge of early Iron Age smiths was complemented here by an occult knowledge that prefigures blacksmiths' undoubted central role in the later (ethno-historical and ethnographic) Mande production of the *nyama*-laden landscape. Why the "illogical" effort to import ore (and charcoal) into the floodplain, if not to perform the function of the Mande Adept in augmenting the occult power by the act of transforming earth, through fire, into iron? Why this locale? Was there an even more ancient, anticipatory power ascription to the locale that smiths, among the first colonists, were attracted to exploit? Later, the waterways of Jenne and Jenne-jeno would be famous (and feared) for their exceptionally high concentrations of *baa-faaro* (water spirits, further natural-world/occult-world manifestations of high-*nyama* potential) (R. McIntosh 1998: 98–99, 177). Could earlier manifestations of analogous visions of the (proto-) Mande landscape be dimly perceived here, through the veil of over two thousand years? And if so, does this not imply that this dangerous occult knowledge was already monopolized and organized by secret occult sodalities – corporations of smiths or hunters or aquatic-monster hunters (and other ritual specialists) ancestral to the later Komo and Porro societies? We can only speculate.

But, while on a roll, let us look just for a moment at the later smith's workshop in unit LX-N at Jenne-jeno. House 10 (S. McIntosh 1995: 39–40, 49, figs. 2.29, 2.30, 2.40) dates to between the tenth and twelfth centuries AD (S. McIntosh 1995: 60): see figure 4.2. By this point in the second long season of excavations at the *tell* site of Jenne-jeno, in 1981, the workers and supervisors were highly attuned to the presence of intact mud-brick wall stumps emerging out of less-consolidated wall collapse material surrounding and covering remains of houses. Still, the complexity of this structure taxed all of our excavation skills. Just by pure chance the house itself rested roughly in the center of unit LX-N (Large Exposure-North) which, along with LX-S adjoining to the south, comprised the largest (10 m × 6 m) exposure dug into Jenne-jeno. At roughly 1 meter 30 centimeters depth from the surface we began to encounter three ashy features, with curious triangular burnt-clay enclosures around them. These turned out to be the external smithing furnaces – not pyrotechnically appropriate for smelting (that is, not allowing the reducing, high carbon monoxide environment needed for smelting ore), but really quite

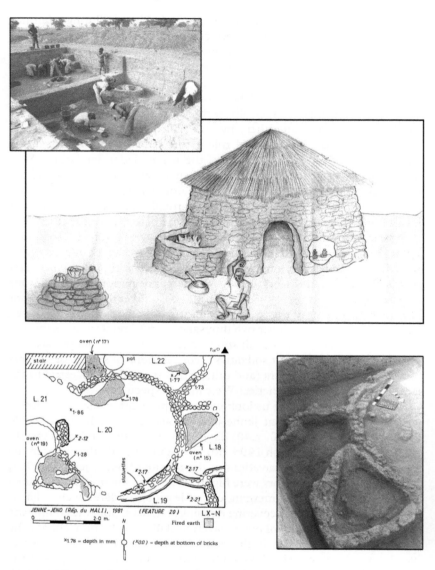

Fig. 4.2. Smith's workshop (House 10, Jenne-jeno, unit LX-N), with protective statuette pair

superbly constructed for iron refining. The soils beneath the overlaying wall collapse level, the soil built up during the use of the workshop, was full of small slag – distinctively smithing slag, without the admixture of smelting slag that characterized the iron-production levels of Phase I/II in other Jenne-jeno units.

More astonishing was the find, excitedly pointed out by Salumoy Traoré, our specialist mud-brick-wall finder (!), as he traced the shallow circular wall stump, of a male–female terracotta statuette pair embedded within the southern wall of the structure (near the entrance). Protective figurines; iron-cult objects? Figure 4.2 provides an artist's reconstruction of how the workshop might have looked, with the smith hard at annealing outside. And the surprises did not end there. In the adjoining unit, LX-S, and clearly associated only meters away were a large cache or pile of undressed large sandstone slabs and four small ash pits (significance unknown). Careful excavation and recording of the thirty-nine-piece sandstone feature (see fig. 4.3) revealed a jumble of evocative goodies: a fragment of a free-standing terracotta statuette; a serpent-appliqué pot lid; another serpent-decorated pot containing thirty-eight rounded sandstone grinders and a polished granite Late Stone Age handaxe; other pots; waster iron; and, around the edges of the cache, a perimeter of oblong dried clay brick. Thirty-nine sandstone slabs and thirty-nine stone tools within; surely that was no coincidence. Sadly the occult significance of "thirty-nine" has been lost to the veil of time. Feature 21 rested atop (and was associated with) a "fire pit" containing burnt earth and bricks and a large fire-damaged bowl.

While the ritual nature of this sandstone feature was never in question, its use was a mystery. Then, several years later, I read of a Dogon (a nearby Mande people) smiths' rainmaking shrine (a *toru*) with obvious structural similarities to Feature 21 (R. McIntosh 1998: 186; S. McIntosh 1995: 278). Smiths, occult and pyrotechnical Adepts, taking charge of the physical phenomenon of the Mande landscape (R. McIntosh 2000b). Pretty clear at AD 1000–1200; however, is extrapolation permissible back to 250 BC? You see, perhaps, the essential frustration of archaeological inference!

Lastly, House 10 and Feature 21 are just continuations of a trend, starting earlier, in later Phase III, of a concentration of smithing (soon to include bronze smithing) in the "Large Exposure" region of Jenne-jeno. Slag, crucibles, tuyère fragments, etc. are dumped in large volumes in enormous ash pits. Susan McIntosh writes:

It is reasonable to ask if we are not seeing some kind of fundamental reorganiza-tion of either metal production or town structure, or both, between Phase I/II and late Phase III, involving a change from short-term, shifting production centers to

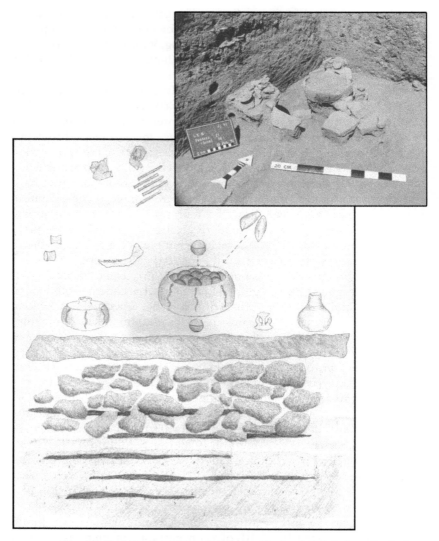

Fig. 4.3. Smith's ritual "altar," Feature 21 of unit LX-S, from Jenne-jeno

the long-term installation of smiths in specific locales, or *quarters*, perhaps as members of organized specialist producer groups. (S. McIntosh 1995: 278)

As an archaeologist, I invoke Preponderance of the Evidence: strong for specialist smiths at the beginning of the settlement; stronger still as the urban sequence evolves.

And blacksmiths are not the only metallurgical specialists yielded by the Jenne-jeno sequence. We have already reviewed the dilemma caused, in terms of identifiability of long-distance traders, by the appearance of copper, ultimately from distant Saharan sources. Copper (or its bronze alloy) first appears in early Phase III (S. McIntosh and R. McIntosh, I: 165, 1980 table 9.37). Now, mere appearance of copper does not necessarily imply the presence of copper-working specialists. However, on-site bronze smithing can be identified, by at least the eighth century AD, by the discarded crucibles (with tin-bronze still affixed) and mold fragments of those levels (S. McIntosh 1995: 264, 275–77). Of course, iron specialists *could* also learn to work copper, but our larger cross-cultural experience and, certainly, West African custom, argues against this. Not a Preponderance of the Evidence for a specialist bronze smithing corporation by the eighth century, but what we might label good Inferential Testimony of the Evidence!

Gold – yet another trade item of distant origin (this time, from the southern forests) (UNESCO 1991: Sheet 1; see also Devisse 1990; Mauny 1961: fig. 58). The first gold appears at Jenne-jeno in the late Phase III deposits underlying the Phase III/IV-transition city wall at the far northern NWS location (S. McIntosh 1995: 267). This object, an earring, is "locked" *in situ* by the overlying massive wall structure; it cannot have trickled down from later levels. In later times, Jenne was famous for its goldsmiths (LaViolette 1987, 1994). Indeed, as early as al-Mas'udi in the tenth century and, most prolifically, with al-Bakri in the eleventh and Idrissi in the twelfth centuries, the Middle Niger (and Jenne-jeno/Jenne) was known to the Islamic world as the "Island of Gold" (S. McIntosh and R. McIntosh 1980, II: 457; S. McIntosh 1981). We would be on shaky ground arguing for an *in situ* goldsmithing corporation in the late first millennium (although it is certainly not *precluded* by the evidence). Only the rashest of archaeologists would construct an entire corporation out of a single earring.

Yet, what do we do with the late Phase I/II (400 AD or earlier) find from the site of a "pottery goldweight," judged by the goldweight specialist Timothy Garrard to have been chipped and rounded to the weight of one-quarter Islamic ounce (7.0 g, and close to the traditional Jenne gold-weight standard of 7.1 g) (S. McIntosh and R. McIntosh 1980, I: 161–62)? Clearly, this could not be making reference to an Islamic ounce, centuries before the birth of Mohammed – but perhaps the Islamic goldworking culture and an earlier trans-Saharan corporation shared an antecedent scale of weights that carried on uninterrupted. This is Inferential Testimony of the Evidence – but pretty weak.

Any number of other archaeological "recognitions" of specialists fall somewhere on the spectrum from High Preponderance of the Evidence (such as the presence of smiths at early Jenne-jeno) to (weak) Inferential Testimony of the Evidence (goldsmiths conjured from a single "pottery goldweight"). The Phase I/II ceramics are "extremely well made" (S. McIntosh and R. McIntosh 1980, I: 156), far beyond the present capacities even of envious members of the potters' corporation in the town of Jenne today. Does this constitute (lesser?) High Preponderance of the Evidence, or (robust?) Inferential Testimony of the Evidence? The "guild" of Jenne masons is still renowned throughout West Africa today. Mason corporation members are hired widely for their skill in making mosques (since the twelfth century, according to local tradition, or as late as the fifteenth century, according to others) (Bourgeois 1987; LaViolette 1987: 293; Maas and Mommersteeg 1994: 80–83; Prussin 1986: 46–47). They, after all, created the famous Jenne mosque – the largest solid mud structure in the world. Do we first pick them up archaeologically at the first appearance of their signature cylindrical mud brick (*djenney-féré*) of the seventh or eighth century at Jenne-jeno (S. McIntosh 1995: 18)? Or must we await the first (archaeologically demonstrable) experiments in multi-story building in the eighteenth or early nineteenth century in the SM-O unit (Site du Musée – Ouest, Structure 5) in Jenne itself (S. McIntosh *et al.* 2003: 178)? Just what evidence can we trust as reliably indicating to us the clear functioning of specialist occupations (quite distinct from specialist corporate groups, although the two are clearly linked), as opposed to serving as far more inferential proxy measures of the activities of specialists?

Further, Frank (2002: 125–28) makes the very plausible but equally difficult to verify assertion that the famous anthropomorphic and zoo-morphic terracotta statuary of the Upper Delta and Macina were most likely to have been produced by specialist craftspersons. Extrapolating back to the tenth century AD or earlier, in the case of these art pieces, she argues that women – as long-term Mande Adepts who worked with *nyama*-charged clays and earth – were the most likely candidates. Again, the specific attribution to individual potters or even to their gender is speculative, but surely scholars can come to some level of consensus about the corporate nature of specialist production of the terracottas.

This last issue, proxy measures of specialists, must be addressed to end this discussion of how archaeologists recognize occupations, specialists performing those occupations, and occupationally defined corporate groups. I have experimented (R. McIntosh 1989) with frequency of the terracotta figurines and appliqué art on ceramics as a proxy measure of social complexity. Figure 4.4 presents the twenty terracotta statuettes or fragments and the sixteen humans or animals represented in appliqué that we possess from *in situ*, stratigraphically secure contexts, dated by

Episodes	Terracotta statuettes			Terracotta appliqué				Total representational art	Other Clay 'toys' of domestic animals
	Statuettes in original context	Fragments in situ	Total	Human motif	Snake motif	Other animal	Total	Total terracotta	
c. AD 1200–1350 Settlement decline *Triumph of Islam*	2	4	6	-	-	-	0	6	(6)
c. AD 1000–1200 Population and building explosion *Crisis of Proximity*	6	3	9	2	8	2	12	21	(13)
c. AD 500–1000 Maximum areal extent and prosperity *Clustering: Identity and Distance*	-	5	5	1	3	-	4	9	(28)
c. 250 BC to AD 500 Foundation and growth *Low Conflict Specialists*	-	-	0	-	-	-	0	0	(19)

Fig 4.4. Frequency of representational art recovered at Jenne-jeno

the full suite of radiocarbon determinations. (This is opposed to the hundreds, if not thousands, of orphans lost to science, looted from similar Middle Niger sites.)

The frequency of terracottas correlates with episodes of settlement change (not necessarily with the phase chronology, which is primarily [not exclusively] a reflection of changes in ceramics). The data in figure 4.4 can tentatively be interpreted as supporting the idea of a gradual growth in the ambiguity of belonging and a production of symbols to resolve that ambiguity. By this hypothesis, the symbol production increased by the mid-first millennium as the settlement fully celebrated its urban status, until around AD 1000. Then, population and "corporate discourse" burgeoned dangerously and the entire traditional belief system came under threat by an intrusive, but unifying, belief system in the form of Islam.

Broad cross-cultural experience with "corporate belonging" provides certain expectations about how behavior and canons of "self-identification" change as society becomes more complex – and about how symbolically charged objects function at such times. These objects serve as instruments of communication by making reference to the socially constructed realities of the social life and histories of their makers' communities. The artisan taps a larger symbolic reservoir shared, at least partially, with his or her contemporaries.

By exploring this symbolic legacy, artisans and artists may play a special role in the representation, and even in the creation, of new cultural perceptions required by economic, social, and political changes. By those very acts of exploration and representation, objects come to reflect socio-cultural change and simultaneously to assume a role described by Vansina:

Is art always a passive epiphenomenon? As new metaphors were created, new tools became available for social and cultural use ... every development [in art] could be used to stress differences between social strata, and innovation was encouraged when the urge was felt to express such increased differences. Art works as concrete symbols could crystallize unfocused ideas and mobilize people ... Art is an epiphenomenon but epiphenomena can sometimes take the lead by the effects they produce. (Vansina 1984: 157–58)

If Vansina is correct, and under empirical circumstances for which we must control carefully, we can be alerted to growing complexity in a society by a change in the diversity of symbolic expression.

What has this to do with the Jenne-jeno terracotta statuettes and appliqué art? In the process of emerging complexity (including urbanism at Jenne-jeno), ever-increasing numbers of sub-groups engage in the erection of legitimizing myth, ideologies, symbols, and the like from larger cultural heritage or legacy of beliefs and their material representations. Thus, the dawning of urbanization at multiple Middle Niger localities created an arena for the playing out of social strategies on unprecedented scales. In some contexts of emerging complexity, cooperation among newly formed corporate groups can be enforced by a coercive elite. There is a substantial literature about why, in these cases, one would expect a simplification and canonization of symbolic expression (Davis 1983; Hornung 1982). In emerging complex societies where evidence of centralization and coercion is absent, as at burgeoning Jenne-jeno, tensions arise as more people, each with greater potential for conflicting claims upon identity, come together. In this context, one would predict a proliferation of elaborate symbols constraining the concept of belonging to this or that sub-group (R. McIntosh 1989; R. McIntosh and S. McIntosh 2003).

These subgroups are, of course, best thought of as corporations, each generating a sense of belonging by right of common possession of or access to "property" (Cochrane 1971). Here, I have taken the inclusive view of common corporate property as including intellectual or spiritual or ritual property. This is a position entirely consistent with the argument of chapter 2 that nodes or aspects of the landscape can be viewed as corporate property. Recall the case of Kangousa and that silver hammer reminding all passers of prior claims to that point of the topography. Access to legitimizing myth, symbols, art, shrines, sacred places in the landscape – all can constitute a satisfactory claim for corporate belonging. Such intellectual property speaks to oneself and to others of one's place in the world. The creation of such objects renders them, in some cases, archaeologically recoverable and, hence, as part of a kaleidoscopic lens held up by the investigator to the process of urbanism. Because of the predicted cacophony of "corporate discourse" at early cities, we might expect to find a crescendo of communication in the art and symbol portion of the archaeological record.

Interestingly, the cacophony of representational art dies away with the advance of Islam. However, new symbols enter the "corporate discourse." At two points in the 9-meter *tell* sequence at the SM-O excavations at Jenne town, we found large fragments of pots inscribed with an 8×8 "magic square," with words of a benedictory verse from the Koran (*Sura* 106). Both contexts were the foundation trenches of new buildings and in one, the magic-square pot was embedded in a mass of rice (a traditional way to bless a new dwelling, even today). Both contexts were buildings associated with Koranic schools or with powerful Muslim families (Imam al-Hadj Alman Korobala of Jenne, pers. comm. 2000).

Baukassou Traoré, my long-time foreman, took one look at the magic squares and casually spun off a translation of their function. He made them all the time, on paper to be sure, not on broken pottery. When not excavating, Baukassou is also a master mason and a Koran instructor. Every time a new house is built or restored, a paper with the same *sura* written on it is immured in the foundation. What a perfect illustration of the power of symbols to communicate ambiguity of belonging – Baukassou as mason, Islamic instructor, member of a long-term Djenneké (town elite) family – and archaeological foreman!

Before we turn to the excavated sequence for the Middle Niger cities, let us review the rude Typology of Discrimination of corporate belonging:

High Preponderance of the Evidence (e.g. early smiths at Jenne-jeno and Dia): number of specialists can be counted with confidence.

Inferential Testimony of the Evidence (e.g. potters at earliest Jenne-jeno; bronzesmiths from the eighth century AD; women artisans making anthropomorphic terracotta statuary): circumstantial evidence for the presence of specialization is reasonable to good, but enumerating them borders on the speculative.

Proxy Measure of Corporate Groups (e.g. traders in metals, ores, and salt at earliest Jenne-jeno; inferences from the frequency of represen-tational art): gives only a qualitative feeling of the increasing or decreasing index of complexity of occupations and society.

"Invisibility Function" (comparing archaeological discrimination from documentary sources of how ancient peoples themselves viewed their corporate makeup): range between Additive and Exponential increase (one specialist $= 1^1 = \{1$ corporate identities$\}$; two specialists $= 2^2 = \{4$ corporate identities$\}$; but, three specialists $= [3 = 3]$ to $[3^3 = 9] = \{6–9$ corporate identities$\}$; $[4 + 4]$ to $[4^4] = \{8–16$ corporate identities$\}$; $[10 + 10]$ to $[10^{10}] = \{20–$near ∞ of corporate identities$\}$). Is there a theoretical upper limit to the number of corporations in any urban setting, even with a population of 5,000 or 50,000? The problem of "constraining ambiguity of belonging" no longer sounds so abstract and pointy-headed! It becomes an issue absolutely critical to the archaeologist's ability to func-tion within the "heterogeneity" function of our definition of urbanism.

Anchors and variability: the core sequence

The lead into this book was the story of Discovery – rather, that moment of "discovery of Jenne-jeno to the world" in the presence of the future Archaeologist President of the Mali Republic, Dr. Alpha Oumar Konaré. The real problem became how to discriminate, from mound topography and surface features alone, without any prior sub-surface examination of the Jenne-jeno deposits, good places to test the differences within the ancient population. Recall our urban definition: the city is a locale "with a qualitatively more heterogeneous population." Job number one is to document, through time, the presence and elaboration of heterogeneity in the evolving urban community.

Fair enough. However, even before one can document variability in the archaeological record (heterogeneity of population expressed in the signature and ancillary waste products, trash, discard and rejects [so much for the romance of archaeology!] of our various corporate groups), the archaeologist must know the basic characteristics of that material record. In other words, an anchoring foundational culture history must be constructed for the community (or regional urban landscape). This foundational culture history is the standard against which variability is measured – which is quite different from first searching for the "typical" and only later investigating "deviation"(more in the nature of computing central tendency and dispersion: Thomas 1986: 72–85).

Mind you, there are some archaeologists who sniff dismissively at those who still construct the anchoring sequences that are the spine of any archaeological culture history. These terribly superior archaeologists are all from privileged parts of the globe where, slowly and methodically – back into the nineteenth century in many cases – earlier generations of archaeologists dug the core sites, recorded and published artifact sequences, seriated and Chi-squared thousands of ceramics, and laboriously extracted radiocarbon samples. These ancestors did all the tedious heavy lifting. And their efforts allow their dismissive progeny now to operate on a higher, more Olympian and theoretical plane of existence (Flannery 1982).

We simply do not have that luxury (anywhere in Africa), even in the Middle Niger which is one of the best, most cosmopolitan-covered parts of the continent (R. McIntosh 2001: 32–34). Anywhere an archaeologist begins work, she or he must reconcile the fundamental tension between two duties. The first is to document the true nature and variety of behaviors of the ancient peoples – *Variability*. The second is to construct a core sequence of artifact change, of chronology (through relative [e.g. ceramic seriation] and calendrical [e.g. through calibrated radiocarbon determinations, or an archaeomagnetic curve]), and of the cultural history of the site – *Anchoring Sequence*. Too much of the latter and we slip back into the bad old days of diagnostic artifacts, "fossiles directeurs" (diagnostic artifacts), and "sondages" (solitary test pits, the "telephone booths" of an earlier Mesoamerica) that held back Middle Niger archaeology for far too long during the colonial and immediate post-colonial period (R. McIntosh 2001: 23–25). This, then, was the source of our frank terror as we emerged over the rim of Jenne-jeno and gazed for the first time upon the vastness, the surface chaos of that humongous site. The question then becomes: How to meld the need to document variability in the urban record with the obligation to construct a core, anchoring sequence?

Basically, that has occupied the next twenty-five-plus years. That question has involved the disbursed but complementary efforts of several teams of archaeologists, Malian and expatriate, working at several key sites all around the Middle Niger. Halting though these early steps may be, there have been two results of all this attention. The appreciation of the complex Historical Ecology urban process(es) in the Middle Niger has undoubtedly been helped by the fact that there are few other places in the world where so many national styles of research commingle – Malian, French, English, Norwegian, German, Swiss, Belgian, American, and Dutch (R. McIntosh 2001: 22, 34). And although negligible by the standards of the other arid-lands floodplain civilizations – Egypt, the Indus, or Mesopotamia – the core cultural historical sequence, anchored at a few sites investigated by repeat, multi-stage projects, is probably better than any other Iron Age domain in sub-Saharan Africa.

Like the "discovery" of Jenne-jeno, the selection of these specific sites for the anchoring sequence was, frankly, surreptitious. One can easily imagine that other *tell*s, some perhaps as yet undiscovered, would yield as good as or even a better understanding of the core sequence of processes involved in the emergence and maturation of Middle Niger urbanism. Such is the nature of culture history, anywhere in the world. That having been said, figure 4.5 presents one way to look at our present understanding of the principal stages in the self-organization of the human and physcial landscape around the theme of urbanism. This figure divides the period of cities unto subjective stages that differ from the paleoclimatic modes, on the one hand, and from the Jenne-jeno and Jenne ceramic phase chronology, on the other. One can imagine even tighter subdivisions to this anchoring sequence – but that would imply an archaeological resolution on the processes involved that would be less than honest. Jenne-jeno and Jenne are emphasized in the construction of this anchoring sequence, just because of the greater volume of the work done at these two sites, and because the absolute (radiocarbon) dating programs at the former is by far the most robust.

Figure 4.5 begins, optimistically, with the "proto-urban" processes documented in the previous chapter. Specifically, the period dating roughly 800–400 BC sets the stage for urbanism. (It is entirely possible that future research will push back true Middle Niger urbanism well into this phase – we are not yet there, however.) The end of the Late Stone Age sequence in the Méma (MacDonald 1994) and the beginning of that "dead delta's" Iron Age sequence (Togola 1993) represent the time when

Fig. 4.5. Anchoring sequence of Middle Niger urbanism

the Pulse Model predicts the qualitatively higher elaboration, possibly showing radically abrupt, phase transform self-organization, to the trends of "diversification with complementarity." Out of a previous Late Stone Age landscape of increasingly specialized subsistence producers, a radically new clustering evolves, by which reciprocating specialists voluntarily come together for exchange and social reciprocity for, progressively, longer and longer seasons of each year. The predicted pre-clustering of the roughly pre-800 BC terminal "death throe (climate) oscillations" would morph into the proto-clusters of semi-sedentary multi-component hamlets we believe we see at Late Stone Age sites such as Akumbu, Bérétouma, and Kolima. The Pulse Model predicts that analogous proto-clusters might be found also in the Middle Niger's other "dead delta," the Azawad. We just have too little prior research in that inhospitable basin to confirm this at the present.

One of the persistent problems of West African prehistory is the scarcity of sites documenting, continuously and *in situ*, the transition from exclusive stone-tool users to the earliest addition of iron. We now believe we know where to find superb specimens for examination (Togola 1993)! These are the high mound sites of the Méma, with later, first millennium AD material stratified over the characteristic finely made ceramics and levels rich in fish as well as domestic and hunted animal bone of the earliest iron-using peoples, of the last half of the last millennium BC. In several cases documented in survey by Togola (1993: 66), these sites have an apron of earlier Stone Age material at their flanks. In other words, iron was added to an *in situ*, indigenous community (adopting this new technology as part of their several strategies to deal with the rapidly changing climate and persistently declining resource base). Or, new iron-using colonists selected the same locales as earlier Late Stone Age peoples, often plopping down on the conveniently built-up deposits (hence, above higher than normal flood) of their predecessors.

Sadly, the "proto-urban" implications of this Méma scenario have yet to be tested for the 800–400 BC, "Ecological Clustering Maturation," stage of figure 4.5. Téréba Togola made a stab at the (later) urban cluster of Akumbu, but he simply lacked the time and resources to complete his units at these enormously high mounds. His AK 1 unit at the Akumbu A mound (not even the highest) was forced to close out at 7.9 meters depth, still only in the middle reaches of the Iron Age! His AK 3 unit at the 8-meter-high Akumbu B mound (in a locale with the best chance of coming down upon the Stone Age antecedent levels) was closed out, still in the early Iron Age, at only 2.75 meters depth. In many parts of the world, archaeologists would sell their souls (or those of their graduate students) for 2.75 meters of exquisitely stratified deposits! Here, archaeologists just commiserate with Togola! Similarly, another unit (AK 5), by the author, into Akumbu B mound was aborted in 2000, due to banditry, after only 2.05 meters. Not exactly as romantic as the Curse of the Mummy, but the Curse of the Méma means that we keep sinking units fated to give us a mere taste of the Late Stone Age–Iron Age transition, before coquettishly driving us away. And the Akumbu mounds are by no means the largest in area. Certainly in terms of accumulated depth of deposits, Akumbu B looks squat in comparison to many!

Until basic survey and excavation can begin again in the now-dry western basin (and in the long-neglected Azawad Basin), apparently our best chance for a window on this 800–400 BC "proto-urban" period will come from the Dia site of the Macina. New excavations report early deposits dating back to the early first millennium BC (Bedaux *et al.* 2001). Dia basks in its (self-proclaimed) reputation as the center of Soninké migratory and merchant diasporas. These population dispersals were critical to the development of the Wangara–Dyula commercial corporation (S. McIntosh 1981). Dia also proclaims itself the earliest city of the Middle Niger (Dieterlen 1959: 125; Monteil 1971: 30–32; Solvaing 1983). Monteil (1971: 31) relates specific oral traditions from Jenne that the earliest agriculturalists (Nono) in the Upper Delta came from Bassikounou ("gateway" from the Aouker plains fronting Dhar Tichitt and Dhar Oualata to the Middle Niger), via the Méma. Thence they first founded Dia, and then Jenne. Appropriately, the origin traditions speak of the meeting and the formation of a reciprocal alliance between Marka (Nono) rice specialists and an elusive, prior "race" subsisting only on fish and wild plants (represented in the town today by the Bozo Koanta lineage).

Exploratory archaeology at the site began in 1986–87 with three test units at two of the archaeological mounds flanking modern Dia. One unit was sunk into at Mara (considered locally to have been the "original" settlement) and two at the larger, 49-hectare Shoma site (including a trench through the ancient city wall) (Haskell *et al.* 1988) (see fig. 4.6). During the 1998–2004 research conducted under Malian, Dutch, French, and English co-directorship, twelve more units were sunk into the Dia Urban Cluster (Bedaux *et al.* 2001).

Returning to the theme of anchoring and variations on the culture historical sequence, the purpose of the preliminary season was to compare the Dia stratified sequence with the better-understood Jenne-jeno sequence (c. 75 km distant), with which the surface material was so superficially similar. Thin-walled, finely prepared ceramics (identical to Phase I/II "Fineware" at Jenne-jeno, called "Delta fabric ware" by the later excavators) rested atop sterile levee soils at 4.4 meters depth at Mara and, from between 2.8 and 4.2 meters at Shoma. Interestingly, at the latter, the earliest Fineware levels showed a horizontal micro-stratigraphy of occupation interdigitating with thin clay lens – which might indicate a very early occupation of successive (seasonal?) discontinuous habitation (Haskell *et al.* 1988: 31). Was the live delta still just drying out, such that

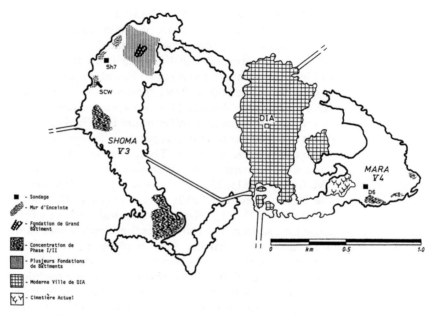

Fig. 4.6. The Dia cluster

the earliest colonists had to flee periodic "pluvial" floods a few years each decade or several times each century? And where exactly did these earliest inhabitants come from?

The preliminary season's yield from Dia replicated the Phase I/II to Phase V ceramic sequence at Jenne-jeno, with little variation and with little, *prima facie* from the artifacts, to suggest that occupation began much earlier than at Jenne-jeno (third century BC). (Subsequent seasons have pushed the foundation well back into the first millennium BC – illustrating why anchoring sequences should never be based on just one, or even a few, test units.)

Interestingly (from the *Variability* perspective), levels with the earliest Fineware ceramics were deep and, comparing lower Mara with lower Shoma, were remarkably dissimilar (Haskell *et al.* 1988: 101, 137–38). We therefore undertook a survey of the Dia hinterland (a 2 km radius from the modern town) in order to test whether this impression of multi-component and clustered occupation extended to the hinterland as well (discussed in the next chapter). The sheer volume of the earliest ceramics at both mounds flanking today's town of Dia, as well as at many of the satellite sites of the hinterland, suggested that early Iron Age occupation was considerable. During the preliminary season, one could perceive little deviation from the anchoring Jenne-jeno artifactual sequence, yet enough internal variation to suggest corporate (ethnic?) heterogeneity amongst the first inhabitants. And when did urbanism at Dia begin? The crying need after this preliminary season was for more extensive excavation, with radiocarbon dates to firm up chronological conclusions from the artifacts.

The challenge was ably answered by the joint Malian–European team, excavating at Shoma (Bedaux *et al.* 2001). They recognize five horizons, with two abandonment interruptions (from 300 BC to AD 300 – a time of sporadic seasonal occupation only – and, more emphatically, from the twelfth through the fourteenth centuries AD). The earliest horizon deposits yielded radiocarbon dates from 800 to 300 BC. Unfortunately, this represents precisely the period of isotopic radiocarbon production that prevents use from calibrating any single date to any calendrical-year period narrower than that half-millennial span. What this means for the archaeologist is that all or any of the dates could, with equal probability, be from early in the millennium or at its end (S. McIntosh and R. McIntosh 1986b: 413–17). Such a pity, because these early levels also yield sherds familiar from the Méma (and Tichitt) Late Stone Age (a few of the Kobadi tradition and maybe 30 percent of the Faita – MacDonald's putative transitional latest Late Stone Age and beginning Iron Age!). The thin-walled "Fineware" (or "Delta fabric ware") begins in Horizon I and continues, strongly represented, through horizons dating to AD 300–800 (Horizon III) and AD 800–1100 (Horizon IV).

Just when did urbanism begin at Dia? The eight units sunk to date at the 100-hectare urban complex of Dia–Shoma–Mara (see fig. 4.6) certainly do not preclude a settlement of urban proportions by 500 BC. All these units have "Fineware" in their lower reaches. Whereas at Jenne-jeno, "Fineware" is narrowly restricted to 250 BC–AD 350 (S. McIntosh 1995: 153–54), at Shoma this ceramic has a majority run of well on 2,000 years, and so cannot be considered to be a chronological marker. Some Fineware was even chopped up and incorporated (as a form of grag to prevent cracking?) into the bricks of the city wall, now dated to the last horizon, fifteenth to seventeenth century AD. We will require many more primary-association radiocarbon dates from units all over the clustered mounds comprising ancient Dia to determine just how large an area was occupied by the mid-first millennium (or earlier) BC. And recall our definition of a city (not size, but corporate diversity): certainly by AD 800–1100 there was a frenzy of burial states (ethnic insignia?) and the presence of specialized herders and fisherfolk (Bedaux *et al.* 2001: 844–46). But just how much earlier

Fig. 4.7. From the surface, the Jenne-jeno unit LX swamped by the vastness of the *tell*'s surface.

can we document specialization, corporate elaboration, and the special relationship of a town with its hinterland?

The story picks up in earnest at earliest Jenne-jeno. Oral tradition is persistent enough, on both sides (at Dia and at modern Jenne!) of foundation from colonists from Dia, that this is a reasonable hypothesis perhaps one day to become testable using hard archaeological data. Before summarizing the earliest part of the Jenne-jeno sequence, I must pick up the theme of anchor and variation by briefly reviewing the twenty-five-year, evolutionary logic of how locales upon this 33-hectare mound were selected for excavation. Work is ongoing; as of this printing there have been twenty-two units excavated stratigraphically (plus another twenty-nine at near satellite sites – see below). An additional thirteen mechanically drilled cores demonstrate very localized stratigraphy (R. McIntosh *et al.* 1996).

I use two contrasting images to illustrate the need, by all archaeologists, to possess a native appreciation of sampling and probability when assessing the elusive calculus of evolving *Variability*. In an earlier time, a simpler age, archaeologists would be content to sink one master unit into a site deemed to be "typical" of the region or prehistoric culture – the artifacts from that lone unit becoming the "diagnostics" of the culture history sequence thus revealed. Lonely, stark in their isolation, these master units at type sites dominated the archaeological literature from the discipline's birth well into the 1960s. But just as the deepest, most voluminous unit at Jenne-jeno is terrifying in its frank puniness compared to the vastness of the site's 33-hectare surface, so too would the enormity of information collected from that unit have misled, in subtle ways, had it not been complemented by twenty-one other units dispersed over the wastes of Jenne-jeno (see fig. 4.7). Compare this impression of scorched Sahelian solitude with the vision of *Variability* given its due in figure 4.8.

The sampling strategy at the site was grounded in a complement of (1) culture history (which areas were most likely to give a full sequence, to be little disturbed and with the greatest yield of radiocarbon and artifacts, as well as "ecofacts" [animal bones and plant remains]) and (2) functional variability across the mound (see S. McIntosh and R. McIntosh 1980; S. McIntosh 1995). Also very important was information about the location of the original settlement and about the later expansion and contraction of occupation. Thus, four units sunk into the highest part of the mound, that precinct with the highest concentration of houses, anchored the sequence. These units (on fig. 4.8, M1 and M2 of 1977 and the adjoining LX-N and LX-S of 1981) provided the entire 1,600-year sequence, with minimal disturbance (from animal burrowers or human looters).

Other units helped test alternative hypotheses of either initial settlement in cluster, with later agglomeration, or initial founding of one large settlement (see fig. 4.9). The latter, contrary to our initial gut feeling, proved to be correct. Some units, designed to test these two hypotheses, also served to give sub-surface documentation to the localized variability witnessed on the surface: CTR showed funerary features on its surface (and deep evidence of long funerary use) and ALS tested a massive, undifferentiated mass of mud brick (eventually, a post-collapse agglomeration of walls, wall stumps, and other architectural collapse of at least two neighboring houses).

Most units, however, were placed in such a way as to spread out information from all parts of Jenne-jeno, but also to relate to specific apparent functional differences in the mound deposits as seen on the surface. In 1977, JF1 sampled a "cemetery" of funerary urns (at the urging of Dr. Konaré) and JF2 tested the assumption that the farthest fringes of the mound represent secondary slough of eroded material from higher on the mound. In 1981, NWS tested the area around and beneath the city wall, while HK sampled the far southern, almost featureless "hook" of the site. WFL (like KIS the following season) tested an area that was coming under intense scrutiny by looters. What did they know that we did not? In 1996–97, sampling was driven partially by the season's funding (an anti-erosion and salvage effort by the World Monuments

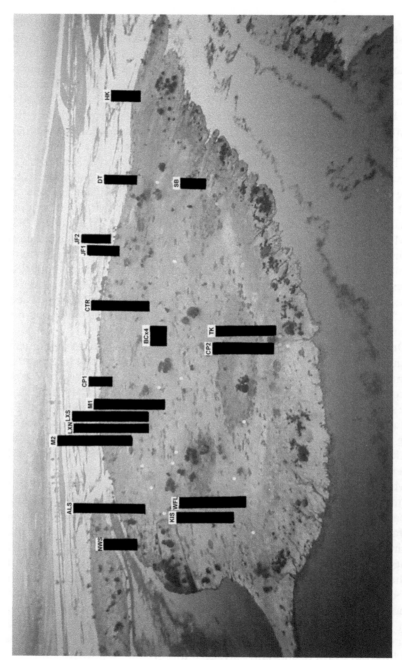

Fig. 4.8. Sampling variability: units and cores at Jenne-jeno.

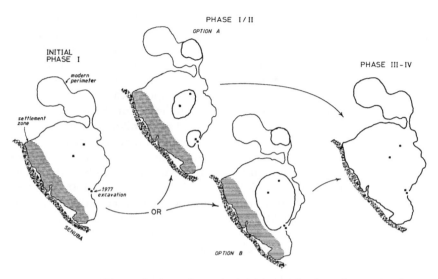

Fig. 4.9 Alternative hypotheses for initial colonization: clustered or large singularity

Fund and the Mission Culturelle de Djenné). That season's CP1 and CP2 (vertical exposures of interior deposits laid bare by penetrating gullies) primarily served to gather information from deposits destined to erode away during the following rainy season. But unit SB sampled another and quite different manifestation of the city wall; DT was sunk into a peripheral region with the highest surface concentration of Phase I/II material and primary evidence of iron production. Finally, for her 1997 doctoral research, SMU student Mary Clark excavated BCSW and BCSE into enigmatic brick rings (testing whether they served as granary supports) and into a linear architectural feature (unit BCNW) (Clark 2003).

The upshot of all this concern with anchoring sequence, tempered by sensitivity to variability (culture history and complexity), is an understanding of the ever-"complexifying" way of life of the Jenne-jeno peoples. These were the data allowing an understanding here of the next stage of the anchoring sequence (fig. 4.5), "Early Cities" of around 400 BC–AD 400, an understanding unmatched in most parts of the African continent. In the many parts of Jenne-jeno now taken down to sterile floodplain deposits, occupation began in the third century BC. Future excavation may well push that foundation date back in time. Archaeologists must always remember that sampling is a crap-shoot and the very next excavation may emasculate any conclusions (such as this) based on negative evidence.

The previous "proto-urban" stage of around 800–400 BC must have been a period of significant migration from the now-Sahara into the Sahel, generally, and into the accessible parts of the Middle Niger floodplain, specifically. This migration surely continued into the "Early Cities" stage. The entire last millennium BC was also, most assuredly, a period of cultural consolidation and considerable complexification. As a consequence, considering the last half of the millennium, Susan McIntosh can speak of a "culture area" (characterized by a uniform style of pottery and art, similar settlement patterns, and common funerary ritual; and, we might add, considerable sub-continental trade) throughout the Upper Delta and Macina (Dia) and into the Méma (Akumbu, Boundou Boubou) and Lakes Region (KNT2) (S. McIntosh 1995: 360–62). The "Early Cities" phase here roughly coincides (give a century or two on either side) to the Upper Middle Niger Fineware phase (coincident with the Jenne-jeno Phase I/II: S. McIntosh 1995: 361–64 and fig. 3.40), with the very distinctive "chinaware" so suggestive of very early ceramic specialist production.

The origins of the earliest Jenne-jeno ceramics are uncertain, but are generally considered to be Saharan (S. McIntosh 1995: 361–64). The Late Stone Age assemblages with closest affinity are those of late Tichitt and Kobadi (earliest in the Méma), and this accords nicely with oral traditions, in Jenne, about the origins of the first sedentary groups to have founded Dia, and then Jenne (Monteil 1971: 31). The permanent colonization of the four "live" deltas of the Middle Niger must have been accelerated by the stable dry period, with annual precipitation reaching −20 percent of the 1930–60 baseline, that dates around 300 BC (and perhaps as early as 500 BC in the far north) to AD 300. S. McIntosh (1995: 373–74) and R. McIntosh (1993) discuss why the Jenne area appears to have been avoided by or inaccessible to Late Stone Age peoples and why, once the settlement began around the third century BC, Jenne-jeno expanded rapidly. The site's area is at least 12 hectares and, recent excavations suggest, was more likely on the order of 20 hectares by the end of the "Early Cities" phase. By that time, precipitation was improving steadily.

The first colonists were fully equipped with iron (smelted and smithed on site), pottery, and with the subsistence knowledge to grow rice (*Oryza glaberrima*), bulrush millet (*Pennisetum americanum/glaucum*), and sorghum (*Sorghum* spp.). The latter two were minority pursuits, compared to rice cultivation and even to the gathering of wild plants. Additionally, they were skillful and wide-ranging fishermen, gatherers of wild plants (heavily of wild millet, *Brachiaria ramosa*), and hunters (including crocodile). Cattle, sheep, and goats complete the menu that was dietarily complex and nutritionally complementary. Agricultural and fishing intensification apparently was never attempted (in sharp contrast with the history of the other great arid-lands, floodplain civilizations).

These earliest city dwellers were scarcely isolated. We have already reviewed the implications of inter-regional imports, in large volumes and weight, of sandstone grinders and iron (ore and perhaps blooms). Semi-precious stone for personal adornment came from further afield in the Sahara. And we need, eventually, to explain the presence in these levels of a tiny glass bead, of composition only known from south and southeast Asia, contemporary with the Han dynasty (S. McIntosh 1995: 252–55, 390–91). One cannot make an entire trade network from one tiny bead, however secure its find context might have been. However, this bead, pregnant with implications, and the (counter) non-appearance of nutritionally obligatory salt, remind us of how little we know about long-distance trade in the last millennium BC and the first AD.

We really know nothing of the social organization of the first inhabitants. We must still test, at Jenne-jeno itself and at its immediate satellites (see the next section of this chapter), whether there were differentiated and archaeologically discernable subsistence groups and occupation corporations (such as blacksmiths), as seems likely. The best we can say with confidence is that the founding population was not inconsiderable and that it expanded rapidly. There was some tendency to clustering, even during this phase (the adjacent settlement of Hambarketolo was founded soon after Jenne-jeno). However, the settlement had (conservatively) expanded to at least 25 hectares by the beginning of the next urban phase ("Urban Prosperity") and to its full area of 33 hectares before AD 800. By this date, Jenne-jeno was a full and heterogeneous agglomeration of craftsmen, herders, farmers, and fisherfolk of different flavors. It boasted a city wall of around 2 kilometers in circumference – the only public architecture yet found, but whether used for classic defense or for flood control is unknown. All excavation suggests a dense use of space, with consequently a high density of population *and* a high coefficient of corporate diversity of that population. Archaeologists shrink (with justification) from making population estimates; let us just guess at a *low-end figure* of 10,000–26,000 people in Jenne-jeno and the 1-kilometer radius satellites (see below) by AD 800 (S. McIntosh 1995: 395).

The period of approximately AD 400 to 1000 or 1100, our so-called "Urban Prosperity" period, coincides with the ceramic Phases III and lower IV at Jenne-jeno. The Middle Niger basked in a stable improvement in rainfall (AD 300 or 400 to 700) and a stable plateau of precipitation at levels around +20 percent of modern baseline (AD 700 to 1000 or 1100). The community was at its maximum of complexity. That is reflected in

the expansion and reorganization of people (and evidently of corporations) in the Jenne-jeno Urban Complex within a 4-kilometer radius.
(The Urban Complex is the subject of the concluding section of this
chapter.) The mid-first millennium AD saw the importation of copper,
from mines at closest 350 kilometers (Gaoua, Burkina Faso) or 500
kilometers (Nioro and Sirakoro, Mali and Gorgol Noir, Mauritania)
distant. A looming question is: Just when did contacts with North
Africa and the Mediterranean commence? From Phase III comes a
natron glass bead of typical Roman manufacture (either Egypt or Italy).
The climatic optimum would certainly have encouraged the desert crossing
(Devisse 1990). Gold is found *in situ* sometime before AD 850–900.
S. McIntosh (1981) gilds the trade argument by her assertion that, by
the tenth century, the Middle Niger was the "Island of Gold" of the Arab
chroniclers. From early in the urban prosperity phase, a distinctive
"Tellem footed bowl" appears all along the Niger, from the gold-producing
regions, eventually, to the southwest to the Méma, the Niger Bend, and
the Bandiagara escarpment. The footed bowl even appears along with the
many occult items, in the "altar" associated with the blacksmith's workshop of Jenne-jeno unit LX (fig. 4.3). One must not make too much
of one ceramic. But this strongly suggests a riverine exchange system
based on the unpreserved (grains, fish oil, animal skins, alcoholic
hydromel, Saharna salt, etc.) and also upon preservable but unremark-
able non-luxury items (stone, iron, ceramics) (Bedaux 1980; S. McIntosh
1995: 391–92).

Specialists reorganized and became even more sophisticated.
S. McIntosh has suggested (1995: 386) that Jenne-jeno copper use evolved
into bronzesmithing by AD 850, bronze being replaced by brass by 1000.
She also suggests a reorganization of iron production sometime after AD
400. Smelting and smithing were done together at the site before that date.
Afterwards, blacksmiths exclusively occupied with non-reductive smithing
inhabited quarters in the town and smelting was done off-site (either at the
distant ore sources or at some of the specialized satellites of the Jenne-jeno
Urban Complex). Subsistence, however, remained remarkably unchanged
from the earlier period (except for reduction of easily hunted territorial
antelope species). We have already remarked upon the lack of agricultural
intensification. This continued and really was one of the reasons why the
Middle Niger was so late to be recognized as one of the ancient world's
great and original urban civilizations (S. McIntosh and R. McIntosh
1979). Another subsistence fact not expected was the continued high
reliance upon suites of wild plants (and the inattention to, the utter uncon-
cern with domestication of a heavily used wild grain, *Brachiaria*)
(R. McIntosh 1997: 414–15; S. McIntosh 1995: 377–79).

The generalized and wild-enhanced subsistence strategy of the "Urban Prosperity" peoples was good for the stable and even improving climatic conditions before the turn of the second millennium AD. And it proved just as sustainable, just as stable, during the abrupt, surely often catastrophic climatic oscillations of the following "Urban Shake-up" from AD 1000 or 1100 to 1400. Consistent with a widespread settlement and population decline during this period (e.g. the vast depopulation of the Méma by the thirteenth or fourteenth century: Togola 1993), the Jenne-jeno population peaked in mid-phase IV (AD 1100 or 1200) and then declined, apparently rapidly. Decline continued at Jenne-jeno and throughout the Jenne-jeno Urban Complex until around 1400, by which time the site was abandoned.

Occupation was restructured thoroughly in the Upper Delta. Some moved to the non-inundated periphery (Galia and Doupwil, see below), some abandoned the lower rice soils (in favor of the recessional and dry farming dunes and sandy levees?), and the urban population, once clustered, imploded upon fewer (larger?) cities, such as Jenne. Dia witnessed a similar regional reorganization (perhaps even earlier: S. McIntosh 1995: 375–76) and the Méma was virtually abandoned by AD 1300. Lack of excavation hinders our understanding of the effects of climate instability and population shake-ups elsewhere on the peoples of the Lakes Region and Niger Bend. However, the erection of richly appointed tumuli, such as El Oualadji, by the eleventh or twelfth century, shows us our first indications of the rise of polities based upon hierarchical power – what can be labeled the Imperial Tradition (R. McIntosh 1998: 281–86).

Climate must have had a central role in this urban shake-up. But we cannot dismiss the profound changes that might have been brought about by the appearance of the horse in the mid- to later first millennium, by potential pandemic diseases (such as plague) that might have crossed the Sahara to the "virgin" Sahelian human reservoir with the growth of the trans-Saharan trade, with the penetration into all ranks of society of Islam, and of the conquering, hegemonic spirit that drove the "empire" builders of the expansive polities known to the outside world as Ghana, Mali, and Songhai (Levtzion 1973; Levtzion et al. forthcoming). What was the role of the terracotta statuettes that exploded in use during this period? Had the cultural confidence of the townsfolk been so badly shaken that appeals to the supernatural, and to the newly entrant religion of Islam, became a shout, and then a deafening din? Al-Sa'di (1900: 23–26) provides a date of 1180 for the conversion of the Jenne leader, Koi-Konboro, to Islam (in the presence of 4,200 ulémas!). He razed his palace and built the first mosque in its place. All suggesting that the negative demographics of the first centuries of the second millennium

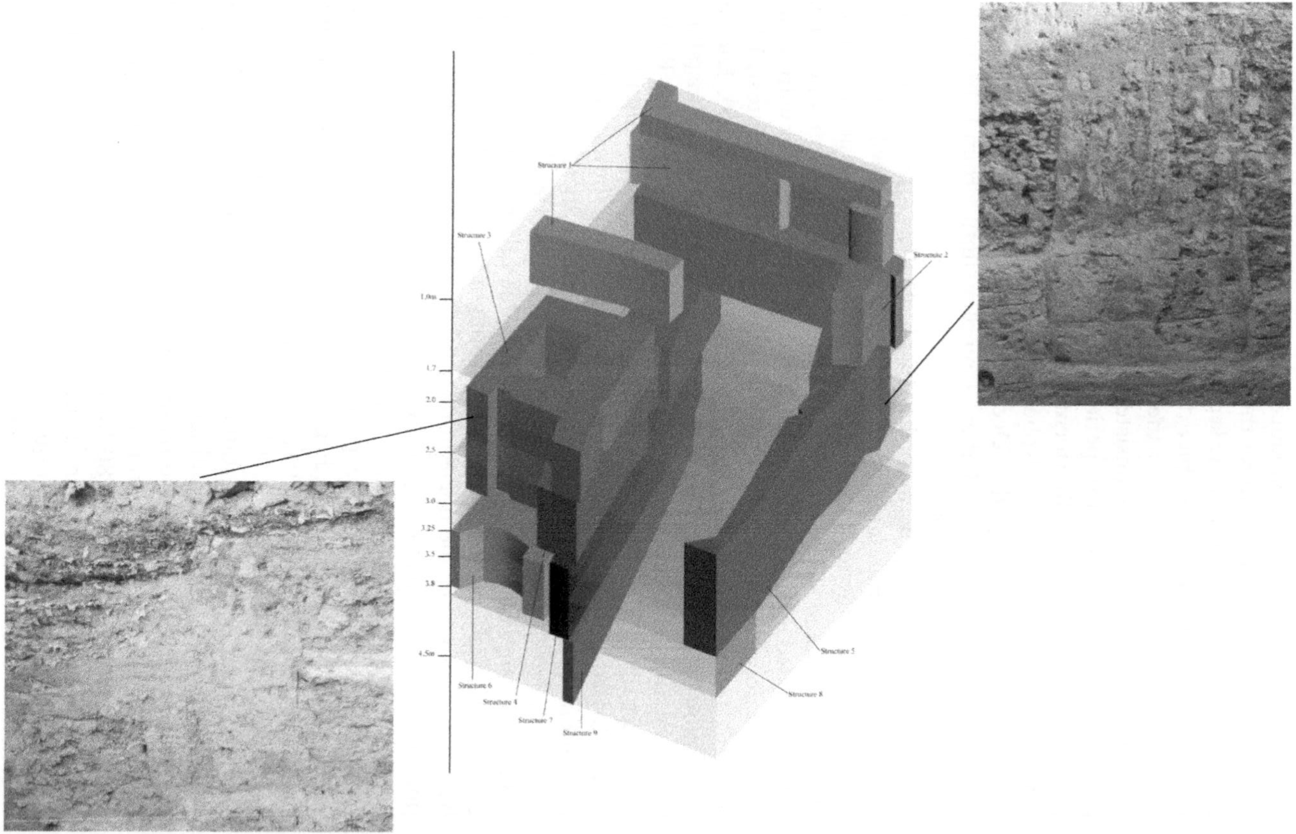

Fig. 4.10. Planimetric reconstruction of the wall complexes at SM-O

worked in favor of the new town of Jenne. Another imponderable is the effect on the long-term regional urban organization of the "late hordes" of militant Bambara millet farmers and equally martial Fulani herders (R. McIntosh 1998: 113–16).

The turbulent regional scene post-1400, and the archaeologically clouded transition from terminal Jenne-jeno to early Jenne is illuminated by Dutch excavations, beginning in 1975, at the sites of Galia and Doupwil (Bedaux *et al.* 1978, 1994: 42–43). The sites are closer to the highland margin of the Upper Delta and date from the eleventh to the sixteenth or seventeenth centuries. Were these sites on the Upper Delta's eastern border founded by ecological (and political?) refugees from deeper in the floodplain (R. McIntosh 1998: 202)? In any event, the Middle Niger floodplain thought by the Guinean historian D. T. Niane (1984: 156) to have been "virtually human anthills" during the apogee of the Ghana and Mali empires were, in fact, by the rise of Mali, instead in the throes of regional instability and, possibly, significantly depopulated.

There were, however, islands of urban stability lapped by these waters of climatic and regional chaos. We continue the Middle Niger's anchoring sequence at a single large excavation, in 1999–2000, at the future city museum of Jenne. This unit, SM-O, was sunk in the shadow of the city's grand mosque, into the ruins of the French colonial medical facilities (S. McIntosh and R. McIntosh 2005; S. McIntosh *et al.* 2003). Coring during an earlier season had indicated that this *dispensaire* (dispensary and *maternité* or child-birthing center, built soon after 1903 and razed in the 1980s) was erected upon a considerable depth of *tell* deposits (R. McIntosh *et al.* 1996). The distinguished marabout (Koranic scholar and saint) family that owns the house immediately south of the museum site claims that the area was located on land originally owned by them and used for a Koranic school, for "centuries before."

Multiple and successive wall complexes provided the framework of interpreting the sequence of activities in this deep unit, 9 meters deep (fig. 4.10). This town is truly paradise for masons. This unit tests accumulations at one part of Jenne during what I have here labeled (fig. 4.5) the "Stable City-Island" period of AD 1400 to around 1600 (end of the Songhai kingdom with the Moroccan victory at Tondibi a few years before) and the "Globalization of Middle Niger Cities" of about 1600 to the moment of Jenne's capture by the French under Colonel Archinard in 1893.

The top 1.5 meters of deposits were composed of the tumbled cement and brick walls of the *dispensaire*. Above the French floor were recent accumulations of trash and blue plastic bags (indicating deposition since c. 1985 – clearly, globalization gone berserk!). Underlying debris (still above the floor) was unambiguously associated with the operation of the dispensary in the first half of the twentieth century (glass ampoules, bottle glass, only one tobacco pipe). The cement floor of the dispensary was found at 1.5 meters. From 2.0 to 6.5 meters depth, we encountered a series of superimposed walls, floor surfaces, pits, and a granary with considerable amounts of rice (fig. 4.10). Two distinct groups of these structures probably date to the nineteenth century and may be related to the aforementioned Koranic school. After a reorientation of alleys and streets, there are separate complexes of late eighteenth–early nineteenth and, again probable seventeenth-century structures. "Globalization" is not too much of an exaggeration for these levels boasting masses of imports, including bottle glass and gunflints, cowries, and over 300 tobacco pipes.

Exotics virtually disappear between 4.5 and 5.0 meters depth. Interestingly, at this depth a second pot with a Koranic magic square and benediction *sura* on a new house appeared in the foundation of a newly constructed house. The date inscribed (519 AH, or AD 1125/1126), curiously, does not refer to the date of the deposits (early to middle seventeenth century?), but it may refer to some much earlier event. Was an earlier benediction ceramic recovered and reused? A well, lined with superimposed, open-bottomed pots, was dug from a depth of 6.4 meters down to 9.0 meters. The water table today begins at 8.5 meters, below which deposits were waterlogged. There were also, significantly, several trash pits dug from the initial occupation surface at 7 meters depth down into the floodplain.

As a first approximation, we place these early deposits somewhere around the fifteenth century (S. McIntosh *et al.* 2003: 175). The ceramics increasingly resemble those of Jenne-jeno late Phase IV (AD 1200–1400), although Phase V (1500–1900) characteristics appear as well. This appears to be the earliest occupation at this locale in Jenne – a limited spatial sample that cannot be extrapolated to indicate the occupation history of the entirety of Jenne. Indeed, tradition in the town claims the SM-O locale to have first been occupied well after other quarters (especially the fisherfolks' Djoboro quarter to the south).

The most recent end of figure 4.5, the immediate pre-colonial and colonial/post-colonial end of the Middle Niger sequence, is supplemented by excavations at the Hamdallahi site (1818–62, capital of the Islamic theocracy of Sékou Amadou) (Gallay *et al.* 1990). More recent still are the ethnoarchaeological studies, principally on ceramics and other crafts, of LaViolette (1987), and an energetic Swiss ethnoarchaeological team (Gallay *et al.* 1994; Huysecom 1994; Huysecom and Mayor 1993; DeCeuninck and Mayor 1994).

But there remains a critical question to ask of the cumulative 2,300-year Jenne-jeno and Jenne anchoring sequence. Where is the citadel? Where are the (now-underground) palaces, temples, the residences of the privileged? True, the grand mosque of Jenne served that function – but only sometime after the turn of the second millennium AD. For perhaps a millennium before, and even longer when one adds the early urban level of Dia, these Middle Niger cities are bereft of classic "signpost to permanence," of the expected monumental tributes to despotic rule. Cities without Citadels?

Perhaps the citadel, the monuments to the gods, and the pleasure palaces are not at the principal settlement. Perhaps the elite and the lordly lived at some remove? Let us now examine the evidence that this was *not* the case, drawn from the satellite sites of clustered Middle Niger cities.

"Polynucleated sprawl": Urban Clusters

The "polynucleated sprawl" is a term used by M. Smith (2003: 4) to describe those cities, modern or ancient, without a clear distinction between the urban and the hinterland. Another way to put it is the "deconcentrated" city (Gottdiener 1985: 4). This spitting in the eye of nucleation is exactly what we have to confront in the case of the early Middle Niger city, and for which the highly evocative term "Urban Complex" has been coined. In the following chapter I will describe, briefly, various campaigns of survey in the hinterlands of the Middle Niger cities. The Urban Complex is somewhere between. Its components are neither fully demarcated behind an urban perimeter (a city wall, for example) nor serving a subordinate position within a regional hierarchy of settlement with the town at the functional apex. The satellite communities orbit at least one, and often more, larger primary settlements ("polynucleated"), but function to enhance the structural heterogeneity of the city. Yet they sustain their physical separateness, their "sprawl."

The essential form of the cluster will be familiar from the Pulse Model "proto-cities" of the Méma.

Once into the urban domain, an interesting problem is presented by the Dia Urban Cluster (fig. 4.11). On the one hand, surface recording of these sites does not give nearly the strong primary evidence for exclusive occupation by one or two specialist communities that we will witness in the Jenne-jeno region. However, the surface evidence for early occupation (Phase I/II, or "Early City" phase, with abundant "Delta fabric, Fineware" ceramics) at easily three-quarters of these settlements suggests that the qualitatively more robust expression of clustering may have become an urban signature here before the Upper Delta. Alternatively, perhaps the near Jenne-jeno satellites were occupied as early, but were abandoned later, so that the late first millennium BC and first centuries AD materials are now hidden under an overburden of Phase III and IV

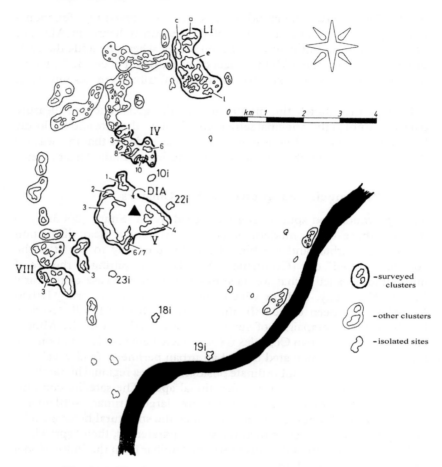

Fig. 4.11. The Dia Urban Cluster

deposits. Also, in contrast to a later abandonment characterizing the Jenne-jeno Urban Cluster, half of the near-Dia sites occupied during Phase III were abandoned before the beginning of Phase IV (AD 900).

Does the fact that many more components of the Dia Urban Cluster were abandoned almost a millennium before the wave of abandonment swept the Upper Delta suggest that the clustering phenomenon began there earlier, only to climax prematurely? Perhaps this early wave of abandonment was related to the strangulation or shifting of the marigots (distributaries) along which the Dia cluster sites are tightly aligned

(Haskell *et al.* 1988: 114–18). However, this was the period of steady and stable climatic optimization. Hydrologists would tell us that, if anything, the distributaries should have been running clear and more vigorous. Susan McIntosh (1995: 375–76) suspects that Dia suffered not from an environmental crisis, but from a profound reorganization of its trade base, between AD 850 and 950. New commercial opportunities would have arisen with the installation of Berber and Ibadite traders in the new southern Saharan trade entrepôt, such as Tegdaoust. "It is likely, in my opinion, that the establishment of these centers disrupted centuries-old trade networks, some predominantly east–west oriented, into which Dia was tied. The famed diaspora of Soninké merchant clans from Dia could well date to this period. As traders quickly fanned out to position themselves strategically in relation to these new opportunities" (1995: 376).

Turning to the relationship of later Jenne-jeno to Dia, Susan McIntosh continues, "Very few sites outside of the present-day town of Dia were occupied [by AD 1200]. The mantle of commercial activity passed, at the time of the diaspora, from Dia to Jenne-jeno within the Upper IND [Inland Niger Delta]. I expect that more than a few families emigrated from Dia to Jenne-jeno to take advantage of that fact" (1995: 376). Whatever the contribution from the Macina, or elsewhere within the (now increasingly climatically distressed) Middle Niger (including, especially, the seriously compromised Méma), clustering remains healthy around Jenne-jeno until several centuries further into the second millennium.

And it is here, at the Jenne-jeno Urban Cluster, or Urban Complex, that the functional (and perhaps symbolic) reasons for this settlement anomaly are best understood (fig. 4.12). Here the phenomenon has been investigated by a multi-phase research program (still continuing). The stages combine initial survey (a walking identification of sites) and surface collection (collecting non-ceramic artifacts, a sample recording of ceramics, and full recording of features, such as houses, smelting furnaces, exposed burials, etc.) with phased-in excavation.

(1) 1977: part of a general, randomized regional survey (to be described more fully in the next chapter) – 20 percent collected (all sites within 4 km verified as sites, as opposed to natural features such as dunes or levees). The sites collected and recorded were selected using a random number process (S. McIntosh and R. McIntosh 1980, II, 1984).

(2) 1981: dedicated 50 percent random surface collection of sites (thirty-three) within 4-kilometer radius of the Jenne mosque – especially recorded to test the impression from 1977 that some or even most sites show "specialist exclusivity" (R. McIntosh and S. McIntosh 1983 and 1993; R. McIntosh 1991).

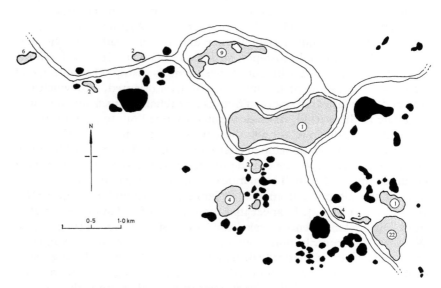

Fig. 4.12. The Jenne-jeno Urban Complex

(3) 1994: mechanical coring at Jenne-jeno (twelve cores), and present Jenne
    (thirty-four cores) and at five satellite sites (R. McIntosh *et al.* 1996).
(4) 1994: 100 percent, closer mapping of sites (sixty-seven, minus
    Jenne, the town cemetery, and Jenne-jeno), especially to map the
    associations of functional features (eg., furnaces, walls, brick circles
    [granaries?]) (Clark 2003).
(5) 1997: refined 100 percent surface recording and excavation of
    thirty-three selected features at ten sites (Clark 2003). These exca-
    vation data are added to the deeply excavated (to sterile floodplain)
    unit, in 1981, into the Hambarketolo (adjacent to Jenne-jeno) and
    Kaniana (adjacent to Jenne) satellites (S. McIntosh 1995).
(6) 1999–2000: excavation (unit SM-O) at present Jenne, at a location
    indicated as promising by the 1994 coring project (S. McIntosh *et al.*
    2003).
(7) Future investment (especially more excavation) into testing M. Clark's
    (2003) general conclusions that support the hypothesis of specialist
    segregation.

Mary Clark's research on the identification of specialization, of corporate distinctions in the archaeological record, and of dating changes to the internal logic of the Jenne-jeno Urban Complex are without equal in the Middle Niger. Of course, she finds a settlement dynamic even more complex than we had ever imagined. In brief, she makes the corollary hypothesis that, within the Urban Complex of seventy sites, there may be reiterated subsystems: multiple focus sites, each with their own orbiting satellites in patterns repeated in other subclusters. In other words, the Urban Cluster is polynucleated. The chronological situation is intriguing, also. Only more excavation at more satellites can resolve the issues of "satellite sites' initial occupation and development of sites or clusters of sites" (Clark 2003: 55). Clark agrees with the conclusion derived from earlier stages of survey that clustering was at its maximum at AD 700 to around 1050 (if not earlier). Between 1000 and 1100, there was an abrupt shift, a phase transform if you will. Before this date specialist economic activities were segregated by site within site clusters; after this date, more varied activities were nucleated on fewer, larger, less-clustered or non-clustered sites (yet with an ever greater diversity of features and with greater morphological diversity within each feature type) (see fig. 5.5).

We can give a final tweaking to our urban definition. The clustered city, then, has become a segmented community of specialists who voluntarily come together to take advantage of the services of others and to exploit the larger market for their products, but who maintain physical separation in order to reinforce their separate identities (see fig. 4.13). From the seventy sites' surface collected, of which ten were excavated (some very rudimentarily, to be sure), we have an indication of a segregation of activities, if not exclusivity. Whereas evidence of all corporate activities was found at Jenne-jeno, at twenty-nine other sites one finds only one, two, or at most three represented. These activities may be subsistence based (fishing) or artisan (metallurgy; weaving) or "miscellaneous" (ritual or symbolic; funerary) – and there is a segregation of that damnably elusive elevated, circular clay feature the "granary/altar" (see fig. 4.14)!

And now let us attempt a first analysis of the clustering rationale: The clustered city was a stable solution (for more than a thousand years) to the complementary ecological problems (physical and social) confronting Middle Niger communities, in the past, as today (R. McIntosh 1991, 2000a; R. McIntosh and S. McIntosh 2003). Firstly, this is a superbly productive environment, but one marked by highly variable rain and flood regimes. Secondly, to combat climatic unpredictability, artisans and subsistence producers become increasingly specialized, yet must be linked together into a generalized economy.

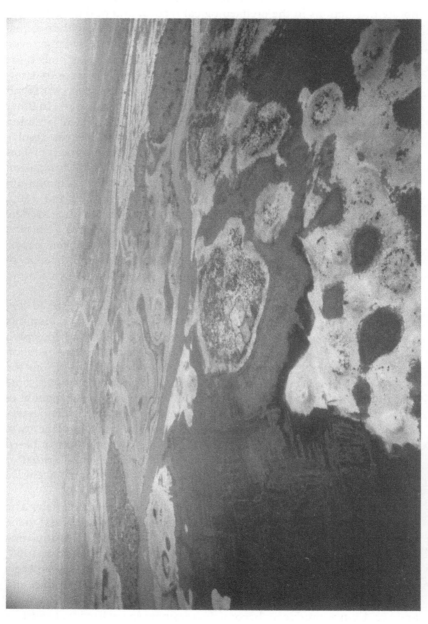

Fig. 4.13. Aerial perspective on the Jenne-jeno Urban Complex (Jenne at far left; Jenne-jeno at far right; all "islands"

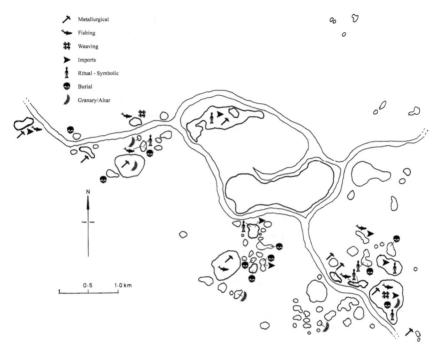

Fig. 4.14. Functional complementarity within the Jenne-jeno Urban Complex

In the apparent absence of elites and coercive control, who keeps the peace in such congeries of corporate groups, particularly when (by c. AD 800) population at the Jenne-jeno Urban Complex may have been considerable? It is highly probable (from the settlement distribution and oral tradition) that most if not all seventy *tell*s of the Jenne-jeno Urban Cluster were occupied simultaneously (at least until the regional wave of abandonment swept through the Middle Niger, no later than AD 1200–1400). The total occupied area in excess of 190 hectares gives a *low-end* population estimate of up to 42,000 persons! Again we must ask, who keeps the peace? An exclusively functional approach to authority is inadequate to answer this critical question. This is why we cautiously enter into the domain of "cognitive archaeology": This was a highly complex society organized horizontally, a heterarchy, with multiple over-lapping and competing agencies of resistance to centralization. The dis-persed clustered city landscape was an instrument of that resistance. Such a view calls up profound Mande views of sacred power-places distributed in a power-grid across the landscape.

Clustering evolves not as a dense agglomeration of population focused upon a single locale – as would be predicted by a long Western tradition of thinking about the origins of the pre-industrial city. Rather, these Middle Niger towns are networks of specialized parts. Urban Complexes, the networks of physically distinct communities, can cover impressive areas – greater than 50 square kilometers in the case of the Jenne-jeno Urban Complex. Clustered cities can form a (peculiar) localized settlement hierarchy within a classic urban regional site hierarchy.

Little by way of purely functionalist explanation of clustering really solves the problem of why native and immigrant groups would persistently choose (nominally) separate settlements over the single unity that dominates Middle Niger cities today. However, are we willing to credit the idea of a socially constructed or socially perceived environment (or, in the sense encouraged by Historical Ecology, a landscape)? In such a socially constructed landscape, the group makes decisions about where to place their communities and how to use the land based upon values and symbolic abstractions. If we can entertain such an approach, then we can begin a test of hypotheses based upon the extrapolated idea of several venerable Mande notions of the grid of occult power (*nyama*) and authority laid over the landscape. These hypotheses can take excavation and survey into novel data fields. Here we tread upon the sacred landscape constructed in deep time.

To understand the rise and interaction of the various corporate groups comprising the clustered city, one must recall our earlier discussion (chapter 3) about alternative routes to authority and to pluri-corporate accommodation amongst the Mande. What is central is how those groups harvest occult knowledge and, hence, power. Authority is harvested by *nyamakalaw*, professional classes of artists and occupational specialists, from a sacred landscape – that spatial blueprint of power in three dimensions. And specialist groups not only accommodate one another. As depicted in figure 3.9, the corporations work together to amplify desired aspects of the landscape – the core of the notion of Mande Ecological Diversity. It seems to me entirely reasonable that there is a very long pedigree to related notions of landscape, occult access to knowledge, and the translation of that knowledge into authority within the community. At its climax, its most mature, the Middle Niger city is where Mande Ecological Diversity reinforces and complements a profound tradition of resistance to power. Possessing merely the cast-aside settlements and the garbage of the ages, how can the archaeologist test the impact of (antecedent) Mande beliefs and values upon behavior at the founding of cities such as Dia and Jenne-jeno? Put a different way, the prehistorian's problem is to verify motivations and intentionality in the remote past.

The test must be done *empirically*. Fail to do so, and even the most elegant explanation remains a just-so story.

All this suggests a future strategy for urban research, not just along the Middle Niger, but in Greater Mande generally, because of two fundamental inadequacies of the functional–ecological explanation. Firstly, where are the elites, the chiefs, the kings, the early state bureaucracies? For after nearly three decades of excavation at Jenne-jeno and at other Middle Niger cities, we have yet to find a king. No court. No palace, nor queen, nor her burial chamber. Indeed, elites and their high-labor investment in burial tumuli (such as El Oualadji in the Lakes Region: R. McIntosh 1998: 223–27) do not appear until the second millennium AD, around the time of the regional depopulation and transformation of urbanism described in the next chapter. No king. No state. To ask once again: Who keeps the peace?

This is the first fundamental complaint raised by the distinctiveness of these towns with the traditional, functionalist "hierarchy as adaptive solution" approach to emerging complex society (critiqued in S. McIntosh and R. McIntosh 1984). To date, excavation at sites such as Jenne-jeno reveals no obvious signs of vertical social stratification, as opposed to the hyper-abundant evidence of (horizontal) social complexification. Where are the public buildings, the monuments, the shrines to state ideologies that classic theory about the rise of the pre-industrial city *tells* us should be present? They are neither at the large site of Jenne-jeno (nor at the larger, 45-ha "site" lurking beneath modern Jenne?), nor are they visible on the surface of any of the scores of Jenne-jeno Urban Cluster components. City without Citadel! One has the strong impression of a highly complex society, with multiple overlapping and competing agencies of authority, decision making, and of highly sustained resistance to centralization. The dispersed cluster city layout was an instrument of that resistance. The "polynucleated sprawl" was far from an artifact of chaos. It had finely focused purposes: sustained ecological resilience and deep-time resistance to power consolidation.

In other words, the satellite sites do not only function in the realm of symbolic property, held communally by all members of certain corporate groups. They can also function, for the inhabitants in the dynamics of their landscape politics and for the archaeologist zooming in from the far distant future, as a lens on processes of resistance to the monopoly of authority and the translation of authority into coercive power.

This notion from the study of Urban Clusters of alternative, multiple paths to authority (in this, recall fig. 1.6) calls up the second fundamental complaint with functional or strictly ecological explanations. Such explanations ignore the persistent Mande view of sacred geography, power-places in the landscape. This forces upon us a very different view of the rationale for the clustered city. The long-term systematics of urban space are shared by environmental concerns and by competition amongst sub-groups within the community for advantageous siting upon the power-grid. In Mande thought, one can gain occult knowledge and harvest power by taking a knowledge quest (*dalimasigi*) to visit distant masters or to power-invested points of the wilderness. Or, one can locate at and extract occult power (preeminently for smiths, by the act of the smelt) from locations loaded with occult power. In local tradition, the flood-plain distributaries encircling both Jenne and Dia are particularly note-worthy for their concentration of *baa-faaro* (water spirits with whom Mande heroes entered into contracts: R. McIntosh 1998: 99, 288–90). In order to understand the rise and sustained interaction of the various corporate groups, one needs to appreciate how they differentially per-ceive the landscape (including the cityscape) as an arena for the playing out (including purposeful augmentation) of occult power. This, then, is the key to landscape as locus of resistance. Heterarchical authority derives from the power grid of the Mande landscape. In ethno-historical and present times, one's place in the world is understood, socially, in terms of a language of the sacred landscape.

In ethno-historical times and the present, the ancient cities of Mande (including, but not limited to ancient Middle Niger cities such as modern Jenne or Dia) occupy a prominent position, in three dimensions, on the sacred landscape. That landscape may be thought of as a local power-grid and a map for navigation for occult knowledge. Thus far, we are entirely in the realm of speculation when we extrapolate earlier versions of these notions, back even to the time of the Mali Empire. The oral traditions of Mali's heroes (Sundjata, Fakoli, and others), heroines (the many *sabu* who wove together the threads of empire consolidation), and villains (poor, misunderstood Sumaworo) (Conrad 1992, 1995; Levtzion *et al.* forthcoming) which present a fairly consistent picture of how authority and the three-dimensional landscape was perceived in the thirteenth century, are mistrusted by some traditionalist historians. Just imagine their skepticism at the project of testing hypotheses about a perceived landscape back several hundred years earlier, not to mention back into the murky Late Stone Age! However, there should be ways empirically to test the proposition that some recognizable (although greatly altered) conception of landscape as a spatial blueprint of power has a very long pedigree in the Middle Niger. If so, corporate groups, through their mythic founders and heroes, or through the agency of the knowledge-traveler well known amongst Mande smiths, sculptors, and bards, would conceivably have been involved in the acquisition and maintenance of occult and political authority by maintaining the integrity of the Urban Cluster.

Seen in this light, is it little wonder that the Dia and, especially, the Jenne-jeno Urban Clusters should have elaborated into such fantastical numbers of components over almost a millennium and a half? And, while the final highly componential form of these cities clearly had its germ in the earlier stages of Middle Niger landscape (of, theoretically, figs. 3.1, 3.2, 3.3 . . .), the city of the Urban Complex is another beast altogether. The dynamics of self-organization have struck again. Why then did the clustering phenomenon collapse and wither away in the first half of the second millennium?

Perhaps the larger settlement patterns of urban hinterlands provide some clues.

5   Surveying the hinterland

Prior strategies

Why, with all the intensity of regard just lavished upon the urban center itself, should we insist upon a complementary strategy of investigating the city's hinterland? Why go even further afield, when an Urban Cluster (such as Jenne-jeno's) can cover in excess of 50 square kilometers and require lifetimes of research to plumb adequately? We are, nonetheless, still beholden to respect the second component of Trigger's definition of a city as a "settlement *that provides a variety of services and manufactures to a wider hinterland*" (1972: 577).

The relationship of the city as provisioner of services and manufactures to the simpler, less corporation-rich communities of its integrated hinterland, and the reciprocal flow of peoples, of subsistence goods, and of raw or partially manufactured materials to the town must be documented. And it is the dynamic of emergence of that integrated, hierarchical, regional relationship out of the previously undifferentiated landscape of villages and hamlets that defines the urban process. Experience with regional reconnaissance, since the first halting steps in the late 1940s, provides guidelines for how the discipline judges the quality and trustworthiness of survey data. However, we also know that every survey strategy must be tailored to the local conditions – there is no boilerplate in regional analysis.

It is not the place of this volume to review the history of survey methodology. Nor will I recapitulate the sometimes-acrimonious debates about probability versus total coverage (see Falconer and Savage 1995; D.Wilson 1990). Still, there is some advantage to being a Johnny-come-lately! It is so easy to see the failings of predecessors (so hard, unless reinventing the wheel altogether, entirely to appreciate the real cleverness of early experimenters in applying half-formed ideas about regional dynamics of political economy and settlement patterns, not to mention probability theory, to often-excruciating field situations). T. J. Wilkinson (2003: 3–14, 33–45) provides a concise summation of the history of landscape survey in the larger Near East. There, the (continually refined) Mesopotamian surveys detailed in those classics *The Uruk Countryside* (Adams and Nissen 1972) and *Heartland of Cities* (Adams 1981; see also Pollock 1999: 45–78) remain, after all these years, a standard against which any of us working in arid-lands floodplains judge ourselves. Further – although slightly dated but still humbling of us mere mortals – the industry standard remains *The Basin of Mexico* (Sanders *et al.* 1979). In that masterpiece, the authors document a total recording of a 7,000 square-kilometer (larger) hinterland of Teotihuacán in semi-arid central Mexico (at a staggering cost of 500 person-months of time and some $200,000 of 1970s dollars!). The Basin of Mexico project serves, by the excellent experimental application of various probability schemes and sampling strategies to the data known from the 100 percent coverage (appendix E, pp. 491–532), to remind us of the compromised quality of information that attends lack of attention to the twin statistical sons of Laocoön. The first son, Freedom from Bias, pays the ultimate price if not ensuring that the investigators' often-unconscious intuitions do not intrude on data collection. Goodness of Fit, the second, is squeezed to his final agonies for failing to employ probability theory to estimate the concordance of the sample with the target population (Thomas 1986: 95–133). Because of this grunt archaeologist's mantra – all that archaeologists have ever done is to investigate the incompletely preserved remains of past peoples' actions upon the world, as they perceived it – the archaeologist's data will always be a shadow sample of our ultimate "population," the entirety of past behavior and intentionality. Quality of hinterland surveys depends on everything from the nimbleness of the archaeologist's theory, to the voluminousness of her or his purse, to the muscle-tone of that aching rectus femoris and moaning gluteus maximus.

Prior surveys in the Middle Niger have ranged widely in that quality. Initial work, in the colonial period and through the 1970s, tended, frankly, to be judgmental. We do not have to dwell on critique here (see S. McIntosh and R. McIntosh 1984 for the larger West African perspective). Decisions were often swayed by the (understandable) exigencies of transport, logistics, and the desire to visit the biggest, the best, the "most typical" sites. Rarely were decisions made according to systematic (randomized) criteria; despite the aforementioned "industry standards," most researchers in the Middle Niger carried on blithely, collecting non-comparable data. And non-comparability is the key issue. Do the patterns of site location and distribution seen in the sample have anything to do with the actual pattern AND, can other researchers use one's data to carry out an independent comparative analysis between, for example, various basins of the Middle Niger? Cases in point are the laborious and well-intentioned but sadly flawed surveys of the Méma, carried out by Téréba Togola and Michel Raimbault (1991), already discussed in chapter 3, and the Projet d'Inventaire des Sites Archéologique, La Zone Lacustre (Raimbault and Sanogo 1991) in the Lakes Region. Lots of sites were discovered; many kilometers were covered. Ancient cities by the scores, if not the hundreds, and their hinterlands, were trod upon. But just how systematic was the identification of sites? Just how thoroughly was every geomorphological landform investigated? The basic problem is that we just cannot use these surveys' data comparatively to assess the similarity or differences in the urban process between the very different environments of the Middle Niger's six basins. These surveys were as good as the best of the world's judgmental surveys. The flaw was in the strategy of survey itself, being judgmental and not systematic.

Even those who were fully aware of the requirements on the investigator lain down by the obligations of freedom from bias and goodness of fit were sometimes forced by circumstances to make compromises. Togola (1993: 34–40) and MacDonald (1994: 72–4) in their jointly conducted survey of the Méma carried out a vehicular survey (already partially discussed in chapter 3). These are sometimes called (dismissively) "windscreen surveys," in contrast to the preferred pedestrian approach (although driving does have the advantage of allowing more distance to be covered). Due to restricted funds and restricted time, they judgmentally selected important sites or villages as their points of departure. They sometimes walked a radius around the key site, but the cores of the surveys were straight-line transects driven north and south (fig. 5.1). The vehicular survey was productive, with 29 Late Stone Age and 109 Iron Age sites accurately plotted on maps, along with their contextual environmental setting. But the strategy does not allow trends seen in the transects to be extrapolated, except in the most general ways, to the larger region. (In other words, lack of a statistical probability strategy does not allow for a goodness of fit assessment.)

In 1984, Téréba Togola, Susan McIntosh, and I conducted a preliminary reconnaissance of the Timbuktu hinterland and that of Mangabéra, some 90 kilometers further downstream along the Niger (S. McIntosh and R. McIntosh 1986a) (fig. 5.2). Rather than being point-directed, as was the Togola and MacDonald Méma survey, this was entirely geomorphologically driven. Judgmentally, we selected for thorough walking irregular transects, testing various Niger Bend landforms – dunes, the constructed floodplain with its scoured fluvial deposits and more-interior paleochannels. Many new data were recovered and the work might be said to have altered our understanding of the human landscape of the Timbuktu hinterland. We covered roughly 50 percent of the region, but

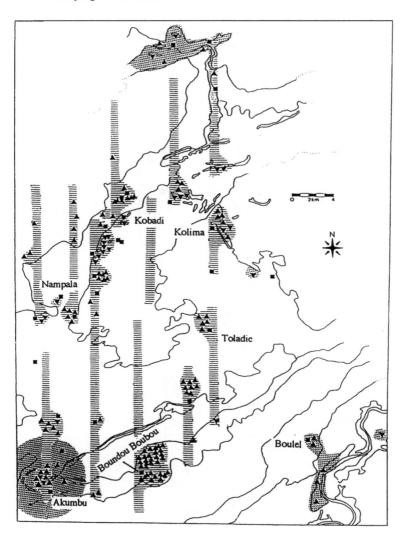

Fig. 5.1. The Togola and MacDonald vehicular survey of the Méma

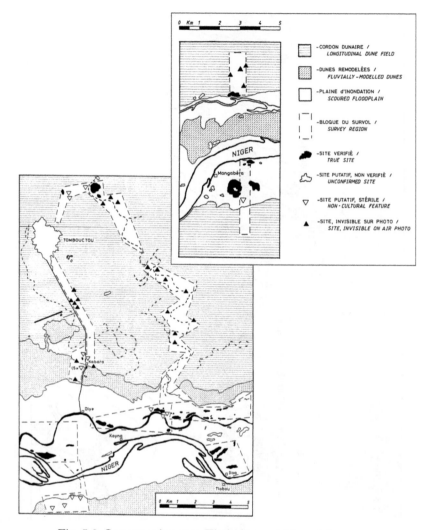

Fig. 5.2. Survey region near Timbuktu and Mangabéra

in a way entirely judgmental. Comparable, extrapolatable results they were not.

Frustrating data, too. Our initial (history-driven) expectation was that present Timbuktu would be a rather late (second millennium AD) desert outlier of the Middle Niger, floodplain-oriented urban civilization, an artifact of the trans-Saharan trade and a parasite on older, indigenous cities to the south. Rather, we found a far denser network of sites oriented to the (constricted) floodplain and the dune-traversing paleochannels. Clearly an artifact of wetter times, was this an urban network anterior to and independent of historical settlements, such as Timbuktu? Or does that fabled town represent just a sad rumor, a depauperate residual of an earlier, denser settlement pattern? And there, far up the paleochannel, the Wadi El-Ahmar, was a town-size site (50 ha), apparently with a ring of satellites, abandoned most probably between AD 900 and 1200. Mangabéra – we struck two wee transects (50 square-kilometer total area) at a point further downstream along the river, just at "random" (haphazardly). Never really expecting to find much in such desolation, there we stumbled upon a depressing number of large, perhaps clustered, *tell*s. Was every stretch of the riverbanks and near dune landscape downstream of Timbuktu as heavily invested with substantial occupation? Our judgmental survey simply will not allow us to say. Does the history of urbanism in the Niger Bend parallel that of the broader-floodplain basins to the south? Our judgmental survey simply will not allow us to say. All we can say is that "the Niger Bend supported urban centers and long-distance commercial activity substantially earlier than the 15th-century date allowed by historical reconstruction" (S. McIntosh and R. McIntosh 1986a: 317). Somehow unsatisfactory, that.

Systematic urban hinterland

Systematic survey can either be total (in some ways preferred, but always costly) or done according to some formalized random probabilistic sampling scheme. The latter was done in the Upper Delta of the Middle Niger, in 1977, as a complement to the first season of excavations at Jenne-jeno (S. McIntosh and R. McIntosh 1980, II). This work has turned into a multi-stage research program, still continuing (fig. 5.3):

1. In 1977, a 20 percent randomized survey of individual floodplain sites and (by transect) of highland features within a 1,083 square-kilometer region north and west of Jenne-jeno. This was eventually extended to a total area of 2,167 square kilometers. The above was supplemented in 1989–91 by systematic geomorphological (Makaske 1998; Makaske and Terlien 1996) and archaeological survey (Bedaux *et al.* 1994: 43; Dembélé *et al.* 1993) of a slightly overlapping, 2,000 square-kilometer region, south of Mopti, west of the Bandiagara border and east of the Niger. Combined, some 1,200 habitation mounds were recorded, many of which are of urban proportions.

2. In 1981, a 50 percent randomized survey of the isolated and clustered sites within a 4-kilometer radius of the Jenne mosque. The seventy

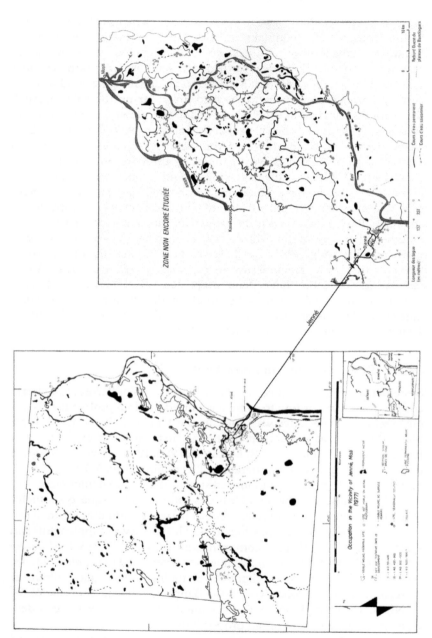

Fig. 5.3. Region of the extensive Jenne hinterland survey

sites were subsequently recognized to comprise the Jenne-jeno Urban
Cluster. Intensive coverage. Subsequently elevated to 100 percent
coverage in 1994 and 1997 by Mary Clark (2003).

3. In 1989 to 1991, the Projet Toguéré undertook a slightly overlapping
   survey to the east of the aforementioned region. The project covered
   some 2,000 square kilometers and over eight hundred sites (and
   sinking unit into two mounds, Diohou and Ladikouna) (Bedaux
   et al. 1994: 43–53; Dembélé et al., 1993: fig. 4) (see fig. 5.3).

This regional survey, although far from complete, has thrown light
upon several of the evolutionary and collapse processes of Jenne-jeno
urbanism (R. McIntosh 1983; S. McIntosh 1995: 393–98; S. McIntosh
and R. McIntosh 1980, II). Of the sites selected by randomized proce-
dures to be surface recorded and the abandonment date estimated from
surface ceramics, almost three-quarters were abandoned by the end of
Jenne-jeno Phase IV (that is, roughly AD 1200–1400). None was abandoned before Phase III (or before roughly AD 400). Most *tell*s boasted
a considerable vertical accumulation above the original floodplain level
(2 meters or more), suggesting some significant length of occupation
before the abandonment date fixed by the surface ceramics. The maximum site density probably dates to Phase III and early Phase IV (second
half of the first millennium and first few centuries of the second millennium AD; although an earlier expression of the urban hinterland is
entirely likely as well). At its maximum, site density in the hinterland of
Jenne-jeno may have approached ten times the density of villages and
small towns in the same region today.

A long history of economic integration of the hinterland is suggested by
application of various geographical models. Such models consider the
size distribution (e.g. rank size) and establish indexes of complexity
(judged from diversity of features and artifacts, by size). The remarkable
homogeneity of the ceramic assemblage of what Susan McIntosh (1995:
360) calls the Upper IND (Inland Niger Delta – that part of the Upper
Delta Basin inclusive of but extending beyond the hinterland of Jenne-
jeno itself) must be taken into account. One must repeat here the frustration
of the Jenne-jeno Urban Complex: Only with much more sub-surface
excavation can we finally know how old and how extensive was the
dynamic of regional integration *at the beginning of Middle Niger urbanization*. There are, however, three interesting processes visible in the
abandonment dynamics:

(1) Ancient sites are first abandoned on dunes and sandy levees, yet a
    higher proportion of modern settlements (37 percent) than ancient
    *tell*s (11 percent) are on these landforms. This may be attributable to
    the fifteenth-century and later migration into the Upper Delta of two

groups (Bambara millet farmers and Fulani herders), both of whom prefer living on sandy highlands. After these sandy landforms, the first soils abandoned are low-lying, high-clay floodplain soils, especially at greater distance from Jenne-jeno.

(2) Ancient sites cluster strongly (only 4 percent isolated), whereas sites still occupied after the fifteenth-century regional reorganization are strongly isolated (93 percent of present villages are isolated, the rest being only paired). The remaining 96 percent of hinterland sites are either paired (15 percent of total) or arranged in clusters of up to fifteen sites.

(3) Later settlements, although far fewer in number, are larger and more uniform in area. Twenty-six percent of all sites are smaller than the smallest modern village. The variation of ancient site size is twice that of villages. Recall Clark's (2003: 204–40) conclusion from the Jenne-jeno Urban Complex region that late Phase IV and post-Phase IV sites, while larger, have a greater diversity of features.

Apparently Middle Niger urbanism was not aborted in the early second millennium (by the high amplitude climatic variability that marks the same period?). Yet there was dramatic and, one might say, abrupt reorganization of population and settlements in the Jenne-jeno urban hinterland. And here comes the joy of recording systematic, comparable survey data from multiple urban hinterlands. We can now compare these abandonment trends to those of the Dia hinterland.

In order to have a comparative perspective on Middle Niger urbanism, we decided in 1986 to conduct an identical, 50 percent randomized regional survey of the Dia hinterland (Haskell *et al.* 1988: 106–39). Using a probability strategy, half of the isolated sites and all sites within half of the clusters within 2 kilometers of Dia were surface recorded (all sites verified, as shown on fig. 5.4). In the end, the sites of the 2-kilometer radius may eventually be recognized as (entirely?) conforming to the Dia Urban Cluster (see fig. 4.11). However, certain larger regional principles of Dia's urban evolution were brought to light.

Compared to the Jenne-jeno hinterland sites, these tend to cleave more tightly and linearly to the waterway systems of the Dia floodplain, without the pattern of small satellites in orbit around a site dominant in size. Here, over 75 percent of the surface ceramics are of the "Fineware, Delta fabric" (at Jenne-jeno, pre-AD 400) – which might imply a far earlier date for abandonment of the Dia hinterland than in the Upper Delta. Recall, however, that the Dia Project (Bedaux *et al.* 2001) found in excavated sequence at Shoma that even their AD 800–1100 horizon yielded "fineware" in the ceramic assemblage. In the event, Phase III ceramics were found on 86 percent of the Dia hinterland sites, but only

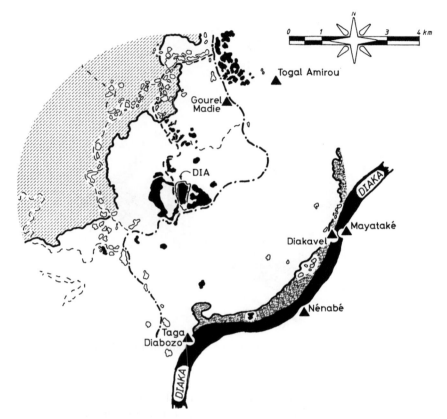

Fig. 5.4. Region of the Dia hinterland survey

38 percent had any ceramics dating after about AD 800 – still indicating an earlier wave of regional abandonment than near Jenne-jeno. Recall also the apparent total abandonment of Shoma from AD 1100 to 1400 (Bedaux *et al.* 2001: 846).

As in the Upper Delta, only higher (sandier) levee sits were abandoned after AD 1400 and villages today show a strong preference for that landform. Today's villages in the Macina are far fewer in number, although somewhat larger in average size, than ancient sites. Overall, the drama of regional landscape transformation, and of very probably massive (order of magnitude?) depopulation plays out here in a trajectory remarkably similar to that in the Jenne-jeno hinterland.

And so, we return to one last iteration of the Lorenz phase transform diagram (fig. 5.5). From the Macina and the Upper Delta Basins, and

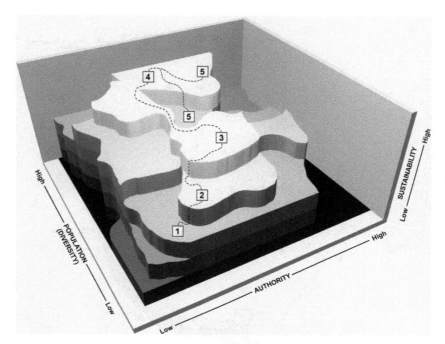

Fig. 5.5. Final phase transform diagram of the Middle Niger urban landscape

emphatically from the Méma, survey suggests lower population numbers. But does population diversity (that is, corporate belonging) really diminish also? And with the rise in the thirteenth century of the Mali Empire, the conquest of Jenne in 1472 by Sonni Ali Ber of the Songhai Empire, and the subsequent impositions of the Ségou kingdom, the *dina* of Sékou Amadou, and French colonial rule (R. McIntosh 1998: 240–303), authority at Middle Niger cities may have been manifested as a dualism. These cities may have retained a great degree of heterarchical autonomy at times, but there is no question that external hierarchical (if not despotic) power was a new part of the landscape. The transition to this new position on figure 5.5, however, was only partially imposed from the outside. This appears genuinely to have been yet another case of an abrupt, indigenous, self-organized manifestation of emergent behavior. Arguably a true phase transform – but can it be called a "collapse," a "reorganization needed to express resiliency" (appropriate to the new climatic exigencies of the time?), or just another expression of deep-time Middle Niger "sustainability"? The ambiguity depicted in figure 5.5

insists that we return, in conclusion, to the thorny issue of resilience and sustainability in a self-organizing urban landscape. And there we confront, head on, the Sustainability Paradox.

Resilience, urban sustainability, and the self-organizing landscape

The Sustainability Paradox runs, essentially, as follows: The self-organizing Middle Niger landscape can charter a self-organizing trajectory of abruptly and unpredictably changing population complexity, with an overall trend to elaborated population diversity *and, at the same time*, maintain a high plateau of sustainability. This despite occupying a bio-physical arena of "chaotic" unpredictability (particularly climatic) and of great risk. This statement is a self-contradicting absurdity only for those who cleave to an older definition of sustainability as celebrating some eponymous, pristine state of social or ecosystemic simplicity and minimal energy transfer from the bio-physical world to humans (Tainter 2000, 2003). How possibly could the peoples of the Middle Niger ascend to the highest sustainability plateau of our Lorenz phase transform diagram (e.g. figs. 1.6 and 1.8d) – and stay there for century upon century, without the dire hand of an elite, an enlightened and far-seeing (from his astral vantage point) despot?

This question, of course, drives the Sustainability Paradox directly on an intersecting course with our paradox of the City without Citadel of chapter 1!

The resolution to the urban Middle Niger Sustainability Paradox is actually rather simple. A resolution is allowed if, at each phase in the trajectory of transforms, people respect and even devise ways to augment the fundamental canons of pluri-corporate conduct. Such are the canons, you will recall, that allow the dynamism of the particular Mande view of landscape amplification (fig. 3.8) and, preeminently in the cities, the complementary acts of corporate creativity (what McNaughton calls entrepreneurship) of Mande Ecological Diversity (fig. 3.9). These rules will always be changing, never in stasis, always a classic example of Middle Niger belief systems and socio-political forms as "layered transformation" (R. McIntosh 1998: xix, 10–22). Ethno-historically we can name some of these canons: *nyama*, *dalimasigi*, undischargeable social debt, and the hero/heroine harvesting of the three-dimensional occult world. It may well be that, in the mists of history-become-prehistory, these had quite different names, quite different formulations. Even so one can make the argument, as do the Mande themselves, that a distinctive conception of "reputation" comes to them as a deep-time legacy (this is the self-same "reputation," you will recall, that allows a resolution of the Tragedy of the Commons).

In other words, the Middle Niger deep-time expectation for sustainability will encompass an ever-amplifying, ever-elaborating number and manifestations of corporate belonging and interconnectedness. It will also, fundamentally and not simply as a corollary, include a deeply ingrained resistance to power hierarchies and to despotism. Corporate elaboration, flexibility of belonging and resistance to rigid, centralized control structures become the key, absolutely, to flexibility (long term and short) in the face of the stresses, unpredictabilities, and objective reality of "chaos" in the natural environment. Put all this in place, and cities are no particular problem. Cities, in fact, become essential to the resolution of the Middle Niger's Sustainability Paradox.

Here we have to clarify the concepts of sustainability and resilience. We subscribe to the somewhat unorthodox "supply-side" definition of sustainability proffered by Allen et al. (2003: 26; see also Tainter 2000, 2003). Their emphasis is upon "maintaining, or fostering the development of, the *systemic contexts* that produce the goods, services, and amenities that people need or value, at an acceptable cost, for as long as they are needed or valued" (my emphasis). Let us dissect this definition. The key phrase is "the *systemic contexts.*" I take this to underscore the social construction of the peoples' productive activities, with particular emphasis upon the matrix of authority within which decisions are made. It certainly includes the larger symbolic environment (social memory, or habitus, depending on the situation) that all the actors occupy. Emphasis upon the systemic contexts is entirely consistent with the emphasis on the recursive interaction between changes in the bio-physical world (including anthropogenic) and in the social world (including the world as perceived) fundamental to Historical Ecology (chapter 2).

Returning to the "supply-side" definition of sustainability, the producers of "goods, services, and amenities," in the Pulse Model of chapter 3, are the precocious specialists. That particular hypothesis is about those circumstances, in the very remote Late Stone Age, that encouraged the gradual emergence of a generalized regional economy based upon the "contractual" exchange of subsistence goods, artisan manufactures, and amenities (and undoubtedly supernatural services) through a network of equals. Of critical importance for the various states of accommodation, the successive phase transforms, of increasing complexity of the Middle Niger peoples, as a test of sustainability, is the continuation of the distinctive social construction of pluri-corporate production and interethnic relations as the Middle Niger flows into becoming a landscape of emerging cities. Cities and, indeed, all manifestations of complex society, are the ultimate challenge for sustainability!

Prehistorians, looking comparatively at the emergence of complex society, have long known that one solution to the problem of providing everyone with the goods and services of an increasingly compartmentalized labor force is hierarchy. In hierarchy, the decisions of the elite few at society's apex are, all to often, reinforced by force. Force, terrorism, and symbolic bombardment are the keel, the hull, and the ribs of the *ex astra* ship of state. The key to long-sustained heterarchy, then, is a built-in mechanism or ethos of resistance to authority-grabs and to power displays.

I have argued here that, in the Middle Niger, a continuity is nested within a layered transformation of the socio-political and the physical landscape. The earlier Pulse Model hamlets, villages, then proto-towns "self-organized" into true urbanism. Throughout and under the ever more "reputation-driven" canons of expected behavior, exchange was conducted in the material and symbolic goods that people themselves came to regard as needed or valued (echoing the sustainability definition of Allen *et al.*). At no point in the archaeological record can we produce evidence that they relinquished their community or corporate authority to figures wielding power (until the massive reorganization in perhaps the twelfth to fifteenth centuries AD). Critically, the "acceptable cost" of Allen *et al.* was negotiated by equals. It was not imposed from on despotic high – to the asymmetrical advantage of some and the detriment of most.

Such a seemingly simple phrase, " . . . that people need or value." But on this phrase turns a vast calculus of needs-criteria that ranges from the most basic biological necessities of life to those esoteric and culture-specific symbolic packages that make life worth living. And the rules for generating the modes of producing these needed and valued elements are deeply rooted in deep-time social memory! I have argued (2000a and 2000b) that earlier transforms of the Mande social memory were alive and well throughout the Middle Niger, the now dead-deltas of the Azawad and Méma included, well within the several millennia through which the self-organizing landscape evolved.

Finally, Allen *et al.* (2003: 26) make it very clear that sustainability (a community's capacity to continue a desired condition of process, social or ecological) is distinct from resilience. Resilience is defined as the ability of a system to adjust its configuration and function under disturbance. A deep-time, archaeological investigation of resilience strategies in a high-risk environment, such as the Méma, is aided enormously by the vast development anthropology (e.g. Raynaut 1997) and prehistoric (e.g. Halstead and O'Shea 1989) literature on risk management and risk buffering. Exchange and reciprocity are important buffering mechanisms. They factor temporal variability against spatial variability – exactly what the not-always-kindly objective realities of life on the Middle Niger demand. Yet elaboration of specialization rarely plays a part in most reconstructions of prehistoric risk management. One more usually reads about solutions of simplification (e.g. Tainter 1988 and 2000: 24–29) or strategies of and manipulating the labor of the weak (e.g. Park 1992). The beauty of this resolution is that specialization, after all, is what the growth of cities – anywhere – is all about. (This encourages the "afterthought" reflections on what the lessons from Middle Niger cities might suggest to prehistorians working in the other great ancient centers of urbanism – northern China, the Nile, and even Mesopotamia – that form the next, our concluding chapter.)

In one sense, then, the analysis of Middle Niger urbanism as a lurching (!) self-organizing landscape concerns the need to reconcile sustainability against resilience in the face of some of the world's most extreme climatic and environmental risk, surprise, and unpredictability. Allen *et al.* (2003: 26) are very clear that the two can conflict, if maintaining resilience also means abandoning sustainability. I submit that the prehistoric Middle Niger was populated by peoples with "social goals [that were] flexible and in harmony with underlying ecological processes" (Allen *et al.* 2003: 26). A demographic decline (such as we see around Dia and Jenne-jeno by the fifteenth century and devastatingly so in the Méma) may simply indicate that many fled adverse or unpredictable conditions in order to maintain an accustomed way of life. It may also, of course, signal a collapse!

Perhaps we also have to ask whether the Méma in demographic demise was sustainable but not resilient – with social goals feasible within the *perceived* parameters inherited from the past, yet not flexible enough to manage the extreme climatic conditions (and perhaps loss of active waterways due to geological processes?) of the early second millennium AD. These are questions that only intensive future research can answer – and remember that we really know next to nothing about the prehistory of the other Middle Niger basins, the Erg of Bara and the Lakes Region/Niger Bend. Cities upon cities yet to be Discovered!

So, the Sustainability Paradox is not such a self-projecting absurdity after all. The self-organizing landscape on a trajectory of emergent and overall increasing population variability can maintain a high plateau of sustainability, even as it goes through phase transforms and even in the face of great environmental risk. If fundamental canons of pluri-corporate reciprocity and respect are maintained, the resolution can, but is not obliged to, have as its consequence the distinctive heterarchical grid of authority that served the Middle Niger city-folk quite well for centuries, perhaps millennia. City without Citadel is not so freakish, after all! And most importantly – *resilience is folded within this local understanding of sustainability.*

Looked at from this perspective, state-driven cities, if one peeks just behind the facade of the monumental and the coercive, are fundamentally fragile. Their society can be prone to collapse, because their hierarchical infrastructure is rigid. Their society can be prone to collapse, because an asymmetrical ideology of social position and authority prevent a collective canon of rules and behaviors celebrating the individual's positive worth as nested within the sustainable commonweal. These societies lack the flexibility to deal with the unexpected. Cities lodged within a state apparatus lack an essential element of sustainability, that degree of "over-engineering" that allows alternative pathways should one section be effaced or should there evolve radical changes in the baseline condition for which the bureaucracy was constructed in the first place. Few citizens, and certainly none of the underclass, feel a "responsibility" to the enterprise. Lacking flexibility; rigidly engineered; not self-generating an "enlarging responsibility." Thank the stars this was not the only option!

The phase transform diagram of figure 1.6 summarizes the very real alternative provided by the heterarchical city. Comprised of specialized components voluntarily united in a generalizing economy, the critical issue is authority. Authority is persuasive and contractual in a system in which force and fear are not the issue, but enormous responsibility to deeper-time values very much is. And fundamentally to heterarchy, the individual's positive sense of self-worth should be nested within the collective notion of sustainable commonweal. Now, all this is fine in the abstract and may even be testable in the empirical world of archaeological dust and data. It has also, most emphatically, had a beneficial effect in the contemporary world.

I close with an observation to warm the heart of any archaeologist. You recall the Malian archaeologist, Dr. Alpha Oumar Konaré, who was there at the moment of "discovery to the world" of Jenne-jeno? In 1992, he was elected not only the first archaeologist head of state, but the first (Archaeologist) President elected in Mali through free elections. He served two terms, being reelected fairly and, as constitutionally mandated, stepped down after his second term (then to become the Chair of the African Union). Mali, under his presidency, has become, rather, the poster-boy of democracy in Africa. And scholars, ambassadors, and think-tankers alike are trying to puzzle out the twin mysteries of why Malian democracy is thriving (1) in the absence of wealth, and (2) in an excess of (so-called) institutional weakness (as the world somewhat condescendingly calls Konaré's complementary push to decentralization) (Z. Smith 2001).

Decentralization – the mistrust and indeed deeply ingrained resistance to statism, to the drive to centralized authority and power of the monolithic, hierarchical nation state. Sounding very Mande?! Indeed, just as the popular revolution of 1991 that brought Konaré to power was a spontaneous manifestation of the Mande streets, Konaré the archaeologist, and his effective *porte-parole* and wife, the Mande historian Dr. Adam Ba Konaré, have consistently used a rhetoric that would be familiar to any reader of this book in their public exhortation towards democracy and decentralization. That is to say, President Konaré has tapped a deep well of cultural understanding about legitimacy of authority to share a new, yet quite venerable, vision of civil society.

Zeric Smith (2001: 76) perhaps best summarizes the enduring legacy of heterachy, resistance to despotism, and Mande canons of "reputation" that seem to be alive and well (so the Drs. Konaré have repeatedly argued) *after all these thousands of years*!

The trust that Malians have in one another demonstrates the importance of a unique political culture that may have provided Mali with a democratic advantage over other African nations. Many aspects of Malian traditional society encourage norms consistent with democratic citizenship, including tolerance, trust, pluralism, the separation of powers, and the accountability of the leader to the governed. These ideas first [not so fast! Probably far earlier! – RJM] appear in the founding epic of the nation, in which Sundjata Keita defeated a tyrant guilty of exercising illegitimate power. Furthermore, traditional forms of social organization and village government have stressed the interdependence of various social groups and power sharing between classes. Patterns of reciprocity, trust, and social solidarity are also found in the traditionally syncretic relationship between Islam and non-Islamic elements, which is accompanied by a strong commitment to religious tolerance.

This is not democracy out of the barrel of a gun (neo-cons, please note); this is democracy out of the well-spring of deep time.

Indisputably central to the foundational epics of Mali (e.g. Conrad 1992; Levtzion *et al*. forthcoming), I would further argue that these ideas of trust, pluralism, the separation of powers, etc. first appear inscribed upon the ancient (urban) landscape of the Middle Niger! And indeed, President Konaré invoked these cities (of which Malians are understandably proud) in multiple public, radio, and televised discourses on his democratic vision. Unique to Mali and to the Mande? Are there no take-away messages for archaeologists investigating the emergence of urbanism elsewhere?

6 Comparative urban landscapes

Alternative cityscapes: Mesopotamia and the Nile

Prehistorians have moved on from an earlier obsession with the apex of urban society, with the king and court, elites and forces of power. The study of almost every civilization represented in the Cambridge Case Studies in Early Societies series has been transformed into inquiries into relations – economic and of authority, social and concerning the web of beliefs – between all segments of these complex communities. The *ex astra* obsessions of earlier urban archaeologists have also descended to ground level. Paleoethnobotany is now as important to their investigation as is recording of elite tomb inscriptions. With this new perspective comes the realization that coercive hierarchy is not the exclusive organizing principle of urban civilization. In some emerging civilizations, the horizontal complexification that has come to be called heterarchy is in evidence long before obvious agencies of centralized control. In other mature civilizations, agencies of hierarchy and heterarchy are nested within each other (see S. McIntosh 1999c; Yoffee 1995: 299–303).

This final chapter will attempt to apply a few of the lessons drawn from viewing the Middle Niger as a self-organizing landscape to three other major Old World urban civilizations. The first two, late pre-literate and early literate Mesopotamia and the Nile during the waning Predynastic (and first days of the Archaic) are undeniably examples of rapidly growing settlements encased within an increasingly martial state milieu. And yet, nested within the traditional city (or non-city, in the case of Dynastic Egypt) lies yet other expressions of urbanism, coexisting in some cases, subordinated in others, perhaps aborted in others. Using the language of the self-organizing landscape, early and middle Uruk period Mesopotamia (roughly, 4000–3500 BC) appears to have been poised on the edge of a social and settlement leap to clustered urbanism. Yet in the end another, more darkly freighted kind of phase transition took place. The city became a place of powerlessness, misery, and oppression for all but the most privileged. At least such was the view until quite recently. Now, with the discovery of alternative, relatively uncentralized later Mesopotamian cities such as Mashkan-shapir (described as a "tapestry of power"), we appear to have a persistent nesting of clustered specialist locales not really consistent with our standard *ex astra* model of centralized control.

In a case of the subordinated city (some might say, the aborted city), enduring canons of kingship and theocratic statecraft had certainly emerged by around 3200 BC along the Nile Valley. However, some of the most interesting research and speculation now concern the chain of parallel, yet competing, "proto-polities" along the Upper Nile of the previous (perhaps) two millennia. Not all began with a king, with a concept of divine godhead already fully formed. What were the self-organizing agencies of ecological and social interaction between these emergent polities, between northerners and southerners (including Nubians), between the new craft specialists, farmers, and traders, between long-term occupants of the floodplain and climatic refugees from the deserts? Robust "proto-cities" (if not fully urban in all cases) emerge in the case of This, Naqada, Hierakonpolis, and almost certainly others – and a form of incipient clustering of specialists can be seen at some. Yet the city, as defined in this book, withers away with the maturation of the Pharaonic state – leading Egyptologists to debate whether earliest Egyptian civilization could really ever be called truly urban (at least until New Kingdom times! Egypt as an aborted cityscape?). Can the theoretical premises behind the "self-organizing landscape" (at interacting scales of analysis) suggest a new way to tackle this problem? No longer can we assert didactically that Egypt appears to have been a state organized from the start on territorial lines not particularly requiring an urban infrastructure (Yoffee 1997: 256–57), Egyptologist John Wilson's "civilization without cities" (J. Wilson 1960). Rather, we begin to see some highly suspicious clustering and precocious specialization in recent research at, for example, Hierakonpolis.

The last example, from late Neolithic Longshan and early Bronze Age (Xia; and earliest Shang?) northern China is more complex. There, recent survey in "peripheral" regions, distant from Sinologists' traditional heartland of dynastic cities, has revealed an unexpectedly early and disturbingly clustered expression of urbanism at its inception. (The Neolithic city plan from Shandong province might, in fact, have been plucked wholesale out of the Middle Niger floodplain!) Clustering carries its signature even into the classically *ex astra* later Shang cities of, for example, Zhengzhou and Anyang. In China, also, there has recently developed a search for alternative pathways to urbanism – that recalls some prophetic words about resistance to centralization, uttered at the time in intellectual solitude, by the venerable archaeologist K.-C. Chang.

Hence, the theme of this chapter will be the global search for alternatives to hierarchy, alternatives that include investigating variability in emerging structures of control. For the progress of comparative approaches to civilization more broadly, it becomes increasingly imperative to find ways to recognize and to describe the horizontal distribution of authority and status at the emergence of complex societies. Hence, one of the objectives of this final chapter is to suggest a broader (but never exclusive) comparative applicability of this book's central theme of long-term trajectories of self-organization in the physical and social landscapes that encouraged the higher levels of complexity we call urbanism, civilization, and regional states. The tale starts at the birthplace of the *ex astra* conception of urbanism, often referred to as the "Heartland of Cities" – Mesopotamia of the (late fifth and) fourth millennium BC.

One can only speculate. If the archaeology of ancient urbanism had started along the Middle Niger, I wonder whether Mesopotamian discoveries would have been interpreted quite differently. And would a very different strategy of field investigation have been undertaken? Would a recent statement by Rita Wright, in her masterful summation of the comparative circumstances of the appearances of the world's indigenous urban civilizations, appear less radical, less threatening to those still cleaving to the *ex astra* ideal?

And ... the development of urbanism and statehood do not always coincide. Whereas at Teotihuacán and in Chinese and Andean cities the two occurred together, this was not the case in the city of Uruk in Mesopotamia. While religious institutions clearly were present, they seem not to have been dominant and there is no evidence for political authority. Thus urbanism occurred in the absence of a strong centralizing state and was able to thrive for at least a brief moment under the control of decentralized local groups. (Wright 2002: 7)

Uruk urbanism without a despotic state; biblical Warka without Citadel! Whatever could Professor Wright be talking about – deep in the heartland of the eponymous ancient city? Well, let us put on our Middle Niger lenses to look at the landscape dynamics of the Uruk hinterland.

The Uruk (the period, from c. 4000 to 3100 BC) in Mesopotamia always struck me as a lost opportunity. Things could have gone so differently, a different path taken, that other bifurcation routing considered, but not followed. The alternative pathways to urbanism were revealed in one of those classic city hinterland surveys, the Warka Survey of Robert M. Adams and Hans Nissen (1972: 9–25, 88–92; Pollock 1999: 55–72, 93–104; Redman 1978: 261–64). In a nutshell: Following the low-density initial penetration of the southern Mesopotamian floodplain by Ubaid peoples settling in moderately sized (average 4 ha or more in size; 14 in

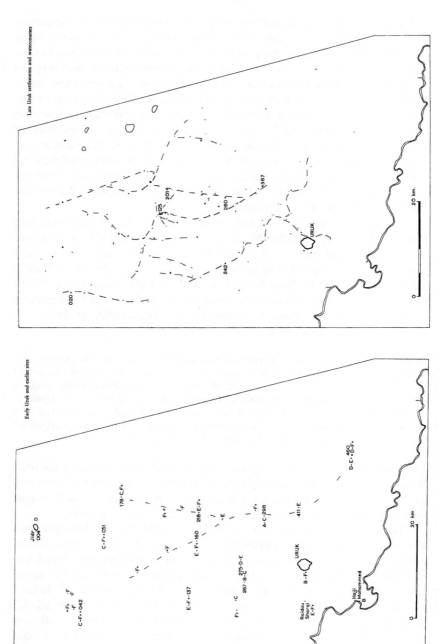

Fig. 6.1. Ubaid and Uruk period settlements from the Warka Survey

the Uruk city hinterland survey region), numbers of settlements and population exploded. There were eighteen settlements by the following early Uruk period, tiny by comparison, except for Uruk itself (unusually, it started to grow and saw major sacred construction projects at the Anu ziggurat and the Eanna temple precinct). By late Uruk there were 108 settlements and rural occupation had peaked (then, or in the Jemdet Nasr period that began 3100 BC and lasted for 200 years). Site numbers then plummet and, certainly, average site size burgeons soon into the following Early Dynastic. By the late Uruk, however, craft specialization is undeniable (Pollock 1999: 96–104), but social stratification is only modestly discernable (Redman 1978: 264–77) – scarcely the oppressive centrally directed and hierarchically organized state economy once argued for by Nissen (1988) and Wright and Johnson (1975) (for *contra*, Adams 1981 and Pollock 1999: 93–94 and below) (fig. 6.1).

These Mesopotamian cities did become elite infested, walled, and highly nucleated: "Urban growth culminated in the late part of the Early Dynastic period. By the mid-third millennium the village-dwelling population had declined to a point where most farmers must have resided in cities" (Pollock 1999: 72). Such was the seduction of the Yahwist interpretation that so permeated nineteenth-century thinkers that this condition of highly nucleated cities, with a rigidly dominant administrative and sacred class supported by unfree subsistence classes and scribal and craft minions, and with a depopulated and dangerous rural hinterland, came to be considered the best, the most primal path to urbanism. Thus it became the ideal urbanization process, to be searched for anywhere else on the globe where indigenous urbanism might be expected. But the Warka Survey data suggest an alternative once considered.

The really striking thing (from the landscape perspective of this book) is the distribution of all those new settlements of the middle and later Uruk. Strongly isolated late Ubaid and early Uruk settlements (distributed equidistantly at c. 4 km along the watercourses) now become strongly clustered (and some multi-component) by late fourth millennium (Adams and Nissen 1972: compare fig. 2, p. 10 to fig. 3, p. 13). These sites are undeniably smaller than the Ubaid settlements (now unimodally size distributed at 1–2 ha, except for exceptional Uruk itself). However, by the dawn of the Early Dynastic only a single future city site was isolated. Another had at least twelve "dependencies" and most had from three to eight or nine satellites, not forgetting the "center." Clustering! – "contiguous distribution reflects the presence of multiple, prevailingly small, closely spaced, presumably interrelated settlements" (Adams and Nissen 1972: 22)! Do we find here the same imperative of corporate differentiation that we see in the Jenne-jeno Urban Complex? Sadly, we do not have verification, one way or the other, from the surface recording, such as Mary Clark's (2003) exquisitely choreographed survey of the Jenne-jeno Urban Complex. Nevertheless, just such an emerging pluri-corporate arena is implied by Pollock's argument that these would have been the formative days of the *oikos* economy, consisting of multiple, interrelated component parts, differentially organized in households, partially in temples and later in large estates (1999: 117–23). New specialization, emerging complexity of kinship and sodality affiliation – growing corporate belonging in a field of loosely organized, horizontally distributed authority. This is starting to sound familiar!

Yet the clusters of the later part of the fourth millennium collapse and implode (Redman 1978: 264–66). Rural depopulation becomes the rule and coercive institutions cast their filthy pallor over the land. And strutting about the Early Dynastic (and later) stage are the self-monumentalizing monarchs, aglitter in their gold and lapis lazuli, aflutter in their celestial legitimization. These monarchs and elites would have appeared every bit as alien as if they had come from another planet, just as bizarre, to our Mande heroes and heroines of resolved Tragedy of the Commons reputation. The classic heterarchy of the Middle Niger, with its landscape expression of clustered urbanism, was the path not taken. Yet, does that mean that an unrepentant statism, a hideously raw *ex astra* control mechanism came into place? Pollock argues: "Institutions located in the emerging towns and cities acted to facilitate the exchange of goods and services among regionally specialized producers rather than to control production ... economic activities remained primarily decentralized, presumably household based, with little direct control exerted by ruling elites" (1999: 94). And this decentralized model takes support from an unlikely quarter – from a major city, even a regional capital, of the late third and early second millennia – Mashkan-shapir.

Pity the poor archaeologist trying to make sense of the surface of these Iraqi *tell*s. *Tell* surfaces are generally a jumble of houses, pits, alleyways, and burials from a score of different periods. Not Mashkan-shapir, given its short occupation of about four hundred years (Stone 1997; Stone and Zimansky 1995). Elizabeth Stone and Paul Zimansky purposefully selected this previously unexcavated (and unlooted) administrative capital of the Old Babylonian Larsa kingdom, abandoned around 1720 BC. The site was perfect for the same kind of minute recording of artifact distribution and surface feature plotting we have already seen at Jenne-jeno and at Mary Clark's work at the surrounding mounds of the Middle Niger polynucleated sprawl (chapter 4). What their recording strategy documented brilliantly was a town plan (and reflection of the underlying economic and authority logic) quite different than one might expect.

Yes, there was a ziggurat temple – to a quite important god (Nergal, god of death) and in its own precinct – but tucked away and segregated. Yes, there are platforms interpreted as an administrative center – but looking anything but the "signpost to permanence" of the expected palace. Mashkan-shapir abounds with many specialists and their workshops and residences of the elite. However, all are jumbled together in discrete residential neighborhoods, but not segregated by wealth or status. For Stone and Zimansky, the case for a highly centralized model for Mesopotamian cities and for a rigidly hierarchical social structure, with unfree craftspersons, looks unconvincing ... "the grounds for seeking the origins of civilization in processes of conquest and coercion seem, at the least, far from compelling" (1995: 123).

Rita Wright runs with Stone's conclusion from Mashkan-shapir of a more consensual view of early Mesopotamian city authority: "the pattern of consensual rule established in the early coordination of microenvironments at Uruk continued to be a force that actively suppressed coercive centralized government" (2002: 9–10). Even here in Mesopotamia we are revisited by an old friend: horizontal authority as agency of resistance to the despotic state. This taps into a larger, growing interpretation by Near Eastern scholars that "local systems of power and authority coexisted with and often resisted centralized governments "(Yoffee 1995: 281; see also 1997). Yet the allure of Weber's "charismatic prince" lives on.

Lives on, but has been given another body blow in the form of a definitive challenge to the old chestnut that early third-millennium settlement simplification (that is, fewer sites, more cities, aborted rural idyll, and suppressed clustering) reflects the consolidation and management of labor for water management (e.g. Redman 1978: 266). In a detailed consideration of Mesopotamia as an anastomosing landscape, T. J. Wilkinson repudiates the belief that bringing water to the emerging city-states' fields involved massive irrigation projects. In his view, the necessary channel system was not created *de novo*, but was the "result of channel management in which key points such as nodes of avulsion ... were the subject of focused teams that cleaned ... only those points that required attention" (2003: 95). By relying on the natural flow characteristics of splays in the floodplain's channel and levee network, local labor pools sufficed. It was not until 1400 BC, the Kassite period, or even the Neo-Babylonian period (600 BC) that corvée labor on a Wittfogelian scale would be witnessed.

We have progressed far from earlier obsessions with coercive control of trade, production, massed unfree labor, and human capital as preconditions to urbanism along the banks of the Tigris and Euphrates.

Thus, in the case of Mesopotamian cities, arguments of *pure hierarchy* or *pure heterarchy* may be overstating the case. Perhaps the Mesopotamians of the later Uruk did not have to tread *either* the total implosive, nucleation path *or* the clustered, dispersed, and decentralized road towards Middle Niger-like Urban Clusters. Perhaps, like President Konaré's vision for Mali's national civil society, ancient Mesopotamia was in a perpetual tension between more horizontal authority and centralizing tendencies that had very different expressions, locally, at different times. Perhaps the aborted clustering of the Uruk countryside was just one landscape expression of the hierarchy–heterarchy negotiations, or of a dynamic harmonic alternating between the two? Perhaps even in the darkest days of Bronze Age despotic rule, there was yet still some hint of horizontal authority nested within (just as local, corporate-based decision making was maintained at Jenne, even during the hegemony of Ségou, of Sékou Amadou, and of the French). When its excavators describe Mashkan-shapir as a "tapestry of power," we are to imagine how a more horizontalized distribution of authority in some domains might coexist with centralization in others. Render unto Caesar ...

The Nile is a more difficult case. Superficially, the heterarchy of horizontal authority and the persistent resistance to centralization of the Middle Niger would seem irrelevant to the story of earliest Pharaonic state and society. Happily, our understanding of the political evolution along the Nile during the Predynastic has undergone a recent massive, and salutary, revision. (Way back when,) in my university Egyptology courses, the Predynastic peoples were presented in the grudging "backdrop" half lecture as stubbornly backward swamp-dwellers, awaiting that day when kingship descends miraculously upon them (by the heroic genius of a Narmer, or perhaps even gifted by travelers from the more civilized Mesopotamia). We now recognize the antecedent "princes" (if largely unnamed) to the Narmer of the First Dynasty. Toby Wilkinson (1999: 28–105) presents the finely spun logic for a far longer, home-grown emergence of regional polities (culminating in Hierakonpolis, Naqada, and This/Abydos along the Upper Nile, with final unification coming from the last) and for the indigenous birth of kingship in all its martial and symbolic glory. From the sadly mangled tombs of these sites, he sees powerful kingdoms as early as the Naqada I period (perhaps as early as 3800 BC) (1999: 49). By Naqada II (Amratian, 3500–3200) times, at the triumvirate, Wilkinson sees elaborate tombs of (anonymous) Dynasty 00 kings – complemented by the emergence of lesser but still significant polities elsewhere north and south along the Nile (e.g. Gebelein, Adadiya). With this rethink of Egyptian Nile Predynastic polities comes a long-over-due reassessment of the Nubian Nile counterparts, such as the kingdom centered at Qustul (O'Connor 1993; Williams 1980). The real meat of political consolidation (territorial as well as hearts and symbolically charged minds) was served up by the named kings of the Dynasty 0 (Naqada III – Gerzian) tombs. And Hassan (1988) reminds us not to dismiss contemporaneous events in Lower Egypt; archaeology with sump-pump is correcting many of the omissions owed to judicious political editing by the southern victors.

Just as interesting is an idea of growing popularity that the unitary state (? of 3150 BC) was preceded, by many centuries before the final battle between Upper and Lower Egypt, by parallel (peer) polities arranged along the Nile like beads on a string (see, esp., Kemp 1989: 45, fig. 13; Lehner 2000: 305–7) (fig. 6.2). As early as 1984 Aldred wrote that by the end of the Predynastic there was "increased clustering of villages into larger territories under the leadership of notables who we may see as proto-pharaohs" (1984: 76). In a regional political model that complements Wilkinson's dynastic hypothesis, This/Abydos, Naqada and, especially, Hierakonpolis found the key to the expansion of these "central places" in a long process of amoeboid-like assimilation of neighbors (Kemp 1989: 31–35, esp. fig. 8, p. 34; T. A. H. Wilkinson 1999: 336).

This parallel polity dynamism of urban growth and state formation was certainly coercive (witness the numbers of *sati* in the burials of the so-called Dynasty 0 and Dynasty 00 tombs). But Kemp (1989) and Trigger (1985: 348) and Hassan (1988:169–75) take that extra step to attribute much of the success of the ultimate Unifier(s) to the skillful manipulation of a deep-time symbolic geography. Deep from within the earlier Predynastic mists (or even earlier?) appear the cultic figureheads of Hierakonpolis (Horus) and of Naqada (Seth). They are reformulated as embodiments of a larger south and north, mixed with the avatars of other localities, symbols of other beads on the Predynastic riverine string, into a pantheon that sustains the Pharaohs in their cosmic struggles for justice, order, and against "chaos" (preeminently, disastrous Nile floods: Friedman 2003: 52; Lehner 2000: 320–21).

On the not-so-positive side, however, this brilliant reformulation of state formation along the Nile treats the issue of urbanization – well, very timidly. With unification, it has been argued, our preferred definition of a city (applicable to the Middle Niger and to most ancient and modern cities) no longer applies to the Nile Valley – such is the drastic reorganization of production and peasant ecology that characterizes the Pharaonic state. Trigger writes: "This helped to perpetuate a pattern of dispersed villages and only relatively small regional administrative centers. Such a development may also explain the preoccupation with rural, as opposed to urban, life that was a distinctive feature of the elite culture of Egypt" (1983: 51). Not exactly the case that post-Unification Egypt became a "civilization without cities" (to recall the famous phrase of Egyptologist John Wilson – that is, with a lack of large population agglomerations,

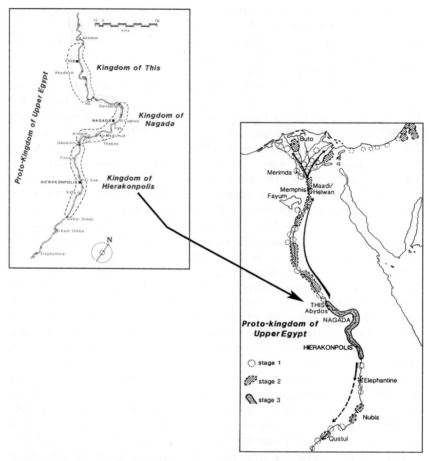

Fig. 6.2. "Beads-on-a-string" emergent polities to proto-states along the
Predynastic Nile

surrounded by city walls and lording over a largely depopulated hinterland, after the Mesopotamian city-state model).

However, many are impressed by the post-Unification state manufacture
(as of an artificial, non-"organic" entity) of the new capital Memphis (and
later fabricated capitals, such as Akhenaten's el-Amarna) and the conse-
quent withering away of the aforementioned triumvirate towns of This/
Abydos, Naqada, and Hierakonpolis (Hassan: 1988: 161–63; Trigger
2003: 132; T. A. H. Wilkinson 1999: 333–34). In this view, Pharaonic cities
become artificial extensions of state logic – cultic, or military, funerary, or

economic. Their plan and foundation are entirely state planned and decreed (the "model communities" of Kemp 1989: 137–80) and Trigger implies that Egypt was the original case of urban manipulation within a "territorial state," in which capitals are more likely to be peripatetic, cities are constructed state enterprises (2003: 131–41). Wilkinson kindly calls this "state interference" (1999: 327)! John Wilson may have got it partially correct – Egypt did become a civilization without the self-organizing city, without the emergent urbanism documented in the Middle Niger.

If so, what led to the abortion of the urbanization process, in mid-stream? Asked another way, might there instead be a variation on the critique leveled at the first excavators of Hierakonpolis, Quibell and Green, apart from their antiquated Social Darwinistic drive to document a spiritual lineage between Victorian civilization and the first literate state of antiquity (Hoffman 1991: 126)? That variation would be our old nemesis the *ex astra* imperative, which can be leveled at those who see a state, perhaps nascent, but already showing its nasty hegemony claws, behind even the first expressions of Egyptian urbanism, however deep within the Predynastic. How else is one to read the instance of Trigger (1985: 348) and even Wilkinson (1999: 324) or Hassan (1988: 162–63) that even the pre-Unification centers of Naqada and Hierakonpolis were not really agglomerations of specialists and agriculturalists (in the spirit even of Trigger's classic 1972 urban definition that we have adopted in this book)? Rather, they were primarily cult centers and emerging administrative foci for the nascent territorial states; centralized storage facilities, a defensive wall, workshops for "royal" craftsmen, scurrying scribes, and monumental temple of palace antecedents would have rounded out the picture. And, after all, late Predynastic Hierakonpolis, the largest of these centers, was rather small – down to a high-density 2 hectares by around 3300 BC (Kemp 1989: 39; T. A. H. Wilkinson 1999: 393).

Contrast this representation of urbanism almost as an afterthought, then, with the view of those dirt archaeologists recently working at Hierakonpolis:

But this does not mean that the overall population density of Egypt was inferior to that of Mesopotamia or any other civilization with great urban centers. The population, within certain districts at least, was almost certainly better distributed over the arable land than in Mesopotamia ... Seen in this light, it was the concentration of a population, possibly around a ceremonial center, triggered by environmental events that provided a group of people of sufficient permanence and size for the emerging political elite to organize. (Hoffman 1991: 309, see also 319)

Indeed, Hoffman *et al.* (1986 and 1987) call the site Egypt's earliest city (by c. 4000 BC) and, by Naqada II (Gerzian) times they estimate a population of 10,000 or more. Attributable only partially to the post-Neolithic Sub-Pluvial (c. 3300 BC) abandonment of extensively distributed settlement from the Hierakonpolis wadi mouth up the Great Wadi some 5 or 6 kilometers, urbanization apparently had even earlier, more diverse causes.

Hoffman began the laborious process of documenting the agglomeration at the edge of the Western Desert as a dense and diverse, deeply layered Predynastic settlement (1991: 127, 155–56). Carrying on after Hoffman's tragically early death, excavator Friedman (2003: 51) represents Hierakonpolis, by at least by 3600 BC, as "a vibrant, bustling city – perhaps the largest in all Egypt – stretching for almost three miles along the edge of the Nile floodplain." Scarcely a vestigial appendage, rather a teeming mass of farmers and fishermen, specialists (beer makers and potters, embalmers, burial mat weavers, and other craftsmen) (Hoffman 1991: 317; Friedman 2003: 52, 54–55).

Speaking of a half-millennium or more before Narmer, Friedman concludes: "These discoveries show that the basic economic infrastructure that later supported pharaonic civilization – large-scale production and specialization – was already developing at this early date" (2003: 52). And, from inside the Great Wadi itself comes evidence of specialist hamlets for the production of ceramics (and stone tools?) (F. J. Harlan 1978) – the Nile and wadi system counterpart of the clustered corporate satellites in orbit about a focal proto-urban center?

Pity poor Hierakonpolis: Mined for centuries for its fertilizing midden soils, cratered by looters since the nineteenth-century emergence of the antiquities and souvenir traffic, abused by the "curious" excavation and recording techniques of Quibell and Green, and now with earlier Predynastic levels reduced to "shapeless heaps" by the elevated post-Aswan Dam water table. Still, might we not entertain an alternative view? Might not a landscape of specialization and a sub-regional integrative relationship of clustered settlements (in other words, the urban hinterland) have preceded or at least developed simultaneously with whatever cultic or symbolic and asymmetrical power landscapes have caught the *ex astra*-occluded eye of later prehistorians and Egyptologists? Taken to a grander scale, what was this process, so elegantly deciphered by Kemp and Wilkinson, of consolidation of the beaded polities along a terminal Predynastic Nile? Was it not the eventual reversal of a far older tendency towards local centrifugal authority (that reasserts itself periodically in the form of nome-based authority at times of Intermediate Period waning of imperial state coherence [Lehner (2000: 335–39)] who makes his argument also in terms of critical systems and self-organizing landscapes)?

One can only speculate. If the archaeology of ancient urbanism had started along the Middle Niger, I wonder whether these Egyptian discoveries would have been interpreted quite differently. And would a very different strategy of field investigation have been undertaken? Would the vast fields of Predynastic deposits at Hierakonpolis and Naqada (and others) have been queried for the emergence of corporateness, and specialization, and landscape writ large – instead of this obsession with despotic power and with finding Narmer's cradle? Would a very different approach to the evolution of Predynastic authority have been more appealing – one that saw the beginning of consolidation perhaps less as a martial and aggressive affair and more as the building of confederations? Was the story of the fourth millennium along the Nile, rather, one of a grand tension between centrifugal, more heterarchical authority and the (eventually victorious) tendency to centralization and hierarchy of power?

One can only speculate. One hopes the basic kind of archaeology – excavation and reconnaissance especially up the wadi – will be done at Hierakonpolis before all the deposits are wasted to greed and to the rising water table. We end on a less pessimistic note: China.

China: the clustered alternative

What a great pity the much-lamented giant of China's prehistory, K.-C. Chang, did not live to witness the verification (to excess) of many of his fondest intuitions about the emergence of cities and states. Feeling much the intruder, but out of tribute to my mentor, I attempted to abstract, from his voluminous original thoughts, three that seem particularly ripe for Middle Niger and China comparisons (R. McIntosh 1991, 1999b). Here we will linger, just briefly, on how data gathered during very recent programs of survey and early city excavations, the offspring of an open China attitude during the past decade, have dealt with Chang's three hypotheses (with the core–periphery issue thrown in for good measure).

The first derives from K.-C. Chang's pioneering work on settlement patterns (1968). Since early, not-terribly-sophisticated, investigations at the later Bronze Age dynasty Shang cities of Anyang and Zhengzhou, archaeologists had puzzled over the non-aggregated distribution of craftspersons' workshops, farming hamlets, and elite residences, clustering in a "point distribution" around the walled royal and ritual precincts. Chang insisted that we suspend all expectations derived from Mesopotamia and see these, undeniable full-state and despotic cities, nevertheless, as a "network of specialized parts" (1986: 363; see 1980: 130, fig. 38 for his "structural model" of Anyang) (R. McIntosh 1991: 206–11 and 1999b: 68–69). Chang (and Keightley 1987: 101–12) made a plea for archaeologists to stop being blinded by the posturing of elites, by their spectacular burials (including *sati*), and monumentality. Instead, archaeologists should consider the possibility of a far earlier time, the dawn of urbanism, when free specialists might have been voluntarily attracted to a shared locale. Most prophetically, he even considered these Shang (period dates, c. 1600 to 1046 BC) capitals as showing residuals of what we would now call intercalated, or nested, hierarchy and heterarchy. Even more audaciously, Chang read in the clustered cities a remnant resistance to centralization, perhaps with the agency of territorial agnatic clans (1986: 303–5), intervillage leagues (1983b: 513–14), and confederation of shamanistic occult leaders (1983a: 44–48 and 1986: 414–22). The alternative to Chang, being trumpeted at the time, was that these clustered cities represented unfree craftsmen forced into segregated "ghetto hamlets" (An 1986: 42–46; Trigger 1985: 347–50; Wheatley 1971: 34–50).

"This is a vision of early urbanism that emphasizes the deep temporal roots of cities as horizontal networks of Ecosocial Interdependence rather than as seats of vertical power, reinforced by monumentality" (R. McIntosh 1999b: 81). Ecosocial Interdependence: the second of K.-C. Chang's precocious thoughts and one that will be familiar to readers of the present book as fundamental to a dynamic, risk-laden, and stress-inducing landscape (Chang 1962: 188 and 1986: 362–63). Chang believed that a northern China, oscillating warm and wet (post-Glacial optimum) and then (after c. 3000 until about the start of the Longshan Neolithic) dry and cooler, would have been under climatic, as well as social (hence, Ecosocial), challenge. This challenge, in part, encouraged collaboration, a complex socio-economic structure made of discrete components, an Ecosocial Interdependence:

But the Yin-Shang settlements had become specialized externally in ecosocial function. Each community no longer worked only for its own survival and wealth, but worked for other communities and was worked for by others as well. The new horizon was marked by the appearance of centers of administration, redistribution, and ceremony, which one may call towns or cities, where officials and priests managed rather than labored. There were also farming and handicrafting hamlets, the inhabitants of which engaged in organized labor co-ordinated under a central control. This phenomenon, the ecosocial interdependence among specialized communities, is to this author one of the most decisive criteria of urbanization, which in turn was brought about by a change of the total social-cultural structure. Insofar as one can see from the archaeological record of this part of the world, no single factor alone makes a civilization appear. (Chang 1962: 188)

Put another way, these later Bronze Age cities may have inescapable signs of the coercive state; but still strong, still vibrant beneath the glitz of temples and palaces are venerable structures of horizontally conceived authority.

To his credit, Chang did not succumb to crass hierarchy bashing! He had a more measured view of what we would today characterize as horizontal authority nested within hierarchical, centralized power. His third concept had a name: "hierarchy segmentation" (Chang 1983a: 11–16, 1983b: 502, 1986: 365–67; see also Keightley 1982: 554). To Chang, this was the glue that kept these clustered cities and the early Chinese states together: In his own words, "In this formulation, cities have their origin first as centers for the transition from folk shamanism to state cult and second as reinforcement to a hierarchical segmentation of the population along the lines of lineages and clan hierarchy that have roots in the Neolithic" (1986: 365).

An individual was assigned a position in society horizontally by membership in kinship descent groups and vertically by clans and lineages that developed differential (vertical) functions and relationship vis-à-vis the ancestors. The earliest state (going back to the earliest of the Bronze Age dynasties, the Xia [2070–1600 BC]) was not at conception a unitary, mechanistic, *ex astra* monster, but rather an alliance of corporate groups. What began as a federation, with the Tzu clan acting more as a *primus inter pares* than as anything else, ended by mid-Shang as something more darkly freighted (if you're anyone but a Tzu!). The later Bronze Age state was an entrenched asymmetry, with the ruler monopolizing much of the critical commerce with the ancestors and spinning off ever more draconian sumptuary laws.

The reader of this book will perhaps not be astonished when I admit that mentorship by K.-C. Chang had an enormous influence on the ideas (and intellectual biases) I brought to the Middle Niger. I had so hoped that Chang could witness the fruits of the eventual opening of China to new theories and urban survey strategies from the outside (R. McIntosh 1991: 209–11 and 1999b: 80–81) and, more importantly, the incredible dynamism resulting when internal and extramural ideas mix and ignite. How pleased he would have been with the results of the growing number of urban region surveys spreading like wildfire over China (summarized in Liu Li 1996; Liu Li and Chen 2001).

The first beast to be vanquished by the new regional survey approach to urban investigations was yet another *bête noire* of Chang's. How he detested the core–periphery conceit that cities, states, and civilization arose in the open plains of the Huanghe (Yellow River) basin and later spread to the barbarian peripheries (Chang 1986: 369; Shelach 1994: 261). This Nuclear Area (or Central Plains, aka Zhongyuan) thesis held that the Xia, Shang, and Zhou dynasties rose and fell sequentially, each in turn shining the light of its ever-more-civilized civilization upon the benighted beyond. Chang argued vociferously that the Zhongyuan should rather be considered as a long-term interaction sphere where the peoples traditionally identified with these dynasties competed, interacted, and shared technical, subsistence, and socio-political responses to shared ecosocial challenges. And, he argued, never ignore the "barbarians"!

Now we can see that the interaction sphere must be expanded far to the coastal Shandong east (Underhill 1994; Underhill *et al.* 1998 and 2002). The same admonition applies far into Inner Mongolia, northeast of Beijing (Shelach 1994, 1997), west – far upstream of the Huanghe River – in the Helan Mountains (Liu Li and Chen 2001: 17; Demattè 1999). And our search for cities must extend down to the middle and coastal reaches of the Yangzi River (to the precocious walled towns of the Qujialing culture area) (Demattè 1999: 129 and Underhill 1994: 197; see also Demattè 1999: 139, fig. 15).

These were just some of the components of the interaction sphere that shared intense competition, copying, and rapid experimentation and innovation – as early as the late Neolithic Longshan (2000 BC or back even to the end of the fourth millennium). In the Longshan, the Zhongyuan was a "crucial matrix" (Liu Li 1996: 237) of chiefdoms and petty polities – and we would be remiss not to mention the Shangqiu Project (collaboration negotiated by K.-C. Chang himself), at the eastern ("barbarous"!) frontier of the Nuclear Area, where the eponymous spiritual seat of all Civilization (Great City Shang, City Song) has been found 5–11 meters beneath the alluvium (Murowchick and Cohen 2001)!

In addition to the important result of breaking the intellectual shackles of the core–periphery concept, these new surveys have discovered to the world some spectacularly early cities! Early (back to 2600 BC), large, and structurally complex settlements are both unwalled and walled (Demattè 1999: 121; Underhill 1994: 203–5), both nucleated and, apparently, dispersed. Walled cities along the middle Yangzi go back to 4000 BC. But what is in a wall? I suspect that K.-C. Chang would gently have chided all the hierarchical enthusiasm shown at the mere mention of walls (are there not reasons other than defense and militarism for constructing a wall – particularly on a flighty, ferocious floodplain?) and at the mere hint of multi-tier settlement hierarchies (Jenne-jeno also has a several-tier regional hierarchy of sites by size).

This warning aside, it is clear that we can talk of true urbanism far to the east in coastal Shandong. There, recent work documents an explosion of settlement by late Neolithic times and apparent rapid (less than half-millennium) consolidation into an urban regional hierarchy focused on the large sites of Liangchengzhen (LCZ) of 246.8 hectares and Dantu of 130.7 hectares (Underhill *et al.* 1998 and 2002) (fig. 6.3). Further west, in the Anyang region of the Zhongyuan itself, Liu Li and Chen (2001: 13, 17–18) argue for an integrated urban hinterland focused upon a 56-hectare primal site as early as 3000 BC.

Recalling the linked arguments by Chang for the "structural (multi-component) model," Ecosocial Interdependence, and "hierarch- ical segmentation," let us take one last look at the Shandong Longshan urban complex in figure 6.3. The LCZ–Dantu cluster is not the only cluster identified in the 400-square-kilometer survey region. Four smaller clusters show the same evidence of being "functionally connected" (Underhill *et al.* 2002: 747–49; also Underhill *et al.* 1998: 463–66). Without deep excavation, the investigators were not able to find quite the same quality of evidence of craft or corporate differentiation as has been documented at the Jenne-jeno Urban Complex. However, Underhill believes that at these, and at the even more nucleated walled towns of the Zhongyuan, crafts and specializations formed distinct clusters (1994: 214). One need not speculate any more. Strategies of extensive, 100 percent or probability-based regional survey, careful surface examination and recording all sites, all periods, and a linked tactic of excavation of elite, non-elite, and specialist mounds or quarters may have begun in China somewhat later than along the Middle Niger. Nevertheless, the similarity of the field remains and landscape patterns in both places makes the advisability of testing K.-C. Chang's notions of heterarchy nested within hierarchy equally compelling in both places.

Exuberant clustering between the Tigris and Euphrates during the Uruk period (only to wither way in the early third millennium); nascent cities on the Nile (with up-wadi specialist hamlets in the case of Hierakonpolis) – only to see "classic" urbanism aborted as the "beads on a string" Predynastic polities consolidate into Pharaonic civilization; and the persistent Ecosocial Interdependence even at full-state Anyang and Zhengzhou. It would be so very easy to unleash one's enthusiasm and say the Middle Niger models of the self-organizing landscape and heter- archy explain it all! No, perhaps there has been too much hubris in the study of ancient cities. Although, in the case of ancient Chinese cities and of Mashkan-shapir, the explanation for the dispersed nature of authority in the Middle Niger has been tapped by local archaeologists, these really are different domains of urbanism. Yet, by assuming a comparative stance, urbanism as a multi-potential process becomes just one of many likely "modes" as society travels along on a long trajectory of response to and interaction with landscape.

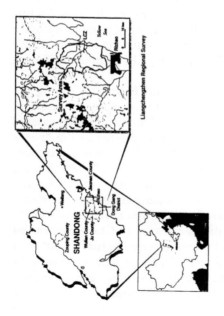

Fig. 6.3. Longshan-period clustered urbanism in coastal Shandong, China

Seen this way, the dominance of the *ex astra* explanation is best seen as an artifact of a different intellectual time. (From its armchair germination by Yahwist-besotted theorists, it was probably too mechanistic, too ideal a concept anyway.) All cities are the nested landscapes of power and authority and of economic and social relations that display their own historical personalities, with clear comparative implications.

I would like to end with a suggestion to keep us from the probable fallacy of an either-or formulation of "heterarchy or hierarchy." I suggest that the long germination of cities in many places, certainly along the Middle Niger and possibly along the Nile, Tigris–Euphrates, and Huanghe also, may be represented graphically by something approximating figure 6.4. The idea here is that complex societies will always display some dynamics of consolidation. The "heterarchs" must always resist the charismatic or ruthless personality types. There will always be cases in which the *primus inter pares* – who is allowed to make decisions, to lead defenses at times of crisis – somehow just never quite wishes to relinquish full authority upon cessation of hostilities. Individuals and even corporations will wage campaigns of invention of tradition. And the agencies of leveling of authority will always be in tension with these agencies of centralization. Seen along a time progression, there is a harmonic (irregular, to be precise) pattern of oscillation back and forth between the ideal expressions of these two states. (The harmonic pattern may be made of smooth changes, or of the abrupt phase transforms more typical, I believe, of these unpredictable, "ecosocially challenged" landscapes.) But the state of the ultimate State, the *ex astra* ideal, presented here in chapter 1, is probably just an extreme and probably would not last very long because of the rigidity, the lack of resilience problem (Risk, Surprise, and Subsistence Security) described at length in chapter 2. True chaos, the cosmic *isfet* so feared by the ancient Egyptians, occupies the opposite extreme, in figure 6.4.

So, the harmonics may slip into discord with a period of extreme hierarchy (and archaeologists have been really clever at finding these periods). Or they may briefly collapse into periods of extreme climatic chaos and political and social pathology. The archaeologists of collapse have been equally obsessive about finding these moments of ancient despair. In the end, I suspect the longer history of the emerging urban landscape is of vibratory oscillation back and forth, with no regular periodicity – lurches, really, between the "purer" heterarchy (whatever that might mean in real terms) and a nested authority. Nested authority – horizontally displayed, overlapping, competing, and counterpoised authority moderated by the assumption (moderated and temporarily, or perhaps just over a circumscribed domain, such as external trade or

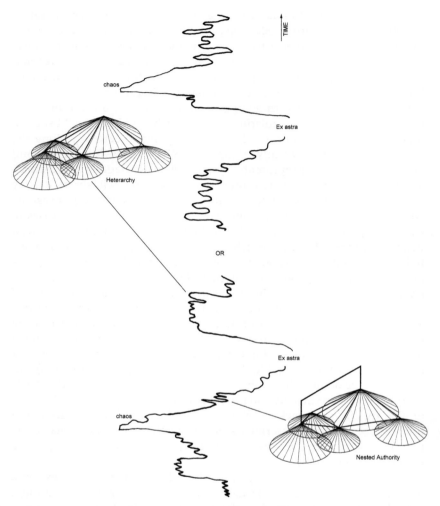

Fig. 6.4. Vibratory alternation of heterarchy and nested authority

foreign diplomacy) by one of a few of the components of society assuming a bit more authority, a mere hint of power. Admirers of the Roman Republic may recognize the dictator Cincinnatus.

The Middle Niger cities may be considered classic expressions of heterarchical social and political relations – complex societies in which the multiple components derive authority from separate, if often over-lapping, sources. The several corporations of these cities provide agencies of resistance and counterbalance to those who would monopolize power. Other urban spheres may have suppressed alternative expressions of

Fig. 6.5. Abana!

authority (ideologically, by the manipulation of monuments and symbols, or by the use of naked terror). But, even in Mesopotamia, along the
Nile, and in northern China, some alternatives lie hidden in the deeper
history of urbanism, or nested even in the most despotic cityscape.

I leave the final word to those Mande who have discovered these
brilliant cities ... figure 6.5.

References

Adams, Robert M. 1966. *The Evolution of Urban Society: Urban Mesopotamia and Prehistoric Mexico*. Chicago: Aldine.
   1981. *Heartland of Cities*. Chicago: University of Chicago Press.
Adams, Robert M. and Hans Nissen. 1972. *The Uruk Countryside. The Natural Setting of Urban Societies*. Chicago: University of Chicago Press.
Albright, W. F. 1953. *Archaeology and the Religion of Israel*. Baltimore: Johns Hopkins University Press.
Aldred, Cyril. 1984. *The Egyptians*, 2nd edition. London: Thames & Hudson.
Allen, T. F. H., Joseph A. Tainter, and Thomas W. Hoekstra. 2003. *Supply-Side Sustainability*. New York: Columbia University Press.
Alley, R. B., J. Marotzke, W. D. Nordhaus, J. T. Overpeck, D. M. Peteet, R. A. Pielke, Jr., R. T. Pierrehumbert, P. B. Rhines, T. F. Stocker, L. D. Talley, and J. M. Wallace. 2003. Abrupt climate change. *Science* 299: 2005–10.
Amblard, Sylvie. 1996. Agricultural evidence and its interpretation on the Dhars Tichitt and Oualata, south-eastern Mauritania. In *Aspects of African Archaeology. Papers from the 10th Congress of the Panafrican Association for Prehistory and Related Studies*, ed. Gilbert Pwiti and Robert Soper, pp. 421–27. Harare: University of Zimbabwe Publications.
An, Chin-Huai. 1986. The Shang city at Cheng-chou and related problems. In *Studies of Shang Archaeology*, ed. Kwang-Chih Chang, pp. 14–48. New Haven: Yale University Press.
Andrews, Anthony P. 1995. *First Cities*. Washington, D.C.: Smithsonian Institution Press/St. Remy Press.
Attarian, Christopher J. 2003. Cities as a place of ethnogenesis: urban growth and centralization in the Chicama Valley, Peru. In *The Social Construction of Ancient Cities*, ed. Monica L. Smith, pp. 184–211. Washington, D.C.: Smithsonian Institution Press.
Balée, William. 1998a. Historical Ecology: premises and postulates. In *Advances in Historical Ecology*, ed. William Balée, pp. 13–29. New York: Columbia University Press.
   1998b. Introduction. In *Advances in Historical Ecology*, ed. William Balée, pp. 1–10. New York: Columbia University Press.
Baro, Mamadou Amadou, Amadou Tidjane Dia, Djibi Ba, Amadou Gacko, and Jean Lebloas. 1987. Recherche sur les systèmes de production rurale dans la Vallée du Fleuve Sénégal. Une mission de prospection des cultures de

Décrue (Walo) dans les régions de Guidimaka, Gorgol, Brakna et Trarza. Report of the Projet de Recherche Agricole en Mauritanie, no. 2. Faculty of Agriculture, University of Arizona, Tucson.

Barth, Frederick. 1956. Ecological relationships of ethnic groups in Swat, North Pakistan. *American Anthropologist* 58: 1079–89.

Bedaux, Rogier M. A. 1980. The geographical distribution of footed bowls in the Upper and Middle Niger region. In *West African Culture Dynamics: Archaeological and Historical Perspectives*, ed. B. K. Swartz and R. Dumett, pp. 247–58. The Hague: Mouton.

Bedaux, Rogier M. A., T. S. Constandse-Westermann, L. Hacquebord, A. G. Lange, and J. Diderik Van der Waals. 1978. Recherches archéologiques dans le Delta intérieur du Niger. *Palaeohistoria* 20: 91–220.

Bedaux, Rogier M. A., Mamadi Dembélé, Annette M. Schmidt, and J. Diderik Van der Waals. 1994. L'Archéologie entre Bani et Niger. In *Djenné. Une Ville Millénaire au Mali*, ed. Rogier M. A. Bedaux and J. Diderik Van der Waals, pp. 41–53. Leiden: Rijksmuseum voor Volkenkunde.

Bedaux, Rogier M. A., Kevin MacDonald, Alain Person, Jean Polet, Kléna Sanogo, Annette Schmidt, and Samuel Sidibé. 2001. The Dia archaeological project. Rescuing cultural heritage in the Inland Niger Delta (Mali). *Antiquity* 75: 837–76.

Bedaux, Rogier M. A. and J. D. Van der Waals, eds. 1994. *Djenné. Une Ville Millénaire au Mali*. Leiden: Rijksmuseum voor Volkenkunde.

Berhaut, Jean. 1967. *Flore du Sénégal*, 2nd edition. Dakar: Editions Clairafrique.

Bernus, Edmond, Patrice Cressier, Alain Durand, François Paris, and Jean-François Saliège. 1999. *Vallée de l'Azawagh*. Paris: Editions SEPIA.

Biersack, Aletta. 1999. Introduction: from the "New Ecology" to the new ecologies. *American Anthropologist* 101 (1): 5–18.

Blanck, J. P. 1968. *Notice des Cartes Géomorphologiques de la Vallée du Niger entre Tombouctou et Labbezanga (République du Mali)*. Strasbourg: Centre de Géographie Appliquée, Université Louis Pasteur.

Blanton, Richard E., Gary F. Feinman, Stephen A. Kowalewski, and Peter N. Peregrine. 1996. A dual-processual theory for the evolution of Mesoamerican civilization. *Current Anthropology* 37 (1): 1–14.

Bourgeois, J. L. 1987. The history of the great mosques of Djenné. *African Arts* 20 (3): 54–63, 909–92.

Bourgeon, G. and R. Bertrand. 1984. Evaluation du milieu naturel des plains alluviales de la Boucle du Niger (Mali) – II. "Potentialités." *L'Agronomie Tropicale* 39: 208–15.

Bovill, E. W. 1970. *Golden Trade of the Moors*, 2nd edition. Oxford: Oxford University Press.

Bradley, R. S. 1985. *Quaternary Paleoclimatology: Methods of Paleoclimatic Reconstruction*. Boston: Allen & Unwin.

Bradley, Raymond S. 1999. *Paleoclimatology. Reconstructing Climates of the Quaternary*, 2nd edition. San Diego: Harcourt.

Brasseur, Gérard. 1968. *Les Etablissements Humains au Mali*. Mémoires de l'Institut Fondamental de l'Afrique Noire, no. 83. Dakar: Institut Fondamental de l'Afrique Noire.

Braun, D. P. and Stephen Plog. 1982. Evolution of "tribal" social networks. *American Antiquity* 49 (3): 504–25.

Breuning, Peter and Katharina Neumann. 2002. From hunters and gatherers to food producers: new archaeological and archaeobotanical evidence from the West African Sahel. In *Droughts, Food and Culture. Ecological Change and Food Security in Africa's Later Prehistory*, ed. Fekri Hassan, pp. 123–55. Dordrecht: Kluwer Academic.

Brooks, George E. 1998. Climate and history in West Africa. In *Transformations in Africa. Essays on Africa's Later Past*, ed. Graham Connah, pp. 139–59. London: Leicester University Press.

Brunet-Moret, Yves, P. Chaperon, J. P. Lamagat, and M. Molinier. 1986. *Monographie Hydrologique du Fleuve Niger*. ORSTOM Monographies Hydrologiques, no. 8. Paris: Institut Français de Recherche Scientifique pour le Développement en Coopération.

Brunfiel, Elizabeth M. 1987. Elite and utilitarian crafts in the Aztec state. In *Specialization, Exchange and Complex Society*, ed. Elizabeth M. Brunfiel and Timothy K. Earle, pp. 102–18. Cambridge: Cambridge University Press.

  1994. Ethnic groups and political development in ancient Mexico. In *Factional Competition and Political Development in the New World*, ed. Elizabeth M. Brunfiel and J. W. Fox, pp. 89–102. Cambridge: Cambridge University Press.

  1998. The multiple identities of Aztec craft specialists. In *Craft and Social Identity*, ed. Cathy Lynne Costin and Rita P. Wright, pp. 145–52. Archaeological Papers of the American Anthropological Association, no. 8. Washington, D.C.: American Anthropological Association.

Brunk, Karsten and Detlef Gronenborn. 2004. Floods, droughts, and migrations. The effect of late Holocene lake level oscillations and climate fluctuations on the settlement and political history in the Chad Basin. In *Living with the Lake. Perspectives on History, Culture and Economies of Lake Chad*, ed. Matthias Krings and Editha Platte, pp. 101–32. Cologne: Rüdiger Kuoppe Verlag.

Bryant, Edward. 1997. *Climate Process and Change*. Cambridge: Cambridge University Press.

Buckle, Colin. 1978. *Landforms in Africa*. London: Longman.

Centre de Suivi Ecologique (Dakar), US Agency for International Development, and US Geological Survey – EROS Data Center. 1996. Framework for Long-Term Monitoring of Senegal's Natural Resources. Unpublished study and map, "La République du Sénégal: Profil Environnemental."

Chang, Kwang-Chih. 1962. China. In *Courses Towards Urban Life. Archaeological Considerations of Some Cultural Alternatives*, ed. Robert J. Braidwood and Gordon R. Willey, pp. 177–92. Chicago: Aldine.

  ed. 1968. *Settlement Archaeology*. Palo Alto: National Press Books.

  1980. *Shang Civilization*. New Haven: Yale University Press.

  1983a. *Art, Myth, and Ritual. The Path to Political Authority in Ancient China*. Cambridge, Mass.: Harvard University Press.

  1983b. Sandai archaeology and the formation of the state in ancient China. In *The Origins of Chinese Civilization*, ed. David Keightley, pp. 495–521. Berkeley: University of California Press.

1986. *The Archaeology of Ancient China*, 4th edition (revised). New Haven: Yale University Press.

Childe, Vere Gordon. 1950. The urban revolution. *Town Planning Review* 21: 3–17.

CIPEA (Centre International pour le Dévéloppement de l'Elevage en Afrique). 1981. *Evolution de l'Utilisation des Terres et de la Végétation dans la Zone Soudano-sahelienne du Projet CIPEA au Mali*. Document de Travail, no. 3 (compiled by Mark Haywood). Addis Ababa: CIPEA (see also Haywood, Mark 1981).

Cissé, Youssouf Tata. 1964. Notes sur les sociétés de chasseurs Malinké. *Journal de la Société des Africanistes* 34: 175–226.

Clark, Mary E. 2003. Archaeological Investigations at the Jenné-jeno Settlement Complex, Inland Niger Delta, Mali, West Africa. Ph.D. dissertation. Southern Methodist University, Dallas.

Cochrane, G. 1971. Use of the concept of the "corporation." *American Anthropologist* 73: 1144–55.

Colombijn, F. 1994. *Patches of Padang: The History of an Indonesian Town in the Twentieth Century and the Use of Urban Space*. Leiden: Centre of Non-Western Studies, Leiden University.

Conrad, David C. 1992. Searching for history in the Sunjata epic: the case of Fakoli. *History in Africa* 19: 147–200.

1995. The Sabu of Dalilu: Sacred Sites and Spiritual Power in Mande History. Paper presented at the annual meeting of the African Studies Association, Orlando, Florida (see also Conrad 1999).

1999. Mooning armies and mothering heroes: female power in the Mande epic tradition. In *In Search of Sunjata. The Mande Oral Epic as History, Literature, and Performance*, ed. Ralph A. Austin, pp. 189–229. Bloomington: Indiana University Press.

2002. *Somono Bala of the Upper Niger. River People, Charismatic Bards, and Mischievous Music in a West African Culture. African Sources for African History*, vol. I. Leiden: Brill.

Conrad, David C. and Barbara E. Frank. 1995. *Status and Identity in West Africa. Nyamakalaw of Mande*. Bloomington: Indiana University Press.

Costin, Cathy Lynne. 1998. Introduction: craft and social identity. In *Craft and Social Identity*, ed. Cathy Lynne Costin and Rita P. Wright, pp. 3–16. Archaeological Papers of the American Anthropological Association, no. 8. Washington, D.C.: American Anthropological Association.

Crumley, Carole L. 1979. Three locational models: an epistemological assessment of anthropology and archaeology. In *Advances in Archaeological Method and Theory*, ed. Michael B. Schiffer. Vol. II, pp. 141–73. New York: Academic.

1994. Historical ecology: a multidimensional ecological orientation. In *Historical Ecology. Cultural Knowledge and Changing Landscapes*, ed. Carole Crumley, pp. 1–16. Santa Fe: School of American Research Press.

1995. Heterarchy and the analysis of complex societies. In *Heterarchy and the Analysis of Complex Societies*, ed. Robert M. Ehrenreich, Carole L. Crumley, and Janet E. Levy, pp. 1–5. Archaeological Papers of the American Anthropological Association, no. 6. Washington, D.C.: American Anthropological Association.

1998. Foreword. In *Advances in Historical Ecology*, ed. William Balée, pp. ix–xiv. New York: Columbia University Press.

Dahl, G. 1979. *Suffering Grass*. Stockholm: University of Stockholm, Department of Social Anthropology.

Davies, Oliver. 1967. *West Africa before the Europeans*. London: Methuen.

Davis, Whitney. 1983. Canonical representations in Egyptian art. *RES: Anthropology and Aesthetics* 4: 20–46.

Dean, Jeffrey. 1996. Demography, environment, and subsistence stress. In *Evolving Complexity and Environmental Risk in the Prehistoric Southwest*, ed. Joseph A. Tainter and Bonnie B. Tainter, pp. 25–56. Santa Fe Institute, Studies in the Sciences of Complexity, Proceedings, vol. 24. Reading, Mass.: Addison-Wesley.

2000. Complexity theory and sociocultural change in the American Southwest. In *The Way the Wind Blows. Climate, History and Human Action*, ed. Roderick J. McIntosh, Joseph A. Tainter, and Susan Keech McIntosh, pp. 89–118. New York: Columbia University Press.

DeCeuninck, Grégoire and Anne Mayor. 1994. La poterie traditionnelle: de sa production à sa consommation. In *Djenné. Une Ville Millénaire au Mali*, ed. Rogier M. A. Bedaux and J. Diderik Van der Waals, pp. 131–38. Leiden: Rijksmuseum voor Volkenkunde.

Delville, Philippe Lavigne. 1997. Sahelian agrarian systems: principal rationales. In *Societies and Nature in the Sahel*, ed. Claude Raynaut, pp. 138–58. London: Routledge.

Demattè, Paola. 1999. Longshan-era urbanism: the role of cities in Predynastic China. *Asian Perspectives* 38 (2): 119–50.

Dembélé, Mamadi, Annette M. Schmidt, and J. Diderik Van der Waals. 1993. Prospections de sites archéologiques dans le delta intérieur du Niger. In *Vallées du Niger. Catalogue Scientifique*, ed. anonymous, pp. 218–32. Paris: Editions de la Réunion des Musées Nationaux.

Deme, Alioune and Susan Keech McIntosh. forthcoming. Excavations at Walaldé. New light on the settlement of the Middle Senegal Valley by iron-using peoples. *Journal of African Archaeology*.

DeMenocol, Peter, Joseph Ortiz, Tom Guilderson, Jess Adkins, Michael Sarnthein, Linda Baker, and Martha Yerusinsky. 2000a. Abrupt onset and termination of the African Humid Period: rapid climate responses to gradual insolation forcing. *Quaternary Science Reviews* 19: 347–61.

DeMenocol, Peter, Joseph Ortiz, Tom Guilderson, and Michael Sarnthein. 2000b. Coherent high- and low-latitude climate variability during the Holocene warm period. *Science* 288 (23 June): 2198–202.

DeMenocol, Peter, W. F. Ruddiman, and E. M. Pokras. 1993. Influences of high- and low-latitude processes on African terrestrial climate: Pleistocene eolian records from equatorial Atlantic Ocean drilling program site 663. *Paleoceanography* 8: 209–42.

Desert Locust Information Service of the Migratory Pests Group. n.d. http://www.fao.org/NEWS/GLOBAL/locusts/LocFAQ.htm.

Devisse, Jean. 1990. Commerce et routes du trafic en Afrique occidentale. In *Histoire Générale de l'Afrique. L'Afrique du VIIe au XIe Siècle*. Vol. III, ed. M. el Fasi, pp. 397–463. Paris: UNESCO.

De Vries, Edwin, Albertus Makaske, Roderick J. McIntosh, and Joseph Tainter, eds. 2005. *Geomorphology and Human Palaeoecology of the Méma, Mali.* Wageningen: Alterra.

Dieterlen, G. 1941. *Les Ames des Dogon.* Travaux et Mémoires de l'Institut d'Ethnographie, no. 40. Paris: Institut d'Ethnographie.

1959. Mythe et organisation social en Afrique occidentale – suite. *Journal de la Société des Africanistes* 29: 119–38.

Dieterlen, G. and D. Sylla. 1992. *L'Empire du Ghana: le Wagadou et les Traditions de Yéréré.* Trans. M. Soumaré. Paris: Karthala.

Droxler, André W., Richard B. Alley, William R. Howard, Richard Z. Poore, and Lloyd H. Burckle. 2003. Unique and exceptionally long interglacial Marine Isotope Stage 11: Window into Earth Warm Future Climate. In *Earth's Climate and Orbital Eccentricity. The Marine Isotope Stage 11 Question,* ed. André W. Droxler, Richard Z. Poore, and Lloyd H. Burckle, pp. 1–14. American Geophysical Union Geophysical Monograph, no. 137. Washington, D.C.: American Geophysical Union.

Dunbar, Robert B. 2000. Climate variability during the Holocene: an update. In *The Way the Wind Blows. Climate, History and Human Action,* ed. Roderick J. McIntosh, Joseph A. Tainter, and Susan Keech McIntosh, pp. 45–88. New York: Columbia University Press.

Durand, Alain. 1982. Oscillations of Lake Chad over the past fifty thousand years: new data and new hypotheses. *Palaeogeography, Palaeoclimatology, Palaeoecology* 39: 37–53.

Emberling, Geoff. 2003. Urban social transformations and the problem of the "first city." In *The Social Construction of Ancient Cities,* ed. Monica L. Smith, pp. 254–68. Washington, D.C.: Smithsonian Institution Press.

Evans, John G. 2003. *Environmental Archaeology and the Social Order.* London: Routledge.

Falconer, Steve and Stephen Savage. 1995. Heartlands and hinterlands: alternative trajectories of early urbanism in Mesopotamia and the southern Levant. *American Antiquity* 60 (1): 37–58.

Flannery, Kent V. 1982. The Golden Marshalltown: a parable for the archaeology of the 1980s. *American Anthropologist* 84: 265–78.

Flight, Colin. 1976. The Kintampo culture and its place in the economic history of West Africa. In *Origins of African Plant Domestication,* ed. Jack R. Harlan, J. M. J. de Wet, and Ann M. Stemler, pp. 211–21. The Hague: Mouton.

Flohn, H. 1975. History and intransitivity of climate. In *The Physical Basis of Climate and Climate Modelling,* ed. anonymous, pp. 106–18. WMO-GARP Publications Series, no. 16. Geneva: World Meteorological Organization.

Folland, C. K., T. N. Palmer, and D. E. Parker. 1986. Sahel rainfall and world-wide sea temperatures, 1901–85. *Nature* 320 (17 April): 602–7.

Fontaine, Bernard and Serge Janicot. 1996. Sea surface temperature fields associated with West African rainfall anomaly types. *Journal of Climate* 9: 2935–40.

Fox, R. G. 1977. *Urban Anthropology: Cities in their Cultural Settings.* Englewood, N.J.: Prentice-Hall.

Frank, Barbara E. 2002. Thoughts on who made the Jenné terracottas: gender, craft specialization and Mande art history. *Mande Sudies* 4: 121–32.

Freidel, David, Linda Schiele, and Joy Parker. 1993. *Maya Cosmos. Three Thousand Years on the Shaman's Path.* New York: William Morrow & Co.

Friedman, Renée. 2003. City of the hawk. *Archaeology* 56 (6): 51–56.

Furon, Raymond. 1929. L'ancien delta du Niger. *Révue de Géographie Physique et de Géologie Dynamique* 2: 265–74.

Gallager, Daphne. 1999. Analysis of seeds and fruits from the sites of Arondo and Ft. Senedebu (Appendix E). In Ibrahima Thiaw, Archaeological Investigations of Long-Term Culture Change in the Lower Falémmé (Upper Senegal region) pp. 385–431. Ph.D. dissertation. Rice University, Houston.

Gallais, Jean. 1967. *Le Delta Intérieur du Niger. Etude de géographie régionale.* Mémoires de l'Institut Fondamental d'Afrique Noire, no. 79. Dakar: Institut Fondamental d'Afrique Noir.

1984. *Hommes du Sahel. Espaces-temps et pouvoirs. Le Delta Intérieur du Niger 1960–1980.* Paris: Flammarion.

Gallay, Alain, Eric Huyesecom, Matthieu Honegger, and Anne Mayor. 1990. *Hamdallahi, Capitale de l'Empire Peul du Massina, Mali. Première fouille archéologique, études historiques et ethnoarchéologiques.* Stuttgart: Franz Steiner Verlag.

Gallay, Alain, Eric Huyesecom, and Anne Mayor. 1994. *Peuples et Céramiques du Delta Intérieur du Niger.* Geneva: Département d'Anthropologie et d'Ecologie de l'Université de Genève.

Galloy, P., Y. Vincent, and M. Forget. 1963. *Nomades et Paysans d'Afrique Noire Occidentale.* Mémoires des Annales de l'Est, no. 23. Nancy: Centre National de la Recherche Scientifique.

Gellner, E. 1983. *Nations and Nationalism.* Oxford: Blackwell.

Gibbal, Jean-Marie. 1988. *Les Génies du Fleuve.* Paris: Presses de la Renaissance.

Gottdiener, Mark. 1985. *The Social Production of Urban Space.* Austin: University of Texas Press.

Gottwald, N. K. 1979. *The Tribes of Yahweh. A Sociology of the Religion of Liberated Israel. 1250–1050 BCE.* Maryknoll: Orbis Books.

Griaule, M. 1948. L'alliance cathartique. *Africa* 18: 242–58.

Grove, Anthony T. 1978 [1967]. *Africa*, 3rd edition. Oxford: Oxford University Press.

1985. *The Niger and its Neighbours. Environmental History and Hydrobiology, Human Use and Health Hazards of the Major West African Rivers.* Rotterdam: A. A. Balkema.

Guitat, Raymond. 1972. Carte et répertoire des sites néolithiques du Mali et de la Haute-Volta. *Bulletin de l'Institut Fondamental de l'Afrique Noire (B)* 4: 896–924.

Haaland, Randi. 1980. Man's role in the changing habitat of Méma during the old kingdom of Ghana. *Norwegian Archaeological Review* 13 (1): 31–46.

Halstead, Paul and John O'Shea. 1989. Introduction: cultural response to risk and uncertainty. In *Bad Year Economics: Cultural Responses to Risk and Uncertainty,* ed. Paul. Halstead and John O'Shea, pp. 1–7. Cambridge: Cambridge University Press.

Harlan, Jack R. 1971. Agricultural centers: centers and non-centers. *Science* 174: 468–74.

1993. The tropical African cereals. In *The Archaeology of Africa: Foods, Metals and Towns*, ed. C. Thurstan Shaw, Paul Sinclair, Bassey Andah, and A. Okpoko, pp. 53–60. London: Routledge.

Harlan, Jack R., J. M. J. de Wet, and Ann B. L. Stemler. 1976. Plant domestication and indigenous African agriculture. In *Origins of African Plant Domestication*, ed. Jack R. Harlan, J. M. J. de Wet, and Ann B. L. Stemler, pp. 3–19. The Hague: Mouton.

Harlan, John Frederick. 1978. Predynastic Settlement Patterns: A View from Hierakonpolis. Ph.D. dissertation. Washington University, St. Louis.

Haskell, Helen, Roderick J. McIntosh, and Susan Keech McIntosh. 1988. *Archaeological Reconnaissance in the Region of Dia, Mali*. Report to the National Geographic Society and Institut des Sciences Humaines.

Hassan, Fekri. 1985. Palaeoenvironments and contemporary archaeology: a geoarchaeological approach. In *Archaeological Geology*, ed. R. Rapp and J. A. Gifford, pp. 85–102. New Haven: Yale University Press.

1988. The Predynastic of Egypt. *Journal of World Prehistory* 2 (2): 135–85.

1996. Abrupt Holocene climatic events in Africa. In *Aspects of African Archaeology*, ed. Gilbert Pwiti and Robert Soper, pp. 83–89. Harare: University of Zimbabwe Publications.

1997. Holocene palaeoclimates of Africa. *African Archaeological Review* 14: 213–30.

2002a. Conclusion. In *Droughts, Food and Culture. Ecological Change and Food Security in Africa's Later Prehistory*, ed. Fekri Hassan, pp. 321–33. Dordrecht: Kluwer Academic.

ed. 2002b. *Droughts, Food and Culture. Ecological Change and Food Security in Africa's Later Prehistory*. Dordrecht: Kluwer Academic.

2002c. Introduction. In *Droughts, Food and Culture. Ecological Change and Food Security in Africa's Later Prehistory*, ed. Fekri Hassan, pp. 1–7. Dordrecht: Kluwer Academic.

Haug, Gerald H., Konrad A. Hughen, Daniel M. Sigman, Larry C. Peterson, and Ursula Röhl. 2001. Southward migration of the Intertropical Convergence Zone through the Holocene. *Science* 293: 1304–07.

Haywood, Mark. 1981. *Evolution de l'Utilisation des Terres et de la Végétation dans la Zone Soudano-Sahelienne du Projet CIPEA au Mali*. Document de Travail, no. 3. Addis Ababa: CIPEA (Centre International pour le Développement de l'Elevage en Afrique).

Hoffman, Michael A. 1991 [1979]. *Egypt before the Pharaohs. The Prehistoric Foundations of Egyptian Civilization*, revised edition. Austin: University of Texas Press.

Hoffman, Michael A., Hany A. Hamroush, and Ralph O. Allen. 1986. A model of urban development for the Hierakonpolis region from the Predynastic through Old Kingdom times. *Journal of the American Research Center* 23: 175–87.

Hoffman, Michael A., Hany A. Hamroush, and Ralph O. Allen. 1987. The environment and evolution of an early Egyptian urban center: archaeological and geochemical investigations at Hierakonpolis. *Geoarchaeology* 2 (1): 1–13.

Hopkins, Anthony E. 1973. *An Economic History of West Africa.* New York: Columbia University Press.

Hornung, Erik. 1982. *Conception of God in Ancient Egypt.* Ithaca: Cornell University Press.

Houston, Stephan, Héctor Escobedo, Mark Child, Charles Gordon, and René Muñoz. 2003. The moral community: Maya settlement transformation at Piedras Negras, Guatemala. In *The Social Construction of Ancient Cities,* ed. Monica L. Smith, pp. 212–53. Washington, D.C.: Smithsonian Institution Press.

Hughes, R. H. and J. S. Hughes. 1992. *A Directory of African Wetlands.* Cambridge: World Conservation Monitoring Centre.

Huysecom, Eric. 1990. *Fanfannyégèné I: un Abri-sous-roche à Occupation Néolithique au Mali: la Fouille, le Matériel Archéologique, l'Art Rupestre.* Wiesbaden: F. Steiner.

1994. Djenné: une région aux productions céramiques très diversifiées. In *Djenné. Une Ville Millénaire au Mali,* ed. Rogier M. A. Bedaux and J. Diderik Van der Waals, pp. 122–30. Leiden: Rijksmuseum voor Volkenkunde.

Huysecom, Eric and Anne Mayor. 1993. Les traditions céramiques du Delta Intérieur du Niger: présent et passé. In *Vallées du Niger,* ed. anonymous, pp. 297–313. Paris: Editions de la Réunion des Musées Nationaux.

Imperato, Pascal. 1972. Nomads of the Niger. *Natural History* 81: 60–68, 78–79.

Ingold, Tim. 2000. *The Perception of the Environment. Essays in Livelihood, Dwelling and Skill.* London: Routledge.

Jacobberger, Patricia. 1988. Drought-related changes to geomorphic processes in central Mali. *Bulletin of the Geological Society of America* 100: 351–61.

Jacobsen, Thorkild. 1976. *The Treasures of Darkness. A History of Mesopotamian Religion.* New Haven: Yale University Press.

Jäkel, Dieter. 1979. Run-off and fluvial formation processes in the Tibesti Mountains as indicators of climatic history in the central Sahara during the late Pleistocene and Holocene. *Palaeoecology of Africa* 11: 13–44.

Janicot, Serge. 1992a. Spatiotemporal variability of West African rainfall. Part I. Regionalizations and typings. *Journal of Climate* 5: 489–97.

1992b. Spatiotemporal variability of West African rainfall. Part II. Associated surface and airmass characteristics. *Journal of Climate* 5: 499–511.

Jantsch, Erich. 1982. From self-reference to self-transcendence: the evolution of self-organization dynamics. In *Self-Organization and Dissipative Structures. Applications in the Physical and Social Sciences,* ed. William C. Schieve and Peter M. Allen, pp. 344–53. Austin: University of Texas Press.

Johnson, Steven. 2001. *Emergence. The Connected Lives of Ants, Brains, Cities, and Software.* New York: Scribner.

Jousse, Hélène and Isabelle Chenal-Velarde. 2001–2002. Nouvelles données sur la faune mammalienne de Kobadi (Mali) au néolithique: implications paléoéconomique et paléoenvironnementales. *Préhistoire et Anthropologie Méditerranéenne* 10–11: 145–58.

Kauffman, Stuart A. 1993. *The Origins of Order. Self-Organization and Selection in Evolution.* Oxford: Oxford University Press.

1995. *At Home in the Universe: The Search for the Laws of Self-Organization and Complexity.* Oxford: Oxford University Press.

Keightley, David. 1982. Shang China is coming of age – a review article. *Journal of Asian Studies* 41: 549–57.

1987. Archaeology and mentality: the making of China. *Representations* 18: 91–128.

Keith, Katheryn. 2003. The spatial patterns of everyday life in Old Babylonian neighborhoods. In *The Social Construction of Ancient Cities*, ed. Monica L. Smith, pp. 56–80. Washington, D.C.: Smithsonian Institution Press.

Kemp, Barry J. 1989. *Ancient Egypt. Anatomy of a Civilization.* London: Routledge.

Knapp, A. B. and Wendy Ashmore. 1999. Archaeological landscapes: constructed, conceptualized, ideational. In *Archaeologies of Landscape: Contemporary Perspectives*, ed. W. Ashmore and A. B. Knapp, pp. 1–30. Oxford: Blackwell.

Knox, P. L. 1995. World cities in a world-system. In *World Cities in a World-System*, ed. P. L. Knox and P. J. Taylor, pp. 3–20. Cambridge: Cambridge University Press.

Koechlin, Jean. 1997. Ecological conditions and degradation factors in the Sahel. In *Societies and Nature in the Sahel*, ed. Claude Raynaut, pp. 12–36. London: Routledge.

Kohler, Timothy A. and George J. Gumerman, ed. 2000. *Dynamics in Human and Primate Societies. Agent-Based Modeling of Social and Spatial Processes.* Oxford: Oxford University Press.

Kostof, Spiro. 1991. *The City Shaped: Urban Patterns and Meanings through History.* Boston: Bulfinch Press.

Kuhn, Thomas S. 1962. *The Structure of Scientific Revolutions.* Chicago: University of Chicago Press.

Kuklick, B. 1996. *Puritans in Babylon. The Ancient Near East and American Intellectual Life, 1880–1930.* Princeton: Princeton University Press.

Kutzbach, J. E. 1981. Monsoon climate of the early Holocene: climate experiment with Earth's orbital parameters for 9,000 years ago. *Science* 214: 59–61.

Kutzbach, J. E. and B. L. Otto-Bliesner. 1982. The sensitivity of the African-Asian monsoonal climate to orbital parameter changes for nine thousand years BP in a low-resolution general circulation model. *Journal of Atmospheric Sciences* 39: 1177–88.

Kutzbach, J. E. and F. A. Street-Perrott. 1985. Milankovitch forcing of fluctuations in the level of tropical lakes from eighteen to zero kyr BP. *Nature* 317: 130–34.

Lamb, Peter J. and Randy A. Peppler. 1992. Further case studies of tropical Atlantic surface atmospheric and oceanic patterns associated with sub-Saharan drought. *Journal of Climate* 5: 476–88.

Launois, Michel. 1996. Locust watch and man–locust confrontation in the Sahel. *Sécheresse* 7: 2.

LaViolette, Adria. 1987. An Archaeological Ethnography of Blacksmiths, Potters and Masons in Jenne, Mali. Ph.D. dissertation. Washington University, St. Louis.

1994. Forgerons, menuisiers, orfèvres et piroguiers-charpentiers. In *Djenné. Une Ville Millénaire au Mali*, ed. Rogier M. A. Bedaux and J. D. Van der Waals. pp. 149–58. Leiden: Rijksmuseum voor Volkenkunde.

Lefebvre, H. 1991. *The Production of Space*. Oxford: Blackwell.

Lehner, Mark. 2000. The fractal house of Pharaoh: ancient Egypt as a complex adaptive system, a trial formulation. In *Dynamics in Human and Primate Societies. Agent-Based Modeling of Social and Spatial Processes*, ed. Timothy A. Kohler and George J. Gumerman, pp. 275–353. Oxford: Oxford University Press.

Le Houérou, Henri Noël. 1989. *The Grazing Land Ecosystems of the African Sahel*. Berlin: Springer-Verlag.

Lepper, B. T. 1995. Tracking Ohio's Great Hopewell Road. *Archaeology* 48 (6): 52–56.

Levtzion, Nehemia. 1973. *Ancient Ghana and Mali*. London: Methuen & Co.

Levtzion, Nehemia, David Conrad, Paulo Farias, Roderick J. McIntosh, and Susan McIntosh. forthcoming. *Emerging Polities of the Western Sudan: Ancient Ghana and Mali*. (Revision of Levtzion, *Ancient Ghana and Mali* [1973].)

Levtzion, Nehemia and J. F. P. Hopkins. 1981. *Corpus of Early Arabic Sources for West African History*. Cambridge: Cambridge University Press.

Ligers, Z. 1957. Têtes sculptées en terre cuite trouvées au Soudan sur les bordes du Niger. *Notes Africaines* 74: 43–46.

Liu Li. 1996. Settlement patterns, chiefdom variability, and the development of early states in North China. *Journal of Anthropological Archaeology* 15: 237–88.

Liu Li and Xingcan Chen. 2001. Settlement archaeology and the study of social complexity in China. *The Review of Archaeology* 22 (2): 4–22.

Lorenz, Edward N. 1970. Climate change as a mathematical problem. *Journal of Applied Meteorology* 9 (3): 325–29.

1976. Nondeterministic theories of climate change. *Quaternary Research* 6: 495–506.

1990. Can chaos and intransitivity lead to interannual variability? *Tellus* 42A: 378–89.

Lovejoy, Paul E. 1985. *Salt of the Desert Sun*. Cambridge: Cambridge University Press.

Lowe-McConnell, R. H. 1985. The biology of the river systems with particular reference to the fishes. In *The Niger and its Neighbours*, ed. Anthony T. Grove, pp. 101–40. Rotterdam: A. A. Balkema.

Maas, Pierre and Geert Mommersteeg. 1994. Une architecture fascinante. In *Djenné. Une Ville Millénaire au Mali*, ed. Rogier M. A. Bedaux and J. D. Van der Waals, pp. 79–94. Leiden: Rijksmuseum voor Volkenkunde.

MacDonald, Kevin C. 1994. Socio-economic Diversity and the Origin of Cultural Complexity along the Middle Niger (2000 BC to AD 300). Ph.D. dissertation. University of Cambridge.

1996. Tichitt-Walata and the Middle Niger: evidence for cultural contact in the second millennium BC. In *Aspects of African Archaeology. Papers from the 10th Congress of the Panafrican Association for Prehistory and Related Studies*, ed.

Gilbert Pwiti and Robert Soper, pp. 429–40. Harare: University of Zimbabwe Publications.

MacDonald, Kevin C. and Phillip Allsworth-Jones. 1994. A reconsideration of the West African macrolithic conundrum: new factory sites and an associated settlement in the Vallée du Serpent, Mali. *African Archaeological Review* 12: 73–104.

MacDonald, Kevin C. and R. H. MacDonald. 2000. The origins and development of domesticated animals in West Africa. In *The Origins and Development of African Livestock: Archaeology, Genetics, Linguistics, and Ethnography*, ed. Roger Blench and Kevin C. MacDonald, pp. 127–62. London: University College London Press.

MacDonald, Kevin C. and Wim Van Neer. 1994. Specialized fishing peoples in the later Holocene of the Méma region (Mali). In *Fish Exploitation in the Past*, ed. Wim Van Neer, pp. 243–51. Tervuren: Musée Royal de l'Afrique Centrale.

McIntosh, Roderick J. 1979. The Development of Urbanism in West Africa: The Example of Jenne, Mali. Ph.D. dissertation. University of Cambridge.

1983. Floodplain geomorphology and human occupation of the upper Inland Delta of the Niger. *Geographical Journal* 149: 182–201.

1989. Middle Niger terracottas before the Symplegades gateway. *African Arts* 22 (2): 74–83, 103–4.

1991. Early urban clusters in China and Africa: the arbitration of social ambiguity. *Journal of Field Archaeology* 18: 199–21.

1993. The Pulse Model: genesis and accommodation of specialization in the Middle Niger. *Journal of African History* 34: 181–220.

1997. Agricultural beginnings in sub-Saharan Africa. In *Encyclopaedia of Precolonial Africa*, ed. Joseph O. Vogel, pp. 409–18. Walnut Creek, Calif.: Altamira Press.

1998. *The Peoples of the Middle Niger. Island of Gold*. Oxford: Blackwell.

1999a. Africa's storied past. Once a "People Without History," Africans explore a vibrant precolonial landscape. *Archaeology* 52 (4): 54–60, 83.

1999b. Clustered cities and alternative courses to authority in prehistory. *Journal of East Asian Archaeology* 1: 63–86.

1999c. Western representations of urbanism and invisible African towns. In *Beyond Chiefdoms. Pathways to Complexity in Africa*, ed. Susan McIntosh, pp. 56–65. Cambridge: Cambridge University Press.

2000a. Clustered cities of the Middle Niger: alternative routes to authority in prehistory. In *Africa's Urban Past*, ed. David M. Anderson and Richard Rathbone, pp. 19–35. Oxford: James Currey and Portsmouth, N.H.: Heinemann.

2000b. Social memory in Mande. In *The Way the Wind Blows: Climate, History, and Human Action*, ed. Roderick J. McIntosh, Joseph A. Tainter, and Susan McIntosh, pp. 141–80. New York: Columbia University Press.

2001. Francophone Africa. In *Encyclopedia of Archaeology. Volume I, History and Discoveries*, ed. Tim Murray, pp. 21–35. Santa Barbara, Calif.: ABC, CLIO.

2003. Climate change and population: history. In *The Encyclopedia of Population*, ed. Paul Demeny and Geoffrey McNicoll. Vol. I, pp. 144–9. New York: Macmillan Reference.

McIntosh, Roderick J. and Susan McIntosh. 1981. The Inland Niger Delta before the Empire of Mali: evidence from Jenne-jeno. *Journal of African History* 22: 1–22

1983. Djenné-jeno, Cité sans citadelle. *La Recherche* 148: 1272–75.

1988. From *siècles obscurs* to revolutionary centuries in the Middle Niger. *World Archaeology* 20 (1): 141–65.

1993. Les prospections d'après les photos aeriennes: régions de Jenné et Tombouctou. In *Vallées du Niger. Catalogue scientifique*, ed. anonymous, pp. 234–48. Paris: Editions de la Réunion des Musées Nationaux.

2003. Early urban configuration on the Middle Niger. In *The Social Construction of Ancient Cities*, ed. Monica L. Smith, pp. 103–20. Washington, D.C.: Smithsonian Institution Press.

McIntosh, Roderick J., Susan McIntosh, and Hamady Bocoum, eds. forthcoming. *Archaeological Excavations and Reconnaissance along the Middle Senegal Valley*. Oxford: BAR.

McIntosh, Roderick J., Susan McIntosh, and Téréba Togola. 1989. Archaeology of the peoples without history. *Archaeology* 42 (1): 74–80, 107.

McIntosh, Roderick J., Paul Sinclair, Téréba Togola, Michael Petrèn, and Susan McIntosh. 1996. Exploratory archaeology at Jenné and Jenné-jeno (Mali). *Sahara* 8: 19–28.

McIntosh, Roderick J., Joseph A. Tainter, and Susan McIntosh. 2000a. Climate, history and human action. In *The Way the Wind Blows. Climate, History and Human Action*, ed. Roderick J. McIntosh, Joseph A. Tainter, and Susan McIntosh, pp. 1–42. New York: Columbia University Press.

eds. 2000b. *The Way the Wind Blows. Climate, History and Human Action*. New York: Columbia University Press.

McIntosh, Susan. 1981. A reconsideration of Wangara/Palolus, Island of Gold. *Journal of African History* 22: 145–58.

1994. Changing perspectives of West Africa's past: archaeological research since 1988. *Journal of Archaeological Research* 2 (2): 165–98.

ed. 1995. *Excavations at Jenne-jeno, Hambarketolo, and Kaniana (Inland Niger Delta, Mali): The 1981 Season*. Berkeley: University of California Press.

1999a. Floodplains and the development of complex society: comparative perspectives from the West African semi-arid tropics. In *Complex Polities of the Ancient Tropical World*, ed. Elizabeth A. Bacus and Lisa J. Lucero, pp. 151–65. Archaeological Papers of the American Anthropological Association, no. 9. Washington, D.C.: American Anthropological Association.

1999b. Modeling political organization in large-scale settlement clusters: a case study from the Inland Niger Delta. In *Beyond Chiefdoms. Pathways to Complexity in Africa*, ed. Susan Keech McIntosh, pp. 66–79. Cambridge: Cambridge University Press.

1999c. Pathways to complexity: an African perspective. In *Beyond Chiefdoms. Pathways to Complexity in Africa*, ed. Susan Keech McIntosh, pp. 1–30. Cambridge: Cambridge University Press.

2001. West African Neolithic. In *Encyclopedia of Prehistory. Volume 1: Africa*, ed. Peter N. Peregrine and Melvin Ember, pp. 323–38. Dordrecht: Kluwer Academic.

McIntosh, Susan, Daphne Gallagher, and Roderick J. McIntosh. 2003. Tobacco pipes from the excavations at the Museum Site, Jenne, Mali. *Journal of African Archaeology* 1 (2): 171–99.

McIntosh, Susan and Roderick J. McIntosh. 1979. Initial perspectives on prehistoric subsistence in the Inland Delta (Mali). *World Archaeology* 11: 227–43.

1980. *Prehistoric Investigations in the Region of Jenne, Mali.* Cambridge Monographs in African Archaeology, no. 2, 2 volumes. Oxford: BAR.

1983. Current directions in West African prehistory. *Annual Review of Anthropology* 12: 215–58.

1984. The early city in West Africa: towards an understanding. *The African Archaeological Review* 2: 73–98.

1986a. Archaeological reconnaissance in the region of Timbuktu, Mali. *National Geographic Research* 2 (3): 302–19.

1986b. Recent archaeological research and dates from West Africa. *Journal of African History* 27: 413–42.

1992. The Middle Senegal Valley Project: preliminary results from the 1990–91 field season. *Nyame Akuma* 38: 47–61.

1993. Cities without citadels: understanding urban origins along the Middle Niger. In *The Archaeology of Africa. Foods, Metals and Towns*, ed. T. Shaw, P. Sinclair, B. Andah, and A. Okpoko, pp. 622–41. London: Routledge.

2005. Results of recent excavations at Jenné-jeno and Djenné, Mali. In *Proceedings of the 11th Panafrican Congress of Prehistory and Related Studies, Bamako*, ed. Kléna Sanogo and Téréba Togola, pp. 469–81. Bamako: Institut des Sciences Humaines.

McNaughton, Patrick. 1988. *The Mande Blacksmiths. Knowledge, Power and Art in West Africa.* Bloomington: Indiana University Press.

1991. Is there history in horizontal masks? A preliminary response to the dilemma of form. *African Arts* 25 (2): 76–85, 99–100.

Mainguet, M., L. Canon, and M. C. Chemin. 1980. Le Sahara: géomorphologie et paléomorphologie éoliennes. In *The Sahara and the Nile*, ed. Martin A. J. Williams and Hughes Faure, pp. 17–35. Rotterdam: A. A. Balkema.

Makaske, Bart (Albertus). 1998. Anastomosing Rivers. Forms, Processes and Sediments. Ph.D. dissertation. University of Utrecht, the Netherlands.

Makaske, Bart (Albertus) and Mark Terlien. 1996. *Le Développement Géomorphologique de la Partie Méridionale du Delta Intérieur du Niger.* Interuniversitair Centrum voor Geo-ecologisch Onderzoek, Report ICG-96/2. Amsterdam: ICG.

Maley, Jean. 1983. Histoire de la végétation et du climat de l'Afrique nord-tropicale au Quaternaire récent. *Bothalia* 14 (3 and 4): 377–89.

Maley, Jean. 2000. Les variations des niveaux du la Tchad au cours du dernier millénaire. Rôle des conditions climatiques régionales et des apports régionales. Comparison avec le lac Navisha et Afrique orientale. *Méga-Tchad* 1–2: 21–26.

Mann, C. C. 2002. 1491. *The Atlantic Monthly* 289 (3): 41–53.

Manzanilla, L. 1997. Early urban societies. Challenges and perspectives. In *Emergence and Change in Early Urban Societies*, ed. L. Manzanilla, pp. 3–39. New York: Plenum Press.

Masson-Detourbet, A. 1953. Terres cuites de Mopti. *Notes Africaines* 60: 100–2.

Matthews, V. H. and D. C. Benjamin. 1993. *Social World of Ancient Israel, 1250–587 BCE*. Peabody, Mass.: Hendrickson Press.

Mauny, Raymond. 1949. Statuettes de terre cuite de Mopti. *Notes Africanes* 43: 70–72.

   1961. *Tableau Géographique de l'Ouest Africain au Moyen Âge, d'Après les Sources Écrites, la Tradition, et l'Archéologie*. Mémoires de l'Institut Fondamental d'Afrique Noire, no. 61. Dakar: Institut Fondamental d'Afrique Noire.

   1970. *Les Siècles Obscurs de l'Afrique Noire*. Paris: Fayard.

Mazar, A. 1990. *Archaeology of the Land of the Bible, 10,000–586 BCE*. New York: Doubleday.

Meggers, Betty J. 1994. Climatic Fluctuations and Cultural Discontinuity in the Neotropical Lowlands. Paper presented at the Palaeoclimates and Prehistory of the Lowland Tropics of Three Continents panel at the 1992 Pacific Science Congress, Honolulu.

Millinski, Manfred, Dirk Semmann, and Hans-Jürgen Krambeck. 2002. Reputation helps solve the "tragedy of the commons." *Nature* 415 (24 January 2002): 424–25.

Mommersteeg, Geert. 1994. Marabouts à Djenné; enseignement coranique, invocation et amulettes. In *Djenné. Une Ville Millénaire au Mali*, ed. Rogier M. A. Bedaux and J. D. Van der Waals, pp. 66–75. Leiden: Rijksmuseum voor Volkenkunde.

Monod, Théodore. 1943. Découverte archéologique à Djénné. *Notes Africanes* 20: 10.

   1955. A propos des jarres-cercueils de l'Afrique occidentale. *Africanischen Studieren* 26: 30–44.

Monod, Théodore and Raymond Mauny. 1957. Découverte de nouveaux instruments en os dans l'Ouest Africain. In *Proceedings of the 3rd Panafrican Congress on Prehistory, Livingstone 1955*, ed. J. D. Clark, pp. 242–47. London: Chatto & Windus.

Monod, Théodore and G. Palausi. 1958. Sur la présence dans la région du lac Faguibine de venues volcaniques d'âge subactuel. *Comptes Rendus de l'Académie des Sciences de Paris* 246: 666–68.

Monteil, Charles. 1971 [1932]. *Une Cité Soudanais: Djenné. Métropole du Delta Central du Niger*, 2nd edition. Paris: Edition Anthropos.

Morris, I. 1997. An archaeology of inequalities? The Greek city-states. In *The Archaeology of City-States*, ed. D. L. Nichols and T. H. Charlton, pp. 91–106. Washington, D.C.: Smithsonian Institution Press.

Munson, Patrick J. 1981. A late Holocene (c.4500–2300 bp) climatic chonology for the southwestern Sahara. *Palaeoecology of Africa* 13: 97–116.

Murowchick, Robert E. and David J. Cohen. 2001. Searching for Shang's beginnings: Great City Shang, City Song, and collaborative archaeology in Shangqui, Henan. *Review of Archaeology* 22 (2): 47–61.

National Research Council. 1996. *Lost Crops of Africa. Volume I. Grains*. Washington, D.C.: National Academy Press.

N'Diaye, Bokar. 1970. *Groupes Ethniques au Mali*. Bamako: Editions Populaires.

Neumann, Katharina. 1996. The emergence of plant food production in the West African Sahel: new evidence from northeast Nigeria and northern Burkina Faso. In *Aspects of African Archaeology. Papers from the 10th Congress of the Panafrican Association for Prehistory and Related Studies*, ed. Gilbert Pwiti and Robert Soper, pp. 441–48. Harare: University of Zimbabwe Publications.

Neumann, Katharina, Werner Schoch, Pierre Détienne, and Frtiz Hans Schweingruber. 2001. *Hölzer der Sahara und des Sahel. Ein Anatomischer Atlas*. Bern: Verlag Paul Haupt.

Niane, D. T. 1984. Mali and the second Mandingo expansion. In *Africa from the Twelfth to the Sixteenth Century*, ed. D. T. Niane, pp. 117–71. UNESCO General History of Africa, no. 4. Berkeley: University of California Press.

Nichols, D. L. and T. H. Charlton, eds. 1997. *The Archaeology of City-States*. Washington, D.C.: Smithsonian Institution Press.

Nicholson, Sharon E. 1978. Climatic variation in the Sahel and other African regions during the past five centuries. *Journal of Arid Environments* 1: 3–24.

1986. The spatial coherence of African rainfall anomalies: interhemispheric teleconnections. *Journal of Climate and Applied Meteorology* 25: 1365–81.

1994. Recent rainfall fluctuations in Africa and their relationship to past conditions over the continent. *The Holocene* 4: 121–31.

1995. Variability of African rainfall on interannual and decadal time scales. In *Natural Climate Variability on Decade-to-Century Time Scales*, ed. J. Shukla, pp. 32–43. Washington, D.C.: National Academy Press.

Nissen, Hans. 1988. *The Early History of the Ancient Near East, 9000–2000 BC*. Chicago: University of Chicago Press.

O'Connor, David. 1993. *Ancient Nubia: Egypt's Rival in Africa*. Philadelphia: University Museum, University of Pennsylvania.

O'Neill, R. V., D. L. DeAngelis, J. B. Wade, and T. F. H. Allen. 1986. *A Hierarchical Concept of Ecosystems*. Princeton Monographs in Population Biology, no. 23. Princeton: Princeton University Press.

Page, Roderic D. M. 2003. *Tangled Trees. Phylogeny, Cospeciation and Coevolution*. Chicago: University of Chicago Press.

Paris, François, Alain Person, and Jean-Francois Saliège. 1993. Peuplements et environnements holocènes du bassin de l'Azawagh oriental (Niger). In *Vallées du Niger*, ed. anonymous, pp. 378–92. Paris: Editions de la Réunion des Musées Nationaux.

Park, Thomas K. 1992. Early trends towards class stratification: chaos, common property, and flood recessional agriculture. *American Anthropologist* 94 (1): 90–117.

Perinbaum, Marie. 1974. Notes on Dyula origins and nomenclature. *Bulletin de l'Institut Fondamental d'Afrique Noire (B)* 36: 676–89.

Petit-Maire, Nicole. 1986a. Homo climaticus: vers une paléoanthropologie écologique. *Bulletin de la Société Royale Belge d'Anthropologie et de Préhistoire* 97: 59–75.

1986b. Palaeoclimates in the Sahara of Mali. A multidisciplinary study. *Épisodes* 9 (1): 7–16.

Petit-Maire, Nicole and J. Riser, eds. 1983. *Sahara ou Sahel? Quaternaire Récent du Bassin de Taoudenni (Mali)*. Paris: Laboratoire de Géologie du Quaternaire du Centre National de la Recherche Scientifique.

Pollock, Susan. 1999. *Ancient Mesopotamia. The Eden that Never Was.* Cambridge: Cambridge University Press.

Prigogine, I. and P. M. Allen. 1982. The challenge of complexity. In *Self-Organization and Dissipative Structures. Applications in the Physical and Social Sciences*, ed. William C. Schieve and Peter M. Allen, pp. 3–39. Austin: University of Texas Press.

Prussin, Libby. 1986. *Hatumere: Islamic Design in West Africa.* Berkeley: University of California Press.

Quensière, Jacques, ed. 1994. *La Pêche dans le Delta Central du Niger.* Paris: Editions d'ORSTOM, Editions Karthala.

Raimbault, Michel. 1986. Le gisement néolithique de Kobadi (Sahel malien) et ses implications paléohydrologiques. *Changements Globaux en Afrique. Proceedings of the 1986 INQUA Symposium*, pp. 393–97. Dakar: INQUA.

Raimbault, Michel and O. Dutour. 1989. Les nouvelles données du site néolithique de Kobadi dans le Sahel malien: la mission 1989. *Traveaux du Laboratoire d'Anthropologie et de Préhistoire des Pays de la Méditerranée Occidentale 1989*: 179–83.

Raimbault, Michel, Claude Guérin, and M. Faure. 1987. Les Vertébrés du gisement néolithique de Kobadi. *Archaeozoologia* 1 (2): 219–38.

Raimbault, Michel and Kléna Sanogo. 1991. *Recherche Archéologiques au Mali. Prospections et Inventaire, Fouilles et Études Analytiques en Zone Lacustre.* Paris: ACCT and Karthala.

Rautman, Alison E. 1996. Risk, reciprocity, and the operation of social networks. In *Evolving Complexity and Environmental Risk in the Prehistoric Southwest*, ed. Joseph A. Tainter and Bonnie B. Tainter, pp. 197–222. Santa Fe Institute, Studies in the Sciences of Complexity, Proceedings, vol. 24. Reading, Mass.: Addison-Wesley.

Raynaut, Claude, ed. 1997. *Societies and Nature in the Sahel.* London: Routledge.

Raynaut, Claude and Philippe Lavigne Delville. 1997a. The diversity of farming practices. In *Societies and Nature in the Sahel*, ed. Claude Raynaut, pp. 159–83. London: Routledge.

1997b. A shared land: complementary and competing uses. In *Societies and Nature in the Sahel*, ed. Claude Raynaut, pp. 109–37. London: Routledge.

Raynaut, Claude, Philippe Lavigne Delville, and Jean Koechlin. 1997. Relations between man and his environment: the main types of situation in the western Sahel. In *Societies and Nature in the Sahel*, ed. Claude Raynaut, pp. 184–213. London: Routledge.

Redman, Charles L. 1978. *The Rise of Civilization.* San Francisco: W. H. Freeman & Co.

1999. *Human Impact on Ancient Environments.* Tucson: University of Arizona Press.

Rehder, J. E. 2000. *The Mastery and Uses of Fire in Antiquity.* Montreal: McGill–Queen's University Press.

Riser, Jean, Anne-Marie Aucour, and Fousseyni Toure. 1986. Niveaux lacustres et néotectoniques au lac Faguibine (Mali). *Comptes Rendus de l'Académie des Sciences de Paris*, série II 10: 941–43.

Roosevelt, Anna C. 1998. Ancient and modern hunter-gatherers of lowland South America: an evolutionary problem. In *Advances in Historical Ecology*, ed. William Balée, pp. 190–212. New York: Columbia University Press.

Ruddiman, William F. 2001. *Earth's Climate. Past and Future*. New York: W. H. Freeman & Co.

2003. The anthropogenic greenhouse era began thousands of years ago. *Climatic Change* 61 (3): 261–93.

Rzoska, J. 1985. The water quality and hydrobiology of the Niger. In *The Niger and its Neighbours*, ed. Anthony T. Grove, pp. 77–99. Rotterdam: A. A. Balkema.

al-Sa'di (c. AD 1656). 1900. *Ta'rikh es-Sudan*. Trans. O. Houdas. Paris: Leroux.

Sanders, William T., Jeffrey R. Parsons, and Robert S. Santley. 1979. *The Basin of Mexico. Ecological Process in the Evolution of a Civilization*, 2 volumes. New York: Academic.

"Sculpture soudanaise" (anonymous). 1947. *Notes Africanes* 33: 20.

Servant, M. and S. Servant-Vildary. 1980. L'environement quaternaire du bassin du Tchad. In *The Sahara and the Nile*, ed. Martin A. J. Williams and Hughes Faure, pp. 133–62. Rotterdam: A. A. Balkema.

Shelach, Gideon. 1994. Social complexity in North China during the Early Bronze Age: a comparative study of the Erlitou and Lower Xiajiadian cultures. *Asian Perspectives* 33 (2): 261–92.

1997. A settlement pattern study in northeast China: results and potential contributions of Western theory and methods to Chinese archaeology. *Antiquity* 71: 114–27.

Shukla, Jagadish. 1995. On the initiation and persistence of the Sahel drought. In *Natural Climate Variability on Decade-to-Century Time Scales*, ed. National Research Council, pp. 44–48. Washington, D.C.: National Research Council.

Smith, Andrew B. 1980. Domesticated cattle in the Sahara and their introduction into West Africa. In *The Sahara and the Nile*, ed. Martin A. J. Williams and Hughes Faure, pp. 489–501. Rotterdam: A. A. Balkema.

1992. *Pastoralism in Africa. Origins and Developmental Ecology*. London: Hurst & Co.

Smith, Monica L. 2003. Introduction: the social construction of ancient cities. In *The Social Construction of Ancient Cities*, ed. Monica L. Smith, pp. 1–36. Washington, D.C.: Smithsonian Institution Press.

Smith, Zeric Kay. 2001. Mali's decade of democracy. *Journal of Democracy* 12 (3): 73–79.

Solvaing, B. 1983. A propos de Dia et de ses lettres au XIXème siècle. *Annales de l'Université d'Abidjan*, série I 11: 119–35.

Stone, Elizabeth C. 1991. The spatial organization of Mesopotamian cities. *Aula Orientalis* 9: 235–42.

1997. City-states and their centers: the Mesopotamian example. In *The Archaeology of City-States*, ed. D. L. Nichols and T. H. Charlton, pp. 15–26. Washington, D.C.: Smithsonian Institution Press.

Stone, Elizabeth C. and P. Zimansky. 1995. The tapestry of power in a Mesopotamian city. *Scientific American* 272 (4): 118–23.

Sundström, Lars. 1972. *Ecology and Symbiosis: Niger Water Folk*. Studia Ethnographica Upsaliensis, no. 35. Uppsala: Institutonen för Allmän och Jämförande Ethnografi vid Uppsala Universitet.

Sutton, J. E. G. 1974. The Aqualithic civilization of Middle Africa. *Journal of African History* 15: 527–46.

Szumowski, George. 1957. Fouilles au nord du Macina et dans la région de Ségou. *Bulletin de l'Institut Fondamental de l'Afrique Noire (B)* 19: 224–58.

Tainter, Joseph A. 1988. *The Collapse of Complex Societies*. Cambridge: Cambridge University Press.

2000. Problem solving: complexity, history, sustainability. *Population and Environment* 22 (1): 3–41.

2003. A framework for sustainability. *World Futures* 59: 213–23.

Tainter, Joseph A. and Bonnie B. Tainter, eds. 1996. *Evolving Complexity and Environmental Risk in the Prehistoric Southwest*. Santa Fe Institute, Studies in the Sciences of Complexity, Proceedings, vol. 24. Reading, Mass.: Addison-Wesley.

Talbot, Michael R. 1980. Environmental responses to climatic change in the West African Sahel over the past 20,000 years. In *The Sahara and the Nile*, ed. Martin A. J. Williams and Hughes Faure, pp. 37–62. Rotterdam: A. A. Balkema.

Talbot, Michael R. and G. Delibrias. 1980. A new Late Pleistocene–Holocene water-level curve for Lake Bosumtwi, Ghana. *Earth and Planetary Science Letters* 47: 336–44.

Thomas, David. 1979. *Naturalism and Social Science: A Post-empiricist Philosophy of Social Science*. Cambridge: Cambridge University Press.

Thomas, David Hurst. 1986. *Refiguring Anthropology. First Principles of Probability and Statistics*. Prospect Heights, Ill.: Waveland Press.

Tilley, Christopher. 1994. *A Phenomenology of Landscape. Places, Paths and Monuments*. Oxford: Berg.

Togola, Téréba. 1993. Archaeological Investigation of Iron Age Sites in the Méma (Mali). Ph.D. dissertation. Rice University, Houston.

1996. Iron Age occupation in the Méma region, Mali. *African Archaeological Review* 13: 91–110.

Togola, Téréba and Michel Raimbault. 1991. Les missions d'inventaire dans le Méma, Kareeri et Farimaké (1984–1985*)*. In *Recherches Archéologiques au Mali. Prospection et Inventaire, Fouilles et Études Analytiques en Zone Lacustre*, ed. Michel Raimbault and Kléna Sanogo, pp. 81–98. Paris: Karthala.

Trigger, Bruce. 1972. Determinants of growth in pre-industrial societies. In *Man, Settlement and Urbanism*, ed. Peter Ucko, Ruth Tringham, and David Dimbleby, pp. 575–99. London: Duckworth.

1983. The rise of Egyptian civilization. In *Ancient Egypt. A Social History*, ed. Bruce G. Trigger, Barry J. Kemp, David O'Connor, and A. B. Lloyd, pp. 1–70. Cambridge: Cambridge University Press.

1985. The evolution of pre-industrial cities: a multi-linear perspective. In *Mélanges offerts à Jean Vercoutter*, ed. F. Geus and F. Thill, pp. 343–52. Paris: Editions Recherche sur les Civilisations.

2003. *Understanding Early Civilizations. A Comparative Study*. Cambridge: Cambridge University Press.

Underhill, Anne P. 1994. Variation in settlements during the Longshan period of northern China. *Asian Perspectives* 33 (2): 197–228.

Underhill, Anne P., Gary M. Feinman, Linda Nicholas, Gwen Bennett, Fengshu Cai, Haiguang Yu, Fengshi Luan, and Hui Fang. 1998. Systematic, regional survey in SE Shandong province, China. *Journal of Field Archaeology* 25 (4): 453–74.

Underhill, Anne P., Gary M. Feinman, Linda Nicholas, Gwen Bennett, Hui Fang, Fengshi Luan, Haiguang Yu, and Fengshu Cai. 2002. Regional survey and the development of complex societies in southeastern Shandong, China. *Antiquity* 76: 745–55.

UNESCO. 1991. *International Mineral Deposits Map of Africa* (1/5,000,000) (Sheet 1, West Africa). Paris: UNESCO Commission de la Carte Géologique du Monde.

Urvoy, Yves. 1942. *Les Bassins du Niger*, Mémoires de l'Institut Fondamental d'Afrique Noire, no. 4. Dakar: Institut Fondamental d'Afrique Noire.

Van der Leeuw, Sander and Charles Redman. 2002. Placing archaeology at the center of socio-natural studies. *American Antiquity* 67 (4): 597–605.

Van Neer, W. 2002. Food security in western and central Africa during the late Holocene: the role of domestic stock keeping, hunting and fishing. In *Droughts, Food and Culture. Ecological Change and Food Security in Africa's Later Prehistory*, ed. Fekri Hassan, pp. 251–74. Dordrecht: Kluwer Academic.

Vansina, Jan. 1984. *Art History in Africa*. London: Longman.

Vernet, Robert. 1995. *Climats Anciens du Nord de l'Afrique*. Paris: Harmattan.

1998. Chronologie holocène sur une marge saharienne: littoral atlantique et Mauritanie occidentale dans l'ensemble saharien. *Palaeoecology of Africa* 25: 43–8.

2002. Climate during the late Holocene in the Sahara and the Sahel: evolution and consequences on human settlement. In *Droughts, Food and Culture. Ecological Change and Food Security in Africa's Later Prehistory*, ed. Fekri Hassan, pp. 47–63. Dordrecht: Kluwer Academic.

forthcoming. Evolution du peuplement et glissement des isohyètes à la fin de la préhistoire et au début de l'histoire en Afrique de l'Ouest sahelienne. *Mande Studies*.

Vieillard, G. 1940. Sur quelques objets en terre cuite de Djénné. *Bulletin de l'Institut Fondamental d'Afrique Noire (B)* 3: 347–50.

Voute, C. 1962. Geological and morphological evolution of the Niger and Benue valleys. *Annales du Musée Royale de l'Afrique Centrale* 40: 189–207.

Webb, James L. A., Jr. 1995. *Desert Frontier: Ecological and Economic Change along the Western Sahel, 1600–1850*. Madison: University of Wisconsin Press.

Weber, Max. 1968. *Economy and Society*, 4th edition. New York: Bedminster.

Wheatley, Paul. 1971. *The Pivot of the Four Quarters*. Chicago: Aldine.

Wilkinson, Toby A. H. 1999. *Early Dynastic Egypt*. London: Routledge.

Wilkinson, Tony J. 2003. *Archaeological Landscapes of the Near East*. Tucson: University of Arizona Press.

Williams, Bruce. 1980. The lost pharaohs of Nubia. *Archaeology* 33: 12–21.

Wilson, David. 1990. Full coverage survey in the Lower Santa Valley: implications for regional settlement patterns on the Peruvian coast. In *The Archaeology of Regions*, ed. Stanley K. Fish and Stephen A Kowalewski, pp. 117–46. Washington, D.C.: Smithsonian Institution Press.

Wilson, John A. 1960. Civilization without cities. In *City Invincible*, ed. Carl H. Kraeling and Robert M. Adams, pp. 124–64. Chicago: University of Chicago Press.

Wilson, R. R. 1977. *Genealogy and History in the Biblical World*. New Haven: Yale University Press.

Woodhouse, James. 1998. Iron in Africa: metal from nowhere. In *Transformation in Africa. Essays on Africa's Later Past*, ed. Graham Connah, pp. 160–85. London: Leicester University Press.

Wright, Henry T. and Gregory Johnson. 1975. Population, exchange, and early state formation in southwestern Iran. *American Anthropologist* 77: 267–89.

Wright, Rita. 2002. The origin of cities. In *Encyclopedia of Urban Cultures. Cities and Cultures around the World*, ed. Melvin Ember and Carol R. Ember. Vol. I, pp. 3–11. Danbury, Conn.: Grolier.

Yoffee, Norman. 1995. Political economy in early Mesopotamian states. *Annual Review of Anthropology* 24: 281–311.

1997. The obvious and the chimerical. City-states in archaeological perspective. In *The Archaeology of City-States. Cross-Cultural Approaches*, ed. Deborah L. Nichols and Thomas H. Charlton, pp. 255–63. Washington, D.C.: Smithsonian Institution Press.

Zeder, Melinda A. 1991. *Feeding Cities*. Washington, D.C.: Smithsonian Institution Press.

2003. Food provisioning in urban societies. In *The Social Construction of Ancient Cities*, ed. Monica L. Smith, pp. 156–83. Washington, D.C.: Smithsonian Institution Press.

Index

Note: Locators for figures appear in italics.

For EU product safety concerns, contact us at Calle de José Abascal, 56–1°,
28003 Madrid, Spain or eugpsr@cambridge.org.